McGraw-Hill's
COMPLETE
MEDICAL
SPANISH

Practical Medical Spanish for Quick and Confident Communication

Joanna Ríos, Ph.D., and José Fernández Torres

New York   Chicago   San Francisco   Lisbon   London   Madrid   Mexico City
Milan   New Delhi   San Juan   Seoul   Singapore   Sydney   Toronto

3 4 5 6 7 8 9 0   DOC/DOC   3 2 1 0 9 8 7 6 5 4

ISBN 0-07-143979-X

Interior illustrations by Ríos Associates, pages 1–33 and 38–132, except pages 1, 9 (nurse), 11 (doctor and IV stand), 16, 17, 19 (IV stand), 20, 21, 71 (man and woman), 80 (money), 105 by Luc Nisset-Raidon. Susan Spellman, pages 34–37. Luc Nisset-Raidon, pages 133–215.

McGraw-Hill books are available at special quantity discounts to use as premiums and sales promotions, or for use in corporate training programs. For more information, please write to the Director of Special Sales, Professional Publishing, McGraw-Hill, Two Penn Plaza, New York, NY 10121-2298. Or contact your local bookstore.

This book is printed on acid-free paper.

*In loving memory of my wonderful father, who possessed a
great wealth of knowledge, was always encouraging and an
enormous inspiration for me. He was extremely helpful with medical
and scientific terms as well as with editing and proofreading
the manuscript for this book.*
—Joanna Ríos

*In dedication to my mother Dolores Torres Villate, R.N.,
who always encouraged me to pursue my dreams. I will always
love you.*
—José Fernández Torres

Contents

Acknowledgments

We would like to acknowledge Tamara Anahí Ríos, M.S.; Silvia "Yola" Ruanova; Dolores Torres Villate, R.N.; Emilio Fernández Torres, M.S.; and Luvy Bravo de Nuanes, Ph.D., for their help with vocabulary and expressions as used in Mexico, the Caribbean, and Central America.

Special thanks go to Milagros Martínez Bello, M.D., for her assistance with medical terms and proofreading the dialogues for accuracy.

Thanks also to all of the students in the medical field who have taken our courses over the years and have been an ongoing source of information.

Introduction

McGraw-Hill's Complete Medical Spanish is an illustrated medical Spanish text-workbook specifically geared to healthcare professionals, in particular, physicians, physicians' assistants, nurses (including NPs, LVNs, LPNs, MAs), medical attendants, lab technicians, and ancillary medical staff.

The book is composed of ten chapters or lessons. Each chapter introduces grammar concepts (often referred to as "structures," which somehow sounds less threatening), vocabulary, and dialogues that attempt to follow the order in which your patient visit takes place. For example, you will learn to greet a patient, take vital signs, interview him or her, find out the chief complaint, review the medical history, give a physical exam, and then recommend prescription or follow-up instructions. Vocabulary and dialogues for various lab tests are also included. Many significant cultural aspects are also interspersed throughout each chapter, culminating with the last lesson that focuses on "Cross-cultural communication."

Each chapter follows a logical progression and introduces vocabulary by means of pictures that are generally related to a single topic. The initial vocabulary section of each chapter is followed by related exercises, dialogues, and/or crossword puzzles. Grammar concepts are explained in a simple, clear, and concise manner. Although grammar, per se, is not stressed, it is reinforced by constant repetition—the very manner in which we learned our native tongue as children.

The purpose of the illustrations and the suggested method of instruction is to encourage you to avoid translating from Spanish to English and vice versa. Instead, you are encouraged to relate the image or concept directly with the appropriate Spanish word, thus eliminating an entire and irrelevant translation step.

The dialogues are based on vocabulary that has already been presented, so you are familiarized with nearly all the words and phrases that will be encountered in each dialogue. Obviously, the purpose of this book is to teach you to communicate with your Spanish-speaking patients in order to form strong clinician–patient rapport. You will be learning a standardized universal Spanish that also includes many words and expressions that take on different meanings in different countries and regions. Your Latino patients will come from a variety of countries, education levels, socioeconomic backgrounds, and origins (whether urban or rural). Some may be from indigenous groups for whom Spanish is also a second language. The point is that their Spanish accents, some vocabulary, expressions, and cultural traits will differ; yet you will be able to understand the essential, salient aspects of what they express. Just think of the variations that exist in English; nevertheless, you probably understand someone from England, Australia, New Zealand, the southern United States, or New York.

If anything, the Spanish text is weighted slightly toward expressions used in Mexico. This is in large part a reflection of the fact that the majority of the healthcare professionals who have studied in the authors' programs and workshops treat more Spanish-speaking-only patients of Mexican origin than those from any other region. Nevertheless, many expressions from Central America, the Caribbean, and some parts of South America are also included.

It is important to remember that if you smile and say as much as you can in Spanish—even if it is only introducing yourself—most of your Spanish-speaking patients will be relieved and impressed that you are attempting to learn and use their language. Don't worry too much about your accent—your patients will understand, and the more you listen to the accompanying recordings, the more you will improve. Just go for it, and, when necessary, ask for their help. You will find that by remembering just a handful of very basic structures, combined with some of the many cognates (words in Spanish that are similar to words in English) that exist in the medical field, you will surprise yourself with your ability to converse satisfactorily. Above all, keep in mind: *do not translate literally,* and *keep it simple.*

Please note: medicine changes so rapidly that what is an accepted word or concept today may not be so tomorrow. Therefore, while we have changed VD to STDs and now to STIs, please make allowances for other examples of new usage that develop once this book is published. (And, by the way, in Spanish it is still called **enfermedades venéreas**!)

We have tried to be as medically correct as possible, and although we have chosen only a few medical dialogues from certain fields, the conversations offer an example of how to use sentence structure and the "power verb concept." The point of this text-workbook is not to include dialogues of every field for you to memorize, but to teach the basic sentence structures needed to form your own dialogues to suit your own specific needs. If you learn the basic structures, you will be able to fill in the sentences with any word from your specialized area.

If a word, dialogue, or concept related to your specific field is not mentioned or used, simply learn to use the sentence structure (in the simplest form) and add your specialized term. In this way, you will learn how to say whatever you need to and to understand why something is stated as it is in Spanish. This takes you beyond just memorizing and allows you to form your own thoughts in Spanish in order to best communicate with your Spanish-speaking-only patients. Remember to "keep it simple." And don't be afraid to use a dictionary. It's a great invention—and it works!

How to use this course

1. As this is a self-study course, we strongly suggest you start working through the text from the beginning, one section at a time. Don't take things too fast, only to discover that you have not fully assimilated the material. The grammatical structures on which conversational Spanish is based are introduced gradually and are immediately placed in contexts that are relevant to healthcare professionals and applicable to common doctor–patient exchanges.

2. Be sure to complete the exercises. You will notice that the exercises within each section generally become progressively more challenging, starting with a basic reinforcement of the grammar concepts and progressing to exercises that require more challenging cognitive thinking. You may check your answers with the suggested responses in the Answer Key at the back of the book. For easy reference, a verb table is also provided in Appendix A, listing the different verb tense endings and conjugations.

3. Vocabulary lists are there to be learned. You should be accustomed to memorizing and assimilating vast quantities of information. (How else were you able to succeed during "med school" or any medically related field of training?) The vocabulary that is presented has been carefully selected to correspond to common healthcare-related conversations; where longer or more technical vocabulary lists are provided, you may be more selective and ignore terms that are not relevant to your specific field.

4. When you arrive at a dialogue in the text, having first memorized the vocabulary, read it as many times as you feel you need. Then listen to the dialogue on the recording while reading along in the book simultaneously. The first few times, just attempt to obtain the general idea of the dialogue. Do not focus on each separate word (just as you don't concentrate on every word uttered by a radio announcer when listening to a radio station in English); rather, try to "catch" the key phrases.

Repeat words and phrases aloud as much as possible to reinforce the structures and to mimic the accent and intonation. Subsequently, just listen to the dialogue on the recording. As important as studying the healthcare provider's role, however, is listening carefully to the patient's part in the dialogues. This will train you to understand what your patient is attempting to communicate to you. To help you achieve this goal, a variety of accents and intonations are included on the recordings.

If a particular dialogue has driven you crazy and you simply must know what it means in English, you may turn to Appendix C, which contains English translations of all the dialogues and monologues. However, we hope that you use the translations *only as a last resort.*

5. Remember, you can reread sections in the book and replay the recordings as often as you need. Even if it is only for five or ten minutes, regular review will help consolidate your grasp of medical Spanish and boost your confidence. You will then realize how much Spanish you have retained and now understand.

6. Don't be shy! Use the Spanish that you have learned whenever the opportunity presents itself. The more you use it, the more comfortable and natural it will seem. And the more you will build your rapport with your Latino patients.

Good luck!

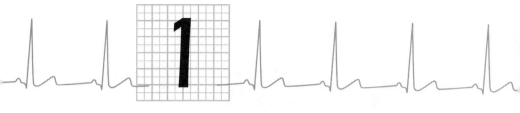

What you will learn in this lesson:

- to greet and introduce yourself to your patient
- the alphabet and three simple rules for pronunciation
- to form singular and plural masculine and feminine nouns (persons, places, or things)
- to form singular and plural forms of the definite article (*the*) and indefinite articles (*a, an, one, some*)
- body parts
- to ask "What seems to be the problem?", "What hurts?", "Where does it hurt?"
- to say "I need . . . ," "You need . . . ," "Do you need . . . ?", and "What/Where/Why/When do you need to . . . ?"

The goal of this lesson is to be able to greet your patients in a culturally courteous manner, make them feel comfortable, take vital signs, ask what brings them to you (chief complaint), or how they're progressing if it is a follow-up visit, and what they need to do next and how often.

1.1 Greetings

Buenos días   Buenas tardes   Buenas noches
(Bway-noss thee-ahs)[1]   (Bway-nahs tarrd-thess)   (Bway-nahs no-chess)

Buenos días means "Good morning" or "Good day" and generally covers from 6:00 A.M. to noon. **Buenas tardes** ("Good afternoon") can vary from country to country. In Mexico, the Caribbean, and Central America it covers from noon to perhaps 6:00 or 7:00 P.M.; while in Spain, it can cover up to 9:00 or so. However, from 7 to 9 P.M., one may begin to say **Buenas noches**, used as "good evening." (The best indicator is when the sun sets.) **Buenas noches** means "Good evening" or "Good night" and refers to sundown until perhaps 2:00 A.M. **La madrugada**, or the "wee morning hours," refers to the remaining hours until approximately sunrise.

Mucho gusto means "Nice to meet you." It is customary to shake hands with everyone upon meeting, greeting, and leave-taking. This applies to everyone: two men, two women, a man and a woman, an adult and a child, or all the children present. (And there probably *will* be many family members and often children present, even at your office.)

One should shake hands with everyone to avoid being seen as extremely rude, cold, and uncaring. An even more kind, caring, and warm gesture is to cup your left hand over the hand you are shaking, which conveys the feeling of trust (**confianza**). It is a quite comforting action seen from the Latin American point of view, and it tends to communicate the feeling that "You are in good hands now." It does not transmit the trite or paternalistic attitude that may be interpreted by U.S. Americans. In Spanish-speaking countries, the proximity between people shaking hands is generally much closer than is customary in the United States. Instead of standing the distance of an arm length apart per person, perhaps a forearm length per person would be more appropriate.

---

[1]Underlined syllable is stressed in phonetic pronunciation.

Often Latin American family members or close friends accompany one another for moral support and concern, even after a crisis has passed. The authors do not intend to generalize or create stereotypes, but often the Latin American family is quite tightly knit and bands together during any emergency or crisis. What may tend to be construed as a crisis for a Latin American may not necessarily be considered a crisis by cultural norms in the United States. Thus the situation or reactions may seem to be more "melodramatic" than those that a person raised in the United States is accustomed to observing.

VOCABULARIO

¡Pase! ¡Pásele![2] (<u>pah</u>-say, <u>pah</u>-say-lay)	Come in!
Siéntese. (see-<u>enn</u>-tay-say)	Sit down.
su (soo)	your, his, her
prefiero (prray-fee-<u>aird</u>-oh)	I prefer
¿prefiere? (prray-fee-<u>airr</u>-ay?)	do you prefer?
soy (soi; *oi* as in *oi*l)	I am
doctor(a) (thoke-<u>torr,</u> thoke-<u>torr</u>-ah)	doctor
enfermero(-a) (en-faird-<u>maird</u>-oh, en-faird-<u>maird</u>-ah)	nurse
Señor, Señora (seh-<u>nyor</u>, seh-<u>nyor</u>-ah)	Mr., Mrs.
señorita (seh-nyor-<u>ee</u>-tah)	Miss (there is no equivalent for Ms.)
¿Cómo está? (<u>koh</u>-moe eh-<u>stah</u>?)	How are you?
Estoy bien, gracias. (eh-<u>stoi</u> bee-<u>en</u>, grrah-see-<u>us</u>)	I am fine, thank you.
¿Y usted? (ee oo-steth?)	And you?
¿Cómo se llama? (<u>koh</u>-moe-say-<u>yah</u>-mah?)	What's your/his/her name?
Me llamo _____. (may <u>yah</u>-moe _____)	My name is _____.
Soy la doctora Ramos. (soi lah thoke-<u>torr</u>-ah <u>rrah</u>-moss)	I am Dr. Ramos.
Soy José, su enfermero. (soi hoe-<u>say</u>, soo en-faird-<u>maird</u>-oh)	I'm José, your nurse.
Mucho gusto. (<u>moo</u>-choh <u>goo</u>-stoh)	Nice to meet you.

---

[2]**Pase** is used in most Spanish-speaking countries; however, in Mexico **Pásele** is often said. Mexicans often attach the word **le** to verbs for no particular reason, for example, **órale, ándale, córrele,** etc. **Le** is in fact an indirect object pronoun, meaning "to you, to him, to her" which you will see in more detail in Chapter 5.

De nada./Por nada. (they nah-the,   You're welcome.
  porr nah-the)
Por favor. (porr fah-bor)   Please.
Gracias. (grrah-see-as)   Thank you.

 DIÁLOGO 1.1 | **Introductions—Greeting your patient**

Now you're ready for your first dialogue. Read it as many times as you feel you need, then listen to it on the recording while reading along simultaneously.

DOCTOR(A)/ENFERMERO(-A)	Buenos días, Señora Gómez. Soy el doctor (la doctora)[3] Pérez. (Soy Bob/Sandra, su enfermero[-a].)
PACIENTE	¡Mucho gusto! *(Both shake hands.)*
DOCTOR(A)/ENFERMERO(-A)	¿Prefiere usted Juana o Señora Gómez?
PACIENTE	Prefiero Juana, por favor.
DOCTOR(A)/ENFERMERO(-A)	Muy bien, Juana. ¡Pásele y siéntese, por favor!
PACIENTE	Gracias, doctor(a). (Gracias, señor[a].)

 1.2 The alphabet

Before moving on, we have to start with the basics of Spanish. One of those helpful necessities is the alphabet (**el alfabeto, el abecedario**).

 PRONUNCIATION

Now listen to the pronunciations on the recording. Pay special attention to the pronunciation of letters that sound alike (*c, s, z*), (*ll, y*), and (*v, b*).

Letter	Pronunciation of letter name	Examples
A	*ah*	(as in *father*) **abdomen, pluma, aspirina**
B	*bay (granday)*	**beber, libro, brazo**
C	*say*	(soft *s* sound) **cerveza, cita, cerebro, cintura**; (hard *k* sound) **cara, corazón, Cuba**

---

[3]Variations, shown in parentheses, do not appear on the recording.

CH	*chay*	mucho, chocolate
D	*they*	diálisis, soda, médico
E	*ay*	qué (like the name *Kay*), vena, enferma
F	*eh-fay*	fácil, familia
G	*hey*	(*h* sound) gente, gis; (hard *g* sound) gas, gotero, gusto
H	*ah-chay*	(*h* is silent) hospital, hora (*ohra*), hola (*ohla*), hielo (*yelo*)
I	*ee*	(like *i* in *machine*) libro, espina, medicina
J	*ho-tah*	(*h* sound) aguja, jeringa, La Jolla, San José
K	*kah*	kilo (borrowed from foreign words)
L	*el-lay*	la, los, líquido
LL	*ell-yay*	(a *y* sound; in some regions *zh*) llamo, silla, costilla
M	*em-may*	mamá, mejilla
N	*en-nay*	no
Ñ	*enn-yay*	(*ny* sound as in *canyon*) mañana, niño, cañón
O	*oh*	(as in *no*) otro, no
P	*p/bey*	(between a *p* and *b* sound) papá, pecho, pestaña
Q	*coo*	(always followed by a silent *u*) que, quien, quijada, bronquios
R	*edd-ay*	(as in *kitty* or *latter*) cara, señora, señorita[4]
RR	*errr-ay*	(initial *r* also trills) Raúl, Rafael, repita, rápido; (*rr*-trill) carro, perro
S	*eh-say*	salud, estómago, saliva
T	*teh* or *deh*	(between a *t* and *d* sound) toma, tijeras
U	*ooh*	(*oo* sound) tu, su, una, pulso, agudo
V	*bay chee-kuh*	veinte, vientre, vacunar, vena, vida
W	*do-blay bay* or *Do-blay oo*	(borrowed from foreign words) kilowatts, Woolworth
X	*eh-kees*	(*h* sound) México; (*ks* sound) extra, excelente
Y	*ee gree-eh-guh*	(as in *youth*) Yuma, yodo, yeso; (*ee* sound) y
Z	*seh-tuh*	(*ss* sound) azul (*assul*), zorro (*ssorro*), lápiz, embarazada

---

[4]In slurred American English, try pronouncing the double *t* in *pretty little kitty, cottage* or the double *d* in *Eddy*. Note the exact spot where the tongue touches the palate. This is the sound needed to pronounce an *r* in Spanish. If you say *cotto* as in cotto salami, you are actually pronouncing *caro* in Spanish.

The most important sounds to remember are the *vowels*:

A (*ahh*)   E (*ehh*)   I (*eee*)   O (*oh*)   U (*oo*)

In Spanish, the vowel sounds are fairly constant. There are no long vowels, short vowels, schwa sounds ("muted" vowels, like *a* in *ago*), or vowel sounds changing in the middle of the word if the word ends in a silent *-e,* as in English. If you can pronounce the Spanish sounds for **a-e-i-o-u**, you can pronounce any Spanish word very easily.

DIPHTHONGS — DIPTONGOS

Diphthongs are combinations of vowels which create different sounds. The following words include two vowels stated rapidly which create one sound.

ua	(*ha*)	Juan	**ia**	(*ya*)	alergia, terapia
ue	(*whey*)	fue	**ie**	(*eeaa*)	diez
uo	(*woa*)	cuota	**io**	(*yo*)	ejercicio

The following words contain two vowels that create two separate vowel sounds, that is, one sound for each vowel.

ai	(*ahee*)	aire	**eu**	(*aaoo*)	Europa
au	(*aoo*)	Paula	**oi**	(*oee*)	estóico
ui	(*wee*)	cuidado			

Cuidado *(Caution)*: Note the difference in pronunciation of the same two vowels (*-ia*) in the following words:

- **farm<u>a</u>cia, art<u>e</u>ria** (*-ia* forms a diphthong at the end of the word; the stress falls on the next to last syllable)
- **disenter<u>í</u>a, vasectom<u>í</u>a, histerectom<u>í</u>a** (the accent places the stress on the *i* and indicates that *-ia* should be pronounced as two separate vowel sounds.)

REGIONAL VARIATIONS

Pronunciation may vary from country to country within the Spanish-speaking world, for example:

- *ll* in Argentina is pronounced as *jh,* as opposed to Mexico (*y*) or Spain (*ly*).
- Some countries skip over syllables or do not pronounce the letter *s* particularly clearly, such as in Cuba, Puerto Rico, and many coastal areas of other countries, where, for example, **peca** and **pesca** are pronounced almost the same (<u>*peh*</u>*-cah*).

- In parts of Spain and the Caribbean countries, the letter *d* is often swallowed or skipped over, for example, in **pegado** (*pegao*) or **cantado** (*cantao*).
- In Puerto Rico an *r* in the middle or at the end of a word is often pronounced as an *l*, for example, with **Puerto** (*Puelto*), **pierna** (*pielna*), **hablar** (*hablal*), **hacer** (*hacel*), while the *rr* or *r* at the beginning of a word is often pronounced as an English *h* sound, for example, with **repita** (*hepita*), **rápido** (*hápido*), **carro** (*caho*), **riñón** (*hiñón*), and so on.

The Spanish vocabulary used in Latin America is basically understood in any of the Spanish-speaking countries. There are, however, some notable variances. For example:

Mexico	El Salvador, Nicaragua, Guatemala	Puerto Rico	English
güero	chele	rubio	*blond*
piernas/patas	piernas/patas/canillas	piernas	*legs*
chamaco/escuincle	cipote/chavalo/patojo	nene/chico	*boy*
estreñido/tapado	estreñido/estítico	constipado/estreñido	*constipated*
excusado/escusado	inodoro	inodoro	*toilet*
estómago/panza	estómago/panza	estómago/pipa	*stomach/belly*
biberón/mamila	pacha	botella/biberón	*baby bottle*
chupón/chupete		bobo	*pacifier, binky*

ACCENT OR STRESS

There are three simple rules to remember.

1. If a word ends in a vowel, *n,* or *s*: stress the next to last syllable.

   mu-cha-cha me-di-ci-na re-ce-tan gra-cias to-ma-mos

2. If a word ends in any consonant except *n* or *s*: stress the last syllable.

   ha-blar re-ce-tar doc-tor en-con-trar pa-pel

3. If a word has an accent mark, stress that syllable (superseding the above rules).

   hí-ga-do cáp-su-la ma-má fá-cil pul-món o-í-do

Notice the difference in pronunciation when the diphthong is accented (**disentería, vasectomía, histerectomía**) and when the diphthong is not accented (**farmacia, arteria, alergia**).

SPELLING

In English, one is constantly faced with various spellings of the same sound (to, too, two) and different pronunciations of the same letter combinations (through, though, thought, tough). However, in Spanish, words are spelled the way they sound, with very few exceptions (especially when compared to English!). Schoolchildren in Latin America are taught to read and spell based on syllables (*ba, be, bi, bo, bu*). The only possible confusion occurs with letters that have virtually the same sound: *b, v: vaso, bazo*; *s, z: casa, caza*; *c, s: censor, sensor*; *ll, y: llega, yegua*; *j, x: tejas, Texas*. Thus, you might hear a Latin American say, for example, **"Vázquez con zeta"** ("Vázquez with a *z*").

If you need help:

¿Cómo se dice...?	How do you say . . . ?
¿Qué quiere decir...?	What does . . . mean?
¡Más despacio, por favor!	Slower, please.
Disculpe, no entiendo.	I'm sorry, I don't understand.
Hablo poco español.	I speak a little Spanish.
Necesito un interprete.	I need an interpreter.
¿Tiene preguntas?	Do you have any questions?

 1.3 Nouns: gender and number

Now that you have become familiar with the alphabet, the next basic point is to learn about masculine and feminine nouns. We'll try to make it as easy and straightforward as possible.

All nouns (persons, places, or things) are either masculine or feminine. There is no method to determine logically to which gender they belong, but most nouns are derived from either Latin or Greek. A general rule of thumb is if the noun (thing) ends in **-a**, it is generally feminine. If the noun ends in **-o** it is generally masculine.

The following are feminine nouns. They often end in **-a** and take the definite article **la**. **La** is the feminine form for the word *the*.

VOCABULARIO | *Singular feminine nouns*

la báscula
(lah <u>bah</u>-scoo-luh)

la jeringa
(lah hair-<u>een</u>-guh)

la aguja
(lah a-<u>goo</u>-huh)

la venda
(lah <u>ven</u>-thuh)

la receta
(lah rre-<u>set</u>-uh)

la medicina
(lah may-thee-
<u>see</u>-nuh)

la cápsula
(lah <u>cahp</u>-soo-luh)

la pastilla
(lah pah-<u>stee</u>-yuh)

la pluma
(lah <u>ploo</u>-muh)

la enfermera
(lah en-fair-<u>mair</u>-uh)

la casa
(lah <u>kah</u>-suh)

la cerveza
(lah serr-<u>vay</u>-suh)

la ventana
(lah ven-<u>taan</u>-uh)

la mesa
(lah <u>may</u>-suh)

la puerta
(lah <u>pwerr</u>-tuh)

la = the (*feminine*)

Generally, feminine nouns (things) end in **-a**.

la mes<u>a</u>	la aguj<u>a</u>

The following nouns are masculine. They often end in **-o** and take the word or definite article **el**. **El** is the masculine form for the word *the.*

VOCABULARIO | Singular masculine nouns

el estetoscopio
(ell ess-tet-oh-<u>skoh</u>-pee-oh)

el otoscopio
(ell oh-toh-<u>skoh</u>-pee-oh)

el depresor
(ell they-press-<u>orr</u>)

el gotero
(ell go-<u>tair</u>-oh)

el microscopio
(ell mee-crow-<u>skoh</u>-pee-oh)

el carro
(ell <u>kah</u>-rroh)

el dinero
(ell thee-<u>nair</u>-oh)

el libro
(ell <u>lee</u>-broh)

el mostrador
(ell moe-struh-<u>thor</u>)

el sombrero
(ell som-<u>brair</u>-oh)

el doctor
(ell thoke-<u>torr</u>)

el martillo
(ell mar-<u>tee</u>-yoh)

el termómetro
(ell tair-<u>moh</u>-meh-troh)

el vaso
(ell <u>bah</u>-so)

el suero
(ell-<u>swear</u>-oh)

---

el = the (*masculine*)

Generally, masculine nouns (things) end in **-o**.

el sombrer<u>o</u>

el termómetr<u>o</u>

CHANGING SINGULAR NOUNS TO THEIR PLURAL FORM

la = "the" feminine *singular*
las = "the" feminine *plural*

Feminine words *generally* end in -**a**.
To form the plural, add -**s**.

la puerta → **las puertas**

 Ejercicio 1A

Change the singular feminine definite article and noun to the plural form, as follows:

EJEMPLO   la mesa → <u>las</u> mes<u>as</u>

1. la casa   → _____ cas_____

2. la pluma   → _____ plum_____

3. la aguja   → _____ aguj_____

4. la bolsa   → _____ bols_____

5. la receta   → _____ recet_____

6. la silla   → _____ sill_____

7. la báscula   → _____ báscul_____

8. la mesa   → _____ mes_____

9. la cerveza   → _____ cervez_____

10. la cápsula → _____ cápsul_____

el = "the" masculine *singular*   **los** = "the" masculine *plural*

Masculine words *generally* end in -**o**. To form the plural, add -**s**.

el helado → **los helados**[5]

---

[5]**el helado** ice cream (**el mantecado** in the Caribbean)

Ejercicio 1B

Change the singular masculine definite article and noun to the plural form, as follows:

EJEMPLO   el sombrero → <u>los</u> sombrer<u>os</u>

1. el carro   →   _____ carr_____

2. el palo   →   _____ pal_____

3. el piso   →   _____ pis_____

4. el vaso   →   _____ vas_____

5. el libro   →   _____ libr_____

6. el termómetro   →   _____ termómetr_____

7. el helado   →   _____ helad_____

8. el gotero   →   _____ goter_____

If a noun ends in -**e**, add -**s** to form the plural.

la pirámide[6] → **las pirámides**

 Ejercicio 1C

Change these singular nouns ending in -**e** to the plural form, as follows:

EJEMPLOS   la madre → <u>las</u> madre<u>s</u>
            el padre → <u>los</u> padre<u>s</u>

1. la base[7]   →   _____ base_____

2. la calle   →   _____ calle_____

3. el nombre   →   _____ nombre_____

4. el trámite[8]   →   _____ trámite_____

---

[6]**la pirámide** the pyramid
[7]**la base** the base
[8]**el trámite** paperwork, red tape

If a noun ends in a consonant, add **-es** to form the plural.

la irritación → **las irritaciones**[9]

 Ejercicio 1D

Change the following nouns and definite articles to the plural form:

EJEMPLOS el corazón[10] → <u>los</u> corazo<u>nes</u>
el riñón[11] → <u>los</u> riño<u>nes</u>

1. la inyección → _____ inyeccion_____

2. el pulmón[12] → _____ pulmon_____

3. la infección → _____ infeccion_____

4. el tamal → _____ tamal_____

5. el frijol[13] → _____ frijol_____

6. la mujer[14] → _____ mujer_____

Indefinite articles also change to agree with nouns in number (singular or plural) and gender (feminine or masculine).

Singular	Plural
una = a, an, one (f.)	**unas** = some (f.)
un = a, an, one (m.)	**unos** = some (m.)

una silla → **unas sillas**
un vaso → **unos vasos**

---

[9]Nouns ending in a consonant that are accented in the singular, such as **corazón**, **riñón**, **pulmón**, and **infección**, lose the diacritical (accent) mark when the plural **-es** ending is added.
[10]**el corazón** heart
[11]**el riñón** kidney
[12]**el pulmón** lung
[13]**el frijol** bean
[14]**la mujer** woman

Ejercicio 1E

Change the following indefinite articles and nouns to the plural form:

EJEMPLOS   una aguja   → <u>unas</u> aguja<u>s</u>
            un termómetro → <u>unos</u> termómetro<u>s</u>

1. una inyección   →   _____ inyeccion_____

2. un papel   →   _____ papel_____

3. una infección   →   _____ infeccion_____

4. una clínica   →   _____ clínica_____

5. un suero   →   _____ suero_____

6. un termómetro →   _____ termómetro_____

Now, repeat exercises 1A–1D by substituting the indefinite article for the definite article; that is, change the singular noun with **una** or **un** to the plural form with **unas** or **unos**.

 1.4 **Parts of the body**

¡Muy bien! Now you're ready to forge ahead. First let's look at the body. For some strange reason, the medical profession likes to learn the name of the body parts, so the following should satisfy that need!

Notes:

- **Oreja** is the outer ear; **oído** is the inner ear. In Mexico, **oreja** is often used only to refer to animal ears.
- In Mexico, **nalgas** is often considered to be a vulgar or street term; the use of **pompis** or **glúteo** is therefore recommended for "buttocks." In the Caribbean, **nalgas** (softened to **nalguitas**) is more acceptable than in Mexico; however, in Central America and South America **el glúteo** or **la cadera** (hip) seem to be the most accepted or, at least, most euphemistic forms.

[🔊] **Las partes del cuerpo**
Vista anterior (front view)

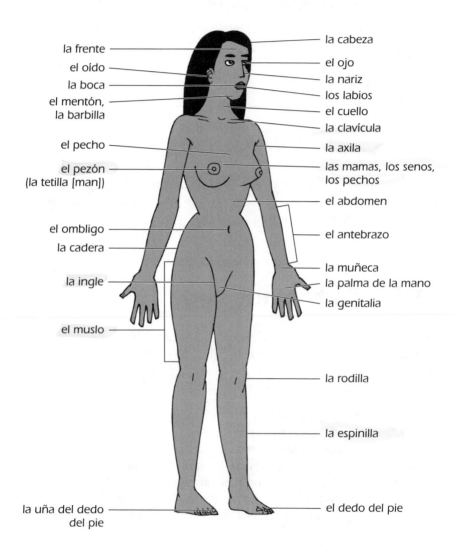

la frente
el oído
la boca
el mentón,
la barbilla

el pecho

el pezón
(la tetilla [man])

el ombligo
la cadera

la ingle

el muslo

la uña del dedo
del pie

la cabeza
el ojo
la nariz
los labios
el cuello
la clavícula

la axila

las mamas, los senos,
los pechos

el abdomen

el antebrazo

la muñeca
la palma de la mano
la genitalia

la rodilla

la espinilla

el dedo del pie

Vista posterior (rear view)

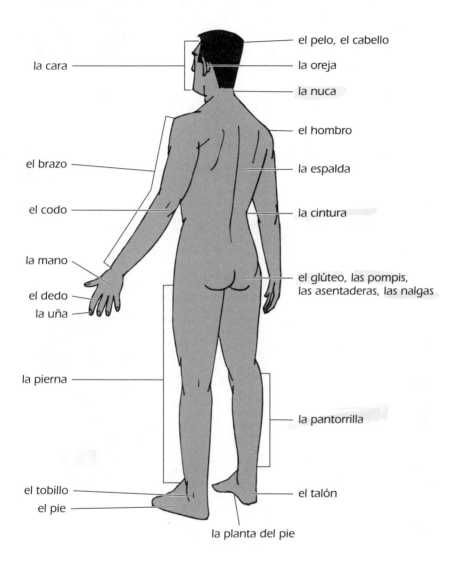

la cara

el brazo

el codo

la mano

el dedo

la uña

la pierna

el tobillo

el pie

el pelo, el cabello

la oreja

la nuca

el hombro

la espalda

la cintura

el glúteo, las pompis,
las asentaderas, las nalgas

la pantorrilla

el talón

la planta del pie

1.5 "What is this?"

Your Spanish-speaking patients will generally be quite impressed with the fact that you speak or are learning their language. Therefore, you may wish to enlist their aid in broadening your knowledge. A good way to do so is to point to something and ask, with a smile and a questioning look, **¿Qué es esto?**

¿Qué es esto?	What is this?
¿Qué es?	What is it? ("It" is understood.)
¿Qué?	What?
es	is, it is
esto	this

✏️ **Ejercicio 1F**

Fill in the blanks with the correct words.

1. ¿Qué es esto?

   Es una _____.

2. ¿Qué es esto?

   Es _____ _____.

3. ¿_____ es esto?

   _____ _____ _____.

4. ¿Qué es _____?

   _____ _____ _____.

5. ¿_____ _____ esto?

   _____ _____ _____.

6. ¿Qué _____ _____?

   _____ _____ _____.

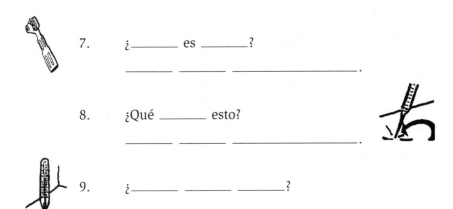

7.   ¿_____ es _____?

     _____ _____ _____.

8.   ¿Qué _____ esto?

     _____ _____ _____.

9.   ¿_____ _____ _____?

     _____ _____ _____.

✏ Ejercicio 1G

¿Qué es esto? "What is this?" Match the Spanish answers with the appropriate picture number.

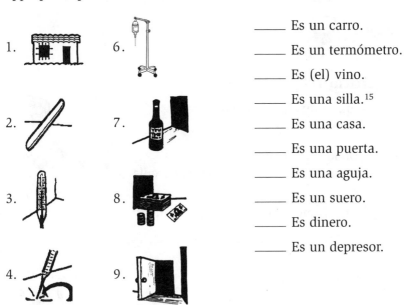

_____ Es un carro.

_____ Es un termómetro.

_____ Es (el) vino.

_____ Es una silla.[15]

_____ Es una casa.

_____ Es una puerta.

_____ Es una aguja.

_____ Es un suero.

_____ Es dinero.

_____ Es un depresor.

---

[15]**la silla** chair

1.6   "Where is . . . ?"

Now that you have mastered the names of the body parts, you will understand your patients' answers when you ask "Where is the pain?" First, however, let's warm up with a few general questions using *where*.

¿Dónde está el vaso?	Where is the glass?
¿Dónde?	Where?
está	is (*used with location*)
en	in *or* on
por	by, over, near
derecho	straight ahead

el vaso grande

el vaso chico

 Ejercicio 1H

Answer the questions in complete sentences.

EJEMPLO   ¿Dónde está el vaso?
El vaso está en la mesa, por la báscula.

 1. ¿Dónde está el sombrero grande?

El _____.

2. ¿Dónde está el vaso chico?

El _____.

3. ¿Dónde está el libro?

El _____.

4. ¿Dónde está el termómetro grande?

El _____.

5. ¿Dónde está la pluma? (*el piso* = *floor*)

La _____ .

6. ¿Dónde está el baño? (*straight ahead*)

El _____ .

1.7 "What do you need?"

¿Qué necesita? — What <u>do you</u> need?
You may not necessarily ask your patient this question, but it's a good way to start learning some regular -**ar** verbs in a simple and somewhat painless manner.

Necesit**o** un termómetro, por favor.	I need a thermometer, please.
Necesit**o** una inyección, por favor.	I need a shot, please.
Necesit**o**	I need
Necesit**a**	You need
¿Necesit**a**?	Do you need?
¿Qué necesit**a**?	What do you need?

Please note **(Observe, por favor [¡Favor de observar!]):**
Necesit<u>o</u> and **necesit<u>a</u>** come from an infinitive verb, **necesit<u>ar</u>** ("to need"). All you need to do is drop the -**ar** ending. Simply add -**o** to say "I need," or add -**a** to say "You need." You can do this with all regular -**ar** verbs in the present tense, which will be explained in more detail in Chapter 3. This is called conjugating.

For healthcare professionals, the most important conjugations are those that end in -**o**, implying "I," or -**a**, implying "you" (for your patient).

Another exciting and simple aspect of the Spanish language is that there are essentially *no auxiliary verbs*, such as "do," "does," "did," etc., as there are in English. For example, to say "Do you need . . . ?", you merely say **¿Necesit<u>a</u>?** in an inquiring tone, which literally means, "Need?" (both the words *do* and *you* are understood).

To say, "¿What do you need?", you simply say **¿Qué necesit<u>a</u>?** or, literally, "What need?" (*you* is understood from the -**a** ending).

To say "¿What do I need?", you simply need to say **¿Qué necesit<u>o</u>?** or, literally, "What need?" (The word *I* is understood from the -**o** ending.)

Ejercicio 11

Answer according to the picture.

EJEMPLO ¿Qué necesita?
  Necesito un vaso chico, por favor.

1. ¿Qué necesita?

  (grande) _____

2. ¿Qué necesita?

  (grande) _____

3. ¿Qué necesita?

  (chico) _____

4. ¿Qué necesita?

  (grande) _____

5. ¿Qué necesita?

  (chica) _____

6. ¿Qué necesito, doctor?

  _____

1.8   **Chief complaint**

After greeting the patient, you often need to ascertain the chief complaint by asking "What seems to be the problem?" or "What brings you here today?"

¿Qué <u>molestias</u> tiene?	What seems to be the problem?, What brings you here today? (literally, What <u>discomforts</u> do you have?)
Me duele. (*singular*)	It hurts me.
Me duele el brazo.	My arm hurts. (*lit.*, The arm is painful to me.)
Me duele la pierna.	My leg hurts. (*lit.*, The leg is painful to me.)
¿Le duele?	Does it hurt you? (*lit.*, Is it painful to you?)
¿Qué le duele?	What hurts you? (*lit.*, What is painful to you?)
¿Dónde le duele?	Where does it hurt? (*lit.*, Where is it painful to you?)

All the questions—**¿Qué molestias tiene?**,[16] **¿Qué le duele?**, and **¿Dónde le duele?**—are commonly asked. **¿Qué molestias tiene?**, however, can refer to pain as well as other problems, such as nervousness, anxiety, insomnia, depression, and so on. The other two questions can only refer to a physical pain. Thus, by inquiring, **¿Qué molestias tiene?**, you are not restricting your patients' answers.

In Spanish, note that it is grammatically correct to use **el**, **la**, **los**, or **las** (the definite articles) with body parts, as opposed to using possessive adjectives **mi(s)** ("my") or **su(s)** ("your"), which are considered to be redundant. However, if you find it easier to use "su(s)," you will certainly be understood.

---

[16]**¿Qué molestias tiene?** = **¿Qué problemas médicos tiene?** = What medical problems do you have? **¿Cómo se siente hoy?** = How are you feeling today? These questions may be used interchangeably.

✎ Ejercicio 1J

Answer the question. (*¡Favor de contestar!*)

1. ¿Qué molestias tiene? (*arm*)

   Me duele _____ _____.

2. ¿Qué le duele? (*eye*)

   Me duele _____ _____.

3. ¿Dónde le duele? (*head*)

   Me duele _____ _____.

4. ¿Qué molestias tiene? (*ear*)

   Me duele _____ _____.

5. ¿Qué le duele? (*back*)

   Me duele _____ _____.

6. ¿Dónde le duele? (*foot*)

   Me duele _____ _____.

7. ¿Qué molestias tiene? (*leg*)

   Me duele _____ _____.

8. ¿Qué le duele? (*ankle*)

   Me duele _____ _____.

9. ¿Dónde le duele? (*knee*)

   Me duele _____ _____.

10. ¿Qué molestias tiene? (*stomach*)

    Me duele _____ _____.

!

¡Observe, por favor!

Me duel**en los** brazo**s**.	My arms hurt.
	(*lit.*, The arms **are** painful to me.)
Me duel**en las** pierna**s**.	My legs hurt.
	(*lit.*, The legs **are** painful to me.)

Ejercicio 1K

Use the English clues in parentheses to answer the questions. (*¡Use las pistas en inglés para contestar las preguntas.*)

1. ¿Qué molestias tiene? (*eyes*)

   Me duelen _____ _____.

2. ¿Qué le duele? (*legs*)   Me duelen _____ _____.

3. ¿Dónde le duele? (*arms*)

   Me duelen _____ _____.

4. ¿Qué molestias tiene? (*ears*)

   Me duelen _____ _____.

5. ¿Qué le duele? (*hands*)

   Me duelen _____ _____.

6. ¿Dónde le duele? (*ankles*)

   Me duelen _____ _____.

7. ¿Qué molestias tiene? (*feet*)

   Me duelen _____ _____.

8. ¿Qué le duele? (*fingers*)

   Me duelen _____ _____.

9. ¿Dónde le duele? (*knees*)

   Me duelen _____ _____.

10. ¿Qué molestias tiene? (*hips*)

    Me duelen _____ _____.

VOCABULARIO

¿Qué molestias tiene?	What seems to be bothering you?
¿Cómo se siente?	How do you feel?
¿Dónde le duele?	Where does it hurt (you)? (*lit.*, Where is it painful to you?)
Aquí/Acá.	Here.
¿Qué le duele?	What hurts you? (*lit.*, What is painful to you?)
¿Cómo sigue?	(*after first visit*) How are you coming along? How is it/he/she (are you) progressing?

DIÁLOGO 1.8 | Beginning a patient interview

This dialogue builds on the situation in Diálogo 1.1.

DOCTOR(A)/ENFERMERO(-A)	Buenos días, Señor(a) Gómez. Soy el doctor (la doctora) Pérez. (Soy Bob/Sandra, su enfermero[-a].)
PACIENTE	¡Mucho gusto! *(Both shake hands.)*
DOCTOR(A)/ENFERMERO(-A)	¿Prefiere usted Juana o Señora Gómez?
PACIENTE	Prefiero Juana, por favor.
DOCTOR(A)/ENFERMERO(-A)	Muy bien, Juana. ¡Pásele y siéntese, por favor!
PACIENTE	Gracias, doctor(a). (Gracias, señor[a].)
DOCTOR(A)/ENFERMERO(-A)	¿Qué molestias tiene? ¿Cómo se siente?
PACIENTE	¡Ay, doctor(a) (señor[a]), me duele la cabeza y me duelen los ojos.
DOCTOR(A)/ENFERMERO(-A)	¿Dónde le duele la cabeza? ¿Qué parte?
PACIENTE	Aquí, doctor(a) (señor[a]).

To end a patient interview:

¡Qué le vaya bien!	May it go well for you. (loosely)
Hasta una semana.	Until one week.
Nos vemos en una semana.	We'll see you in one week.
Cuídese mucho Señor(a) Gomez.	Take good care of yourself, Mr. (Mrs.) Gomez.

To reassure patients:

No se preocupe	Don't worry.

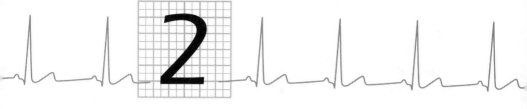

What you will learn in this lesson:

- to count from 1 to 499
- dialogues: taking vital signs, basic discussion of chief complaints, prescription/diet or follow-up instructions, what to do, and how often, if lab tests are needed and when
- to say words related to liquids (to be used with the verb **tomar** "to take/to drink")
- the names of internal organs and parts of the reproductive system
- medical cognates

The goal of this lesson is to be able to take vital signs in Spanish, have a basic discussion of chief complaints, prescription, diet, and follow-up instructions, what should be done, how often it should be done as well as if and when lab tests are required. The goal is also to learn medical cognates and internal body parts, and to be able to recognize some common slang or vulgar terms for body parts that less educated patients might use during their medical interview.

Numbers

It's probably time for a slight respite from all the seriousness here, so we'll break up the monotony with some breathtaking numbers. Just imagine the tools you will now have available to convey information to your patients concerning weight, blood pressure, cholesterol levels, lab results, statistics, and more.

LET'S COUNT! — ¡VAMOS A CONTAR!

1	uno	13	trece	25	veinte y cinco
2	dos	14	catorce	26	veinte y seis
3	tres	15	quince	27	veinte y siete
4	cuatro	16	diez y seis[1]	28	veinte y ocho
5	cinco	17	diez y siete	29	veinte y nueve
6	seis	18	diez y ocho	30	treinta
7	siete	19	diez y nueve	40	cuarenta
8	ocho	20	veinte	50	cincuenta
9	nueve	21	veinte y uno[2]	60	sesenta
10	diez	22	veinte y dos	70	setenta
11	once	23	veinte y tres	80	ochenta
12	doce	24	veinte y cuatro	90	noventa

100	cien; *use* ciento *when 100 is followed by another number, for example*:
110	ciento diez
115	ciento quince
116	ciento diez y seis
120	ciento veinte
131	ciento treinta y uno, etc.

200	doscientos(-as)
300	trescientos(-as)
400	cuatrocientos(-as)
415	cuatrocientos quince
416	cuatrocientos diez y seis
499	cuatrocientos noventa y nueve

 Ejercicio 2A

Write the following numbers in Spanish. *(Favor de escribir los siguientes números en español.)*

1. 15 _____

---

[1]**diez y seis** is also spelled as **dieciséis**, **diez y siete** as **diecisiete**, etc. The form shown here is easier to learn.

[2]**veinte y uno** is also spelled as **veintiuno**, **veinte y dos** as **veintidós**, etc.

2. 28 _____

3. 119 _____

4. 256 _____

5. 374 _____

6. 473 _____

 ## **2.2** **Vital signs**

For preliminaries, the patient is usually weighed and then brought into the **consultorio**, where blood pressure, temperature, and pulse are taken. The following vocabulary should help you conduct such procedures in Spanish. Using almost the same vocabulary as before (with the inclusion of numbers), together with the same sentence structures, you will be able to take the vital signs.

 ### VOCABULARIO | **Taking vital signs**

la enfermera	nurse	**la presión baja**	low blood pressure
primer/primero(-a)	first		
toma	takes	**su (la) temperatura**	your temperature
el peso	weight; a coin		
hoy	today	**también**	also, too
segundo(-a)	second	**muy bien**	very good
tercero(-a)	third	**ahora**	now
¡Favor de subirse!	Please get on!	**bueno(-a)**	good
la báscula	scale	**sobre**	over
Necesito pesarle.	I need to weigh you.	**¡Favor de abrir!**	Please open!
		Ahorita viene[3]	The doctor will
la presión arterial	blood pressure	**la doctora.**	be right here.
el pulso rápido	rapid pulse	**su pulso**	your pulse
lento	slow	**punto**	point
irregular	irregular	**un momento**	a moment, just
la presión alta	high blood pressure		a moment, in a moment

---

[3]**viene** comes (The present tense can be used for near future situations.)

DIÁLOGO 2.2 | **Taking vital signs**

The nurse weighs the patient, checks her blood pressure and pulse, and takes her temperature. *(El enfermero toma el peso, la presión arterial, el pulso y la temperatura.)*

ENFERMERO(-A)	Buenos días, Señora Gómez. Soy Bob (Sandra), su enfermero(-a).
PACIENTE	¡Mucho gusto! *(Both shake hands.)*
ENFERMERO(-A)	¿Prefiere Ud. Juana o Señora Gómez?
PACIENTE	Prefiero Juana, por favor.
ENFERMERO(-A)	Muy bien, Juana. ¡Pase y siéntese, por favor!
PACIENTE	Gracias, señor(a).
ENFERMERO(-A)	¿Es su primera visita?
PACIENTE	No, es la segunda (tercera, etc.).
ENFERMERO(-A)	¡Ah, bueno! Favor de subirse en la báscula. (Súbase en la báscula, por favor.) Necesito pesarle. Muy bien. Usted pesa cincuenta kilos.
PACIENTE	¡Ay, no! ¡Peso mucho!
ENFERMERO(-A)	No, no es mucho. También, necesito tomar su presión arterial—su (el) brazo, por favor.
PACIENTE	Bueno, aquí está.
ENFERMERO(-A)	Muy bien. Es ciento sesenta sobre cien (160/100).
PACIENTE	¿Está bien?
ENFERMERO(-A)	Está un poco alta y ahora el (su) pulso... Bueno es setenta y dos (72). Favor de abrir la boca. (Abra la boca, por favor.) Necesito tomar la temperatura.
PACIENTE	Bueno, señor(a).
ENFERMERO(-A)	Es noventa y ocho punto seis grados (98.6°).
PACIENTE	¿Es normal?
ENFERMERO(-A)	Sí, Juana, está bien, también. Muchas gracias. Un momento y ahorita[4] viene la doctora.

 Ejercicio 2B

Answer the questions based on the preceding dialogue. *(Favor de responder a las preguntas según el diálogo anterior.)*

1. ¿Es la primera visita de la señora Gómez? _____

2. ¿Qué prefiere la paciente—Juana o la señora Gómez?

_____

---

[4]**Ahorita** = right away and **ahora** = now in Mexico. In Puerto Rico and Cuba **ahorita** = now and **ahora** = right now. It is the opposite.

3. ¿Cuánto pesa la señora Gómez? _____

4. ¿Cuál es la presión arterial de Juana Gómez? _____

5. ¿Es normal el pulso y es normal la temperatura de la paciente?

_____

2.3 Question words, relative pronouns, prepositions, and other words

These tiny, seemingly insignificant words serve as a link to forming complete sentences and, equally important, complete questions. And of course, you will need to ask your patients a great many questions.

VOCABULARIO

¿Qué?	What?	**la primera vez/**	the first time/
¿Quién?	Who?	**la última vez**	the last time
¿Dónde?	Where?	**de**	of, from
¿Cuándo?	When?	**a**	to, at
¿Cada cuándo?	How often?	**sin**	without
¿Cuánto(-a)?	How much?	**en**	in, on
¿Cuántos(-as)?	How many?	**para**	for, in order to
¿Cuántas veces?	How many times?	**por**	by, for, through
¿Cómo?	How?	**al día, por día**	per day
¿Cuál?	Which?	**sí**	yes
¿Por qué?	Why?	**si**	if
porque	because	**siempre**	always
¿Hay?	Is there?, Are there?	**nunca**	never
hay	there is, there are	**y**	and
es	is, it is	**o**	or
son	are, they are		

 Ejercicio 2C

Provide answers to the following questions in complete sentences. *(Favor de contestar con frases completas.)*

1. ¿Qué necesita el paciente—una receta o una báscula?

_____

2. ¿Dónde necesito la inyección, doctor, en el brazo o en el dedo?

_____

3. ¿Por qué necesito una receta, doctora? ¿Es porque necesito antibióticos? Sí, _____

4. ¿Cuándo (Cada cuándo) necesito una inyección? _____

   _____

5. ¿Cuántas veces al día (por día) necesito tomar[5] la medicina—tres o
   cuatro veces por día? _____

   _____

6. ¿Cómo necesito tomar la medicina, doctora—en pastillas o cápsulas? _____

7. ¿Cuál prefiere usted—tomar tabletas o cápsulas? _____

   _____

8. ¿Toma usted las pastillas con agua o con cerveza? _____

   _____

LIQUIDS AND SOLIDS

el té	el café	el agua[6]	la leche

la aspirina;   la sopa   el hielo   el helado (Mex. and
el Tylenol™   Central America),
                                           el mantecado (Puerto
                                           Rico, Cuba, Caribbean)[7]

---

[5]**tomar** to take (medicine, measurements, etc.); to drink (water, etc.)

[6]Even though **agua** takes a masculine direct article, the word is feminine. Because the stress is on the first syllable, saying **la agua** is very awkward, so the masculine article is used. Adjectives will match the gender: **el agua fría** the cold water.

[7]For sno-cone, use **el raspado** (Mex.) or **el piragua** (P.R. and Caribbean).

Ejercicio 2D

Write questions in Spanish using the following words. *(Favor de escribir unas preguntas con esas palabras.)*

1. What?   ¿_____?

2. When?   ¿_____?

3. Where?   ¿_____?

4. How much?   ¿_____?

5. How often?   ¿_____?

6. How many?   ¿_____?

7. Which?   ¿_____?

8. Why?   ¿_____?

 Internal organs

INTERNAL ORGANS — **LOS ÓRGANOS INTERNOS**

Now that we have become somewhat familiar with the names of the body parts, it can't hurt to move onward or inward, so to speak, to learn the names of the internal organs and the parts of the reproductive system in Spanish.

Internal organs
Los órganos internos

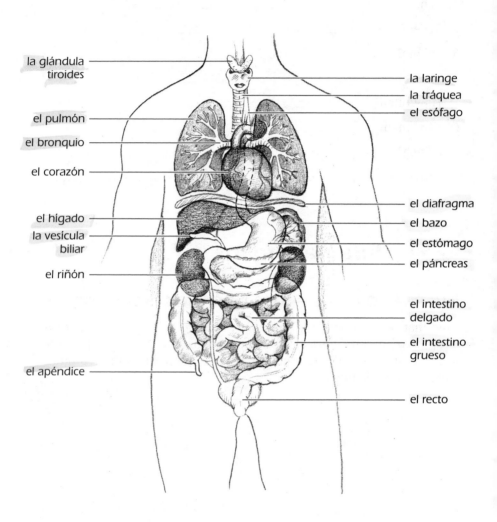

la glándula tiroides

la laringe
la tráquea
el esófago

el pulmón

el bronquio

el corazón

el diafragma
el bazo

el hígado
la vesícula biliar

el estómago
el páncreas

el riñón

el intestino delgado

el intestino grueso

el apéndice

el recto

Male reproductive system
El sistema reproductor (reproductivo) masculino

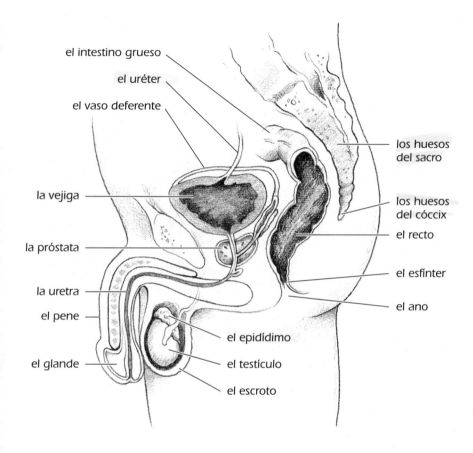

el intestino grueso

el uréter

el vaso deferente

los huesos
del sacro

la vejiga

los huesos
del cóccix

el recto

la próstata

el esfínter

la uretra

el ano

el pene

el epidídimo

el glande

el testículo

el escroto

Female reproductive system
El sistema reproductor (reproductivo) femenino

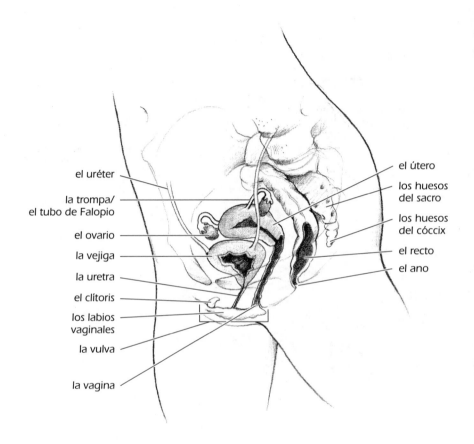

el uréter

la trompa/
el tubo de Falopio

el ovario

la vejiga

la uretra

el clítoris

los labios
vaginales

la vulva

la vagina

el útero

los huesos
del sacro

los huesos
del cóccix

el recto

el ano

The head
La cabeza

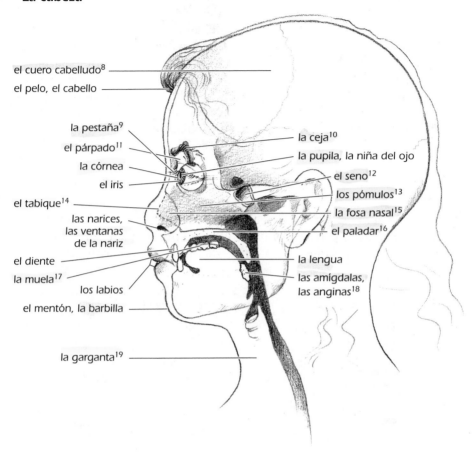

el cuero cabelludo[8]

el pelo, el cabello

la pestaña[9]

el párpado[11]

la córnea

el iris

el tabique[14]

las narices,
las ventanas
de la nariz

el diente

la muela[17]

los labios

el mentón, la barbilla

la garganta[19]

la ceja[10]

la pupila, la niña del ojo

el seno[12]

los pómulos[13]

la fosa nasal[15]

el paladar[16]

la lengua

las amígdalas,
las anginas[18]

Other body parts — **Otras partes del cuerpo**

la piel	skin	**el esqueleto**	skeleton
el vello	body hair	**el cráneo**	cranium
el hueso	bone	**los tejidos**	tissues
la costilla	rib	**la articulación**	joint

---

[8]scalp   [9]eyelash   [10]eyebrow   [11]eyelid

[12]**seno** also means "breast." When referring to the sinuses, a patient will often say **Tengo sinusitis** "I have sinusitis."

[13]cheekbone   [14]nasal septum   [15]nasal cavity   [16]palate

[17]tooth, molar   [18]tonsils   [19]throat

la coyuntura	joint	el prepucio	foreskin
el nervio	nerve	el quiste	cyst
la arteria	artery	el nódulo, la bolita,	nodule, lump
la vena	vein	el bulto	
el vaso	vessel	la torcedura	twist, sprain
el vaso sanguíneo	blood vessel	el desgarre	torn ligament,
los ligamentos	ligaments		pulled muscle
el ombligo	belly button,	el lunar	mole
	umbilicus	la mancha de	birthmark
el cordón umbilical	umbilical cord	nacimiento	
la pelvis	pelvis	la estría	stretch mark

Slang terms

Here are some slang terms that your patients may be accustomed to using. However, you should first try to use the standard form yourself when speaking. If they do not understand, then you may try the slang form.

Slang term	Standard Spanish	English
el pescuezo (animal)	el cuello	neck
el sobaco (vulgar)	la axila	armpit
la barriga, la panza	el estómago	stomach
la pata (animal/furniture)	la pierna, el pie	leg, foot
el cuadril (animal haunch)	la cadera	hip
las chiches, las tetas	los senos	breasts
el pellejo	el prepucio	foreskin

2.5 Cognates

Let's now look at cognates, which are a tremendous ally for any healthcare professional who is learning Spanish. If you will recall, cognates are words that are very similar in two languages, often because they come from the same origin (for example, Latin or Greek). The following cognates are grouped by endings, and once you master the corresponding English and Spanish ending changes to the main root word (which is almost always the same in both languages), you'll be astonished at how many Spanish medical terms you readily recognize.

FORMATION OF SPANISH WORDS
AND THEIR ENGLISH EQUIVALENTS

-tion	**-ción** (f.) These are always feminine in Spanish.		
hallucination	**la alucinación**	constipation	**la constipación**[20]
recuperation	**la recuperación**		**(el estreñimiento)**
sterilization	**la esterilización**	contusion	**la contusión**
laceration	**la laceración**		**(el golpe)**
contraception	**la contracepción**	exception	**la excepción**
indication	**la indicación**	secretion	**la secreción**
relaxation	**la relajación**	irritation	**la irritación**
	(el descanso)	inflammation	**la inflamación**
complication	**la complicación**	immunization	**la inmunización**
dislocation	**la dislocación**		**(la vacuna)**

Exception:
abortion   **el aborto**

-ity	**-(i)dad/-tad** (f.) These are also always feminine.		
sexuality	**la sexualidad**	university	**la universidad**
difficulty	**la dificultad**	identity	**la identidad**
city	**la ciudad**	anxiety	**la ansiedad**
casualty	**la casualidad**[21]	senility	**la senilidad**
mortality	**la mortalidad**	maternity	**la maternidad**

-ce	**-cia/-cio**		
importance	**la importancia**	impotence	**la impotencia**
incontinence	**la incontinencia**	edifice/building	**el edificio**
convalescence	**la convalecencia**	insistence	**la insistencia**
service	**el servicio**		

-ous	**-oso/-osa**		
generous	**generoso(-a)**[22]	nervous	**nervioso(-a)**
cautious	**cauteloso(-a)**	cancerous	**canceroso(-a)**
contagious	**contagioso(-a)**	infectious	**infeccioso(-a)**
poisonous	**ponzoñoso(-a)**		

Exception:
serious   **serio(-a)**

---

[20]**Constipación** is actually a false cognate as it usually means the same as **congestión** (nasally congested). **El estreñimiento** is the standard word for "constipation."

[21]Casualty is more likely to be expressed as **víctima** or **accidentado**. **Casualidad** usually means "coincidence" or "chance."

[22]When referring to a masculine person or thing, the descriptive word will end in **-o**; when referring to a feminine person or thing, the word will end in **-a**.

-ology	-ología (f.)		
immunology	la inmunología	ophthalmology	la oftalmología
biology	la biología	cytology	la citología
hematology	la hematología	dermatology	la dermatología
radiology	la radiología	audiology	la audiología
neurology	la neurología	gynecology	la ginecología
cardiology	la cardiología	pathology	la patología
urology	la urología	bacteriology	la bacteriología

-y	-ia/-io		
dysentery	la disentería	family	la familia
laboratory	el laboratorio	allergy	la alergia
directory	el directorio	epilepsy	la epilepsia
pharmacy	la farmacia	therapy	la terapia
emergency	la emergencia	insufficiency	la insuficiencia
surgery	la cirugía		

Note: When no accent mark is present, **-ia** is a diphthong, forming one syllable; the penultimate syllable is then stressed.

-ical	-ico/-ica		
physical	físico(-a)	obstetrical	obstétrico(-a)
biological	biológico(-a)	political	político(-a)
medical	médico(-a)	physiological	fisiológico(-a)

-tic	-tico/-tica		
neurotic	neurótico(-a)	psychotic	(p)sicótico(-a)
narcotic	narcótico(-a)	spastic	espástico(-a)

-itis	-itis (f.) These words are always feminine.		
arthritis	la artritis	encephalitis	la encefalitis
laryngitis	la laringitis	hepatitis	la hepatitis
bursitis	la bursitis	dermatitis	la dermatitis
conjunctivitis	la conjuntivitis	peritonitis	la peritonitis
colitis	la colitis		

-scope	-scopio (m.)		
stethoscope	el estetoscopio	microscope	el microscopio
otoscope	el otoscopio	fetoscope	el fetoscopio

-ometer	**-ómetro** (m.)
thermometer	**el termómetro**

-ologist	**-ólogo/-óloga**		
pathologist	**patólogo(-a)**	histologist	**histólogo(-a)**
neurologist	**neurólogo(-a)**	bacteriologist	**bacteriólogo(-a)**
ophthalmologist	**oftalmólogo(-a)**	cardiologist	**cardiólogo(-a)**
biologist	**biólogo(-a)**	dermatologist	**dermatólogo(-a)**
cytologist	**citólogo(-a)**	hematologist	**hematólogo(-a)**
embryologist	**embriólogo(-a)**	urologist	**urólogo(-a)**
gynecologist	**ginecólogo(-a)**	pharmacologist	**farmacólogo(-a)**

Note: An -**o** ending generally refers to a male, while an -**a** ending generally refers to a female. If a word ends in "ma," it is often masculine due to its origin from Greek roots, for example el **sistema**, el **diafragma**, el **problema**, el **programa**.

As you can see, many cognates are recognizable by their endings. Other cognates are distinguishable by their initial sounds or different spellings of similar sounds. Notice the similarities in the following groups of cognates.

s + consonant	**es-**		
special	**especial**	spirit	**espíritu**
spasm	**espasmo**	schizophrenic	**esquizofrénico(-a)**
spastic	**espástico(-a)**	scurvy	**escorbuto(-a)**
spasmodic	**espasmódico(-a)**	structure	**estructura**
stomach	**estómago**	Spanish	**español**

-ph-	**-f-**		
telephone	**el teléfono**	phosphorous	**el fósforo**
pharmacy	**la farmacia**	pharyngitis	**la faringitis**

-y-	**-i-**		
dysentery	**la disentería**	hypochondria	**la hipocondría**
hymen	**el himen**	myopia	**la miopía**
hypertension	**la hipertensión**	psychotic	**(p)sicótico(-a)**
hysteria	**la histeria**	psychologist	**(p)sicólogo(-a)**

When you are unsure of the Spanish for a medical word that consists of three or more syllables, you can always go out on a limb and just add an -**o** or an -**a** to the end of the English word. It often works, though not always. However, it's certainly worth a try!

2.6 **Giving instructions**

 VOCABULARIO | **Chief complaints**

After the preliminary examination of vital signs, the doctor will interview the patient, ask what the chief complaint is, and after having reviewed the results of the vital signs examination, will give some instructions.

¿cuando?	when?	**la primera vez**	the first time
vez	time[23] (*in a sequence*)	**la última vez**	the last time
		al día, por día	per day
veces	times	**hacer**	to make, to do
a ver...	let's see . . .	**una muestra**	a sample
no es ni... ni	it's neither . . . nor	**necesita tomar**	you/she/he need(s) to take
técnico(-a)	lab tech(nician)		
la orina	urine	**la sangre**	blood
otro(-a)	other, another	**la recepcionista**	receptionist
para mañana	for tomorrow	**una cita**	an appointment
¿Cada cuándo?	How often?		

 DIÁLOGO 2.6 | **Chief complaints**

DOCTOR(A) ¿Qué molestias tiene? ¿Cómo se siente?

PACIENTE ¡Ay, doctor(a), me duele la cabeza y me duelen los ojos!

DOCTOR(A) ¿Dónde le duele? ¿Qué parte de la cabeza?

PACIENTE Aquí, doctor(a). ¿Qué necesito?

DOCTOR(A) Bueno, a ver.... su presión arterial es un poco alta. Su temperatura es normal y su pulso también. No es ni rápido ni lento. Por el momento, Juana, usted necesita tomar dos aspirinas (Tylenol) para el dolor de cabeza.

PACIENTE ¿Cada cuándo? (¿Cuándo?)

DOCTOR(A) Necesita tomar dos aspirinas (Tylenol), cuatro veces al día. También, el técnico (la técnica) necesita tomar una muestra de su orina y de la sangre.

PACIENTE Bueno, doctor(a), y ¿cuándo necesita usted las muestras?

DOCTOR(A) Primero, Juana, usted necesita hacer una cita con la recepcionista para mañana.

PACIENTE Muy bien, gracias, doctor(a).

---

[23]**vez** time (*singular*), **veces** (*plural; the z changes to c*)

Ejercicio 2E

Answer the questions based on the preceding dialogue. *(Favor de responder a las preguntas basado en el diálogo anterior.)*

1. ¿Qué molestias tiene la paciente? _____

    _____

2. ¿Cómo está la presión arterial de la paciente? _____

3. ¿Qué necesita hacer la paciente? _____

    _____

4. ¿Cuántas pastillas necesita tomar al día? _____

5. ¿Qué necesita hacer el técnico? _____

    _____

 Ejercicio 2F

UN CRUCIGRAMA

Horizontales

1   2   3

Verticales

4   5   6   7

What you will learn in this lesson:

- to conjugate regular -**ar** verbs in the present tense
- the numbers 500–1000
- to conjugate the verb **estar** ("to be," used when referring to health and location)
- to use and conjugate the verb **tener** ("to have," used to indicate possession)
- to ask the patient about specific chief complaints, present problems/ symptoms (utilizing the verbs **estar** and **tener**)
- to attempt to characterize symptoms with your patient
- to create a dialogue of a patient interview
- to politely excuse yourself from the room momentarily

The goal of this lesson is to be able to learn to conjugate verbs and to use them in sentences and in questions to ask what brings the patient here today (chief complaint); to ask how the patient is progressing if it is a follow-up visit; to clarify, quantify, and attempt to characterize the symptoms the patient has; to ask what medications or remedies the patient is presently taking or using; to ask what needs to be done next; and to excuse yourself from the room in a culturally courteous manner.

3.1 Conjugation

Now, we've finally arrived at what you've been so enthusiastically awaiting: *conjugating*! It's really quite simple. Just think, for example, of "conjugated estrogen." You merely take a basic molecular structure and change that base by adding on different molecules, or in this case, adding on different endings to the base root of the verb. (How thrilling!)

First, let's begin by refreshing our memories. Do you remember what an infinitive is? If not, we'll gladly remind you that an *infinitive* in English consists of the word "to" and a verb: to take, to eat, to examine, to walk, to run, and so on. However, in Spanish, an infinitive is comprised of *only one* action word, which ends in either **-ar**, **-er**, or **-ir**. In Spanish, there is no equivalent of the separate word "to."

tomar (to drink, to take)
hablar (to speak)
pesar (to weigh)

These Spanish infinitives end in **-ar** and must be conjugated.

To conjugate an **-ar** verb: drop the **-ar** ending.

tomar − the ending = **tom**

Take the stem **tom** and add:

(yo)	tomO	I	drink
(tú)	tomAS	you (*familiar*)	drink
(él, ella, usted)[1]	tomA	he, she	drinks
		you (*formal*)	drink
(nosotros)	tomAMOS	we	drink
(ellos, ellas, ustedes)[2]	tomAN	they (*m., f.*)	drink
		you (*pl.*)	drink

---

[1]**usted** is often abbreviated as **Ud.**
[2]**ustedes** is often abbreviated as **Uds.**

From the standpoint of a healthcare professional, you would use

tú   to address a child or teenager
Ud.   to address an adult
ellos to refer to a group of males and females or a group of
           males only
ellas to refer to a group of females only

In general, **tú** is called the familiar form of you, and **Ud./Uds.** is called the formal form of you. Now you know!

(yo)	_____o	(nosotros)	_____amos
(tú)	_____as		
(él)		(ellos)	
(ella) }	_____a	(ellas) }	_____an
(usted)		(ustedes)	

Take any regular **-ar** verb, drop the **-ar** and add these endings to the stem to form the present tense:

-o	**-amos**
-as	
-a	**-an**

Ejercicio 3A

Conjugate the following. *(Conjugue lo siguiente.)*

hablar (to speak)

*(yo) habl_____   (nosotros) habl_____

 (tú) habl_____

 (él) habl_____   (ellos) habl_____

 (ella) habl_____   (ellas) habl_____

*(Ud.) habl_____   (Uds.) habl_____

pesar (to weigh)

*(yo) pes____	(nosotros) pes_____
(tú) pes____	
(él) pes____	(ellos) pes____
(ella) pes____	(ellas) pes____
*(Ud.) pes____	(Uds.) pes____

*The **yo** ("I") and **usted/Ud.** ("you" singular, formal) are the most often used forms between a healthcare professional and patients. Therefore, you may wish to focus on these forms more than the others.

Now try using **-ar** verbs in their conjugated forms in the following exercises.

Ejercicio 3B

Substitute the proper verb form and finish the sentence. *(Sustituya la forma correcta del verbo y complete la frase.)*

EJEMPLO   Yo <u>tomo</u> mucha medicina.

1. Él _____.
2. Ella _____.
3. Nosotros _____.
4. Tú _____.
5. Uds. _____.
6. María _____.
7. Todos (*all*) _____.
8. María y³ José _____.
9. Ud. _____.

———
³**y** and

Ejercicio 3C

Substitute the proper verb form and finish the sentence. *(Sustituya la forma correcta del verbo y complete la frase.)*

EJEMPLO   Yo <u>hablo</u> español con los pacientes.

1. Tú _____.

2. Nosotros _____.

3. Él y yo _____.

4. Tú y yo _____.

5. Las enfermeras _____.

6. Ud. _____.

7. Susana y Laura _____.

8. Los doctores _____.

 Ejercicio 3D

Fill in the correct form of **tomar** and the name of the corresponding picture. *(Complete con la forma correcta del verbo **tomar** y la palabra del dibujo correspondiente.)*

1. Yo _____ en la fiesta.

2. Ella _____ en casa.

3. Uds. _____ en la cantina.

4. Nosotros _____ en el restaurante.

5. Pancho y Rosa _____ en la clase.

6. Ellos _____ en el hospital.

7. Tú y yo _____ en el consultorio.

8. Unos pacientes _____ en la clínica.

🖊 Ejercicio 3E

Answer in Spanish in complete sentences. *(Favor de responder en español con frases completas.)*

1. ¿Toman mucho vino en Francia?

_____

2. ¿Qué toma Ud.?

_____

3. ¿Tomamos agua o salsa picante[4] en el desierto?

_____

4. ¿Dónde toman mucho tequila?[5]

_____

5. ¿Toma Ud. mucha medicina?

_____

6. ¿Toman los norteamericanos mucha aspirina?

_____

7. ¿Dónde tomamos la temperatura—en la clínica o en el carro?

_____

8. ¿Cuándo tomas tú el café—por la mañana o por la noche?

_____

NEGATIVES

The answers to some questions, of course, require a knowledge of the negative in Spanish.

¿Toman leche los bebés? Sí, los bebés toman leche.

pero *(but)*: Los bebés <u>no</u> toman cerveza.
Los bebés <u>no</u> toman vino.
Los bebés <u>no</u> toman tequila.

In Spanish, the negative always *precedes* the verb.

 Ejercicio 3F

Change to the negative. (*Cambie al negativo.*)

EJEMPLO   Los bebés toman café.
Los bebés no toman café.

1. Los norteamericanos toman mucha salsa picante.

_____

2. Uds. toman té.

_____

---

[4]**salsa picante** hot (as in spicy) sauce
[5]Hard liquor is generally masculine, e.g., **el tequila, el ron, el mescal, el whiskey**.

3. María toma leche en el carro.

_____

4. Yo tomo vino en la clase.

_____

 Ejercicio 3G

Answer in the negative. _(Respondan en la forma negativa.)_

EJEMPLO   ¿Hablan inglés en México?
          No, no hablan inglés en México.

1. ¿Habla español nuestro[6] Presidente?

_____

2. ¿Hablas tú español en el hospital?

_____

3. ¿Hablan francés en Cuba?

_____

4. ¿Hablamos inglés o español en la clínica?

_____

3.2 Common -ar verbs

There are many regular **-ar** verbs that you will be using in your medical practice. The following are a sample. Memorize only the ones that are relevant to your needs. Remember that to conjugate them in the present tense, simply drop the **-ar** and add the appropriate endings.

-ar endings: present tense

-o	-amos
-as	
-a	-an

_____

[6]**nuestro** our

aislar[7]	to isolate	**desear**	to desire
amputar	to amputate	**desinfectar**	to disinfect
ayudar	to help	**doblar**	to turn, to bend
bajar	to lower, to descend,	**durar**	to last
	to get out/off	**embarazarse**[10]	to become pregnant
bajar de peso[8]	to lose weight	**escuchar**	to listen to
bofetear	to slap	**enfermarse**[10]	to get sick
(*Carib.*)		**enjuagar**	to rinse
buscar	to look for	**entrar**	to enter
cachetear	to slap	**enyesar**	to put a cast on
(*Mex.*)		**esterilizar**	to sterilize
cambiar[9]	to change	**estudiar**	to study
caminar	to walk	**evitar**	to avoid
causar	to cause	**examinar**	to examine
charlar	to chat	**firmar**	to sign
chocar	to crash	**fumar**	to smoke
chupar	to suck	**gastar**	to spend, to waste
consultar	to consult	**golpear**	to hit, beat up
circular	to cycle, to circulate	**guardar**	to take care of,
comprar	to buy		to keep; to stay
congelar	to freeze	**hablar**	to speak
contagiar	to become infected	**indicar**	to indicate
contaminar	to contaminate	**infectar**	to infect
cortar	to cut	**ingresar**	to admit (as in
continuar	to continue		hospital)
cuidar	to care for, to take	**internar**	to hospitalize
	care of	**inmunizar**	to immunize
curar	to cure	**inyectar**	to inject, give a shot
dañar	to hurt, harm	**irrigar**	to irrigate
defecar	to defecate	**lastimar(se)**	to hurt (oneself)
dejar	to leave behind	**lavar**	to wash
dejar de	to stop (**dejar de**	**levantar**	to lift, raise
	fumar, to stop	**limpiar**	to clean
	smoking)	**llamar**	to call
descansar	to rest	**llevar**	to carry, to wear,
desconectar	to disconnect		to take someone

---

[7]**aislar** adds accent marks in most forms when conjugated: **aíslo, aíslas, aísla, aislamos, aíslan.**

[8]**peso** coin, basic currency unit, or weight

[9]When another vowel precedes the -ar ending, that vowel is retained: **cambio, cambias,** etc.

[10]Or **estar embarazada/enfermo(-a)** to be pregnant/sick. Here **estar** must be conjugated, which we'll soon learn to do.

manejar	to drive, to manage	resultar	to result
masajear	to massage	sacar	to take out, to take
masticar,	to chew		(as in photos or
mascar			X rays)
mirar	to look at	salvar	to save (a life)
mojar	to wet	sangrar	to bleed
nadar	to swim	secar	to dry
necesitar	to need	separar	to separate
observar	to observe	terminar	to terminate, end
operar	to operate	tocar	to touch, to knock,
orinar	to urinate		to play (an
pagar	to pay		instrument)
pasar	to pass, to happen	tomar	to drink, to take
pegar	to hit, strike;	trabajar	to work
	to stick, glue	tratar	to treat
pesar	to weigh	tratar de	to try to
platicar	to chat	(+ *infinitivo*)	(+ *infinitive*)
(*Mex.*)		tragar, pasar	to swallow, bolt
preguntar	to ask	saliva	down food
preparar	to prepare	usar, utilizar	to use
quedar	to remain	vacunar	to vaccinate
quemar	to burn	voltear	to turn (around)
quitar	to take off, remove	vomitar	to vomit
recetar	to prescribe	vigilar	to watch, guard
regresar	to return	visitar	to visit
respirar	to breathe		

 Ejercicio 3H

Answer the questions in complete sentences. (*Conteste [Favor de contestar] con frases completas.*)

1. ¿Baja Ud. de peso rápido? _____

2. ¿Escuchan Uds. a los pacientes siempre? _____

_____

3. ¿Examina Ud. a los pacientes? _____

_____

4. ¿El doctor visita a los pacientes en el hospital o en la clase de

   español? _____

5. ¿Pesa Ud. mucho? _____

6. ¿Trabaja Ud. en el hospital o en la clínica? _____

   _____

7. ¿Lleva Ud. una maleta[11] al hospital? _____

   _____

8. ¿Quién toma aspirinas—los pacientes, los doctores o los dos?[12]

   _____

9. ¿Quién toma Tylenol™? _____

10. ¿Los pacientes con problemas de los riñones toman hielo después

    de la diálisis? _____

11. ¿Respira Ud. bien cuando tiene gripe?[13] _____

    _____

12. ¿Vomitan mucho los pacientes en el proceso de la diálisis?

    _____

13. ¿Qué causa la alergia—el polen o los animales en la casa o los

    dos? _____

14. ¿Inmuniza Ud. a los pacientes? _____

    _____

15. ¿Limpia Ud. su carro en el hospital? _____

    _____

16. ¿Toma Ud. aspirina o Tylenol™?[14] _____

17. ¿Respira con dificultad el paciente con asma? _____

    _____

18. ¿Saca Ud. muchas radiografías? _____

    _____

19. ¿Vacuna Ud. a muchos niños? _____

    _____

_____

[11]**la maleta** suitcase
[12]**los dos** both
[13]**tiene gripe** you have a cold, the flu. Other words for a cold or flu are **una gripa,
un resfriado**, and **un catarro** (*all Mex.*).
[14]For the answer, you will need **tengo** "I have" (irregular present tense).

20. ¿Orina Ud. con dificultad? ¿Orina Ud. mucho o poco por lo gene-

ral? (generalmente) _____

 # "Necesitar"

Now that you know something about conjugating verbs, let's look again at the verb **necesitar** (to need), one of the most useful and important -**ar** verbs.

¿Qué <u>necesita</u>?—What do <u>you</u> need?

While you may not necessarily ask your patient this question, this is an effective way to learn how to use regular -**ar** verbs in a simple and somewhat painless manner.

Necesito un gotero, por favor.	I need a dropper, please.
Necesito una receta, por favor.	I need a prescription, please.
Necesito...	I need . . .
Necesita...	You need . . .
¿Necesita?	Do you need?
¿Qué necesita?	What do you need?

Necesito and **necesita** come from the infinitive verb, **necesitar** (to need). As previously mentioned, all you need to do to "activate" the verb is drop off the -**ar** ending; simply add -**o** to say "I need," or add -**a** to say "You need." You can do this with all regular -**ar** verbs, as listed on the previous pages.

Remember: for health care professionals, the most important regular -**ar** verb conjugations are those that end in -**o**, implying "I," or -**a**, implying "you" (for your patient). And there is no need to use the personal pronoun (**yo** "I," **usted** "you," etc.), as this is indicated by the ending.

Another exciting and simple aspect of the Spanish language is that there are essentially no auxiliary verbs such as "do," "does," "did," etc. as there are in English. For example, to ask:

• "Do you need . . . ?," just say "**¿Necesita?**" in an inquiring tone, which literally means, "Need?" (both the words "do" and "you" are understood).

• "What do you need?," just say "**¿Qué necesita?**" or, literally, "What need?" ("You" is understood from the -**a** ending.)

- "What do I need?," just say "**¿Qué necesito?**" or, literally, "What need?" (The word "I" is understood from the **-o** ending.)
- "Where do I need . . . ?," just say "**¿Dónde necesito...?**" or, literally, "Where need?" (The word "I" is understood from the **-o** ending.)
- "When do I need . . . ?," just say "**¿Cuándo necesito...?**" or, literally, "When need?" (The word "I" is understood from the **-o** ending.)
- "How many do I need?," just say "**¿Cuántos(as) necesito?**" or, literally, "How many need?" (The word "I" is understood from the **-o** ending.)

Forming questions can be done in this manner with nearly all verbs. Take a look at the same structures with the verb **tomar**. To say:

- "What do I take?," just say "**¿Qué tomo?**" or, literally, "What take?" (The word "I" is understood from the **-o** ending.)
- "What pills do I take?," just say "**¿Qué pastillas tomo?**" or, literally, "What take?" (The word "I" is understood from the **-o** ending.)
- "What pills do you take . . . ?," just say "**¿Qué pastillas toma...?**" or, literally, What pills take? (The word "you" is understood from the **-a** ending.)
- "When do I take . . . ?," just say "**¿Cuándo tomo...?**" or, literally, "When take?" (The word "I" is understood from the **-o** ending.)
- "How many do I take?," just say "**¿Cuántos(as) tomo?**" or, literally, "How many take?" (The word "I" is understood from the **-o** ending.)
- "How many pills do you take?," just say "**¿Cuántas pastillas[15] toma?**" or, literally, "How many pills take?" (The word "you" is understood from the **-a** ending.)

 Ejercicio 31

Read and then listen to the following brief monologue, and then answer the questions. (*Favor de leer y escuchar el siguiente monólogo y de contestar las preguntas.*)

DOCTOR   Juan, Ud. necesita dos inyecciones por día en el glúteo por un período de diez días para controlar los síntomas de su enfermedad. (*¡Pobre Juan!*)

---

[15]Note that the words **Cuántas** and **pastillas** must agree in number and gender. This means that because the word **pastillas** is feminine and plural, the word **cuántas** must also be feminine and plural.

1. ¿Qué necesita Juan? _____

2. ¿Cuándo o cuántas veces al día necesita las inyecciones?

   _____

3. ¿Dónde necesita las inyecciones? _____

   _____

4. ¿Quién necesita las inyecciones? _____

   _____

5. ¿Por qué necesita Juan las inyecciones? ¿Cada cuándo, cuántas veces al día, por cuánto tiempo y dónde necesita (Juan) las inyecciones? _____

   _____

NECESITAR + INFINITIVE

There is another extremely helpful use of the verb "to need." With the form **necesito**, you can simply add any infinitive verb. For example:

Necesito tomar su temperatura.	I need to take your temperature.
Necesito examinar su oído.	I need to examine your ear.
Necesito inyectar su brazo.	I need to inject your arm (give you a shot in the arm)
Necesito recetar medicina.	I need to prescribe medicine.

Just as in English, when two verbs are used together, the first one is conjugated (**necesito**, "I need") and the second verb remains "untouched" in its infinitive form (**examinar**, "to examine"). Therefore, "I need to examine" becomes, in Spanish, **necesito examinar**. (So, in Spanish as in English, you would not conjugate both verbs by saying "I need I examine.")

Once you get the hang of this simple concept, you can begin to talk up a storm! For example:

Necesito escuchar los pulmones.
Necesito examinar su brazo.
Necesito pesarle.

(Usted) necesita tomar su medicina.
Necesita cuidar la infección.
Necesita regresar en dos semanas.
Necesita examinar los (sus) senos en casa.

This simple concept broadens your horizons considerably as far as what you can now ask and answer! It also makes conjugating immeasurably easier for you. Just conjugate the first verb (**necesito**, for "I need"; **necesita** for "you need, do you need?") and leave the second verb alone in its infinitive form. The other wonderful advantage of this is that it doesn't matter if the second verb is regular or irregular—you don't need to conjugate it. This is a fantastic "shortcut"!

Ejercicio 3J

Translate into Spanish. *(Favor de traducir al español.)*

1. I need to examine your ear. _____

   _____

2. I need to take your pulse. _____

   _____

3. I need to inject your (give you a shot in your) buttocks.

   _____

4. I need to prescribe pills. _____

   _____

5. You need to take your medicine. _____

   _____

6. You need to examine your breasts at home. _____

   _____

7. You need to drink a lot of fluids (liquids). _____

   _____

3.4 "Estar"

¡**Vamos a aprender el verbo** *estar*! Let's learn the verb **estar** ("to be")—an indispensable verb for expressing states of being, illness, wellness, and existence in general! It is slightly irregular, but only in the **yo** form.

estar (to be)	
(yo) **estoy**	I am
(tú) **estás**	you are (*familiar*)
(él, ella, Ud.) **está**	he is, she is, you are (*formal*)
(nosotros) **estamos**	we are
(ellos, ellas, Uds.) **están**	they are, you are (*plural*)

Estar is used for:

1. Health   **¿Cómo está Ud.?/Estoy enferma.**
2. Location **El libro está en la mesa.**

 Ejercicio 3K

Substitute the correct form of the verb **estar** and finish the sentence. *(Escriba [Favor de escribir] la frase con la forma correcta de **estar**.)*

EJEMPLO   Yo estoy enfermo.

1. Nosotros _____.

2. Ellos _____.

3. Juan _____.

4. Yo _____.

5. Los pacientes _____.

6. Tú _____.

7. Rafael y Armando _____.

 Ejercicio 3L

Provide possible answers in Spanish. *(¡Favor de contestar en español!)*

1. ¿Dónde está Ud. hoy? _____

2. ¿Dónde está Tucsón—en Arizona o en California? _____

3. ¿Dónde están los pacientes—en el hospital o en el museo?[16]

_____

4. ¿Estamos en la clínica o en la casa? _____

_____

5. ¿Estás en una cantina o en una silla? _____

_____

6. ¿Dónde está la cerveza—en el vaso o en una jeringa?

_____

!

Expressions with **estar** denoting emotion and health

Singular

estar contento(-a) ☺   estar triste ☹
estar alegre ☺   estar deprimido(-a) ☹
estar nervioso(-a) ☺

Plural

estar contentos(-as) ☺☺   estar tristes ☹☹☹
estar alegres ☺☺☺   estar deprimidos(-as) ☹☹

estar enfermo(-a) = no estar bien
estar borracho(-a) = tomar mucho licor o alcohol
estar crudo(-a) = la mañana después de estar borracho

✎ Ejercicio 3M

Write complete sentences. _(Escriba frases completas.)_

EJEMPLO (Yo) No <u>estoy</u> content<u>o</u> cuando <u>estoy</u> crud<u>o</u>.

1. (Ella) _____.

2. (Uds.) _____.

3. (Martín y yo) _____.

---

[16]**el museo** museum

4. (Tú) _____.

5. (Nosotros) _____.

6. (Los pacientes) _____.

✎ Ejercicio 3N

Answer the questions in complete sentences. *(Responda a las preguntas con frases completas.)*

1. ¿Cómo está Ud. hoy? _____

2. ¿Está Ud. triste cuando no trabaja? _____

_____

3. ¿Estamos contentos cuando escuchamos música? _____

_____

4. ¿Está alegre Ramón si toma mucho vino? _____

_____

5. ¿Están enfermos Uds. cuando fuman puros[17] todo el día?

_____

6. ¿Están borrachos ellos si toman demasiado[18] licor?

_____

7. ¿Están crudos después?[19] _____

8. ¿Está enfermo el doctor hoy? _____

_____

9. ¿Está borracho el maestro hoy? _____

_____

10. ¿Están nerviosos los pacientes la primera vez?[20] _____

_____

_____

[17]**puros** cigars
[18]**demasiado** too much
[19]**después** after(wards)
[20]**la primera vez** the first time

3.5   More numbers

¡Vamos a aprender más números! Let's learn some more numbers! You never know when you will need to inform your patient of numbers this high (well, there are milliliters, of course . . .).

500	quinientos(-as)[21] (the root is **quince**—15)
600	seiscientos(-as)
700	setecientos(-as) (the root is **setenta**—70)
800	ochocientos(-as)
900	novecientos(-as) (the root is **noventa**—90)
1000	mil
1999	mil novecientos noventa y nueve[22]
2000	dos mil
2005	dos mil cinco
2016	dos mil diez y seis[23]

doscien**tos** libr**os** (*m.*)
doscien**tas** libr**as** (lbs.) (*f.*)
trescien**tos** kil**os** (*m.*)
trescien**tas** doctor**as** (*f.*)

3.6   Common symptoms

Since your patients come to see you with some malady, you may want to learn some vocabulary related to common symptoms. This will provide you with the ability to ask probing questions in Spanish in order to pinpoint more information concerning the chief complaints. ("Complaints" is used in the plural here because there will almost certainly be more than just one, which may well be a cross-cultural phenomenon).

¿Se siente...? Do you feel . . . ? / **¿Está...?** Are you . . . ?
Me siento... I feel . . . / **Estoy...** I am . . .

mal	bad	**triste**	sad
alegre	happy	**acelerado(-a)**	jumpy, hyper

---

[21]When numbers in the hundreds precede a noun, they must agree with the noun (the gender and number [singular/plural] must be the same).

[22]Years and addresses are written in this form also—never 19-99 or 15-25.

[23]Also written as **dos mil dieciséis**.

ansioso(-a)	anxious	mareado(-a)	dizzy
asustado(-a)	frightened	hinchado(-a)	swollen[24]
angustiado(-a)	anguished	moreteado(-a)	bruised
acongojado(-a)	overwhelmed	entumido(-a)/	numb
avergonzado(-a)	ashamed	entumecido(-a)	
inquieto(-a)	uneasy, restless	inflamado(-a)	inflamed
soy/estoy	I'm handicapped	adormecido(-a)	sleepy; numb
lisiado(-a)		agotado(-a)	exhausted
bien	good	deprimido(-a)	depressed
débil	weak	preocupado(-a)	preoccupied
enfermo(-a)	sick	incómodo(-a)	uncomfortable
achicopalado(-a)	somewhat	lastimado(-a)	hurt
(Mex.)	depressed	lesionado(-a)	injured
mortificado(-a)	mortified, upset	herido(-a)	wounded
sorprendido(-a)	surprised	maltratado(-a)	abused,
apenado(-a)	embarrassed		mistreated
atónito(-a)	astonished,	mormado(-a),	stuffed-up nasally
	in shock	tupido(-a)	
ronco(-a)	hoarse	(Carib.)	
cansado(-a)	tired	estreñido(-a),	constipated
contento(-a)	content, happy	estítico(-a)	
nervioso(-a)	nervous	constipado(-a)	stuffed-up nasally;
confundido(-a)	confused		congested[25]

Note: When you need to refer to either physical or emotional abuse (such as home violence), the following phrases are useful for conveying the concept. It is best not to use **abusar** because it most commonly means "to take advantage of a situation." It can also mean "to rape" in some contexts. Use **maltratar** for "to abuse" and **violar** for "to rape."

¿Le maltrata su pareja (alguien)?	Does your partner (anyone) abuse you?
¿Le pega o golpea su novio?	Does your boyfriend hit or beat you?
¿Le ofende su esposo?/¿Le maltrata verbal o emocionalmente su esposo?	Does your husband verbally/ emotionally abuse you?

In English you can say "I am dizzy," but in Spanish you use a different construction, equivalent to "I have dizziness." You would there-

---

[24]generally used with body parts

[25]In the Southwest, **constipado(-a)** also means "constipated"—effectively legitimizing an "espanglish" false cognate.

fore use **tener** "to have" instead of **sentir** or **estar**. The following are the common symptoms that are used with **tener**.

🔲 **Tengo...** I have . . . / **Tiene...** You have . . .
¿Tiene Ud....? Do you/Does he/she have . . . ?

vómito (*m.*)	vomit	**indigestión** (*f.*)	indigestion
mareos (*m. pl.*)	dizziness	**flema** (*f.*)	phlegm
sudores (*m. pl.*)	sweats	**la nariz tapada/**	stuffy nose
escalofríos	chills	**tupida** (*Carib.*)	
(*m. pl.*)		**un tintineo,**	ringing, buzzing
espasmos (*m.*)	spasms	**un zumbido**	(in the ears)
tos (*f.*)	cough	**moretones** (*m.*)	bruises
cólicos (*m. pl.*)	colic or menstrual	**frío** (*m.*)	cold
	cramps	**calor** (*m.*)	hot
calambres	cramps (*muscle*)	**sed** (*f.*)	thirst
(*m. pl.*)		**hambre** (*f.*)	hunger
retortijones	cramps	**la nariz suelta**	runny nose
(*m. pl.*),	(*abdomen*)	**angustia** (*f.*)	anguish
(re)torcijones		**ardor** (*f.*)	burning, stinging
comezón (*m.*)	itching	**miedo** (*m.*)	fear
picazón (*m.*)	itching	**agotamiento** (*m.*)	exhaustion
rasquera (*f.*)	itch (*itching*)[26]	**susto** (*m.*)	fright, scare
granitos (*m. pl.*),	pimples, acne	**el cuerpo**	aching all over,
acné (*f.*)		**cortado** (*Mex.*)	flu-like
la garganta	inflamed throat		symptoms
inflamada		**huesos fracturados**	broken bones
glándulas (*f. pl.*)	swollen glands	**(quebrados,**	
inflamadas		**rotos)**	
fiebre (*f.*),	fever	**salpullido** (*m.*),	diaper rash;
calentura (*f.*)		**sarpullido** (*m.*)	heat rash
¿Tiene apetito?	Do you/Does	**ronchas** (*f. pl.*),	rash
	she/he have	**erupciones**	
	an appetite?	(*f. pl.*)	
ojos (*m. pl.*)	watery eyes	**urticaria** (*f.*)	rash, hives
llorosos		**náusea** (*f.*),	nausea
hormigueo (*m.*)	tingling	**asco** (*m.*),	
diarrea (*f.*)	diarrhea	**basca** (*f.*)	
agruras (*f. pl.*)	heartburn		

---

[26]**rasquera** is derived from **rascar**, "to scratch." It may be used incorrectly by some patients to mean "itch/itching."

Note: **lisiado(-a), descapacitado(-a),** or **disabilitado(-a)** (*Mex.*), "hand-icapped," may be used with **soy, es,** etc. (from the verb **ser**). As un-P.C. as it may seem, some countries use the terms **minusválido(-a), imposibilitado(-a), incapacitado(-a),** or **deshabilitado(-a).** The term **cojo(-a),** "lame," is often used for someone with a limp.

Generally, patients will use the following structures when referring to having a symptom.

Tengo dolor de _____.	I have a pain in _____.
Tengo inflamación de _____.	I have swelling of/in _____.
Tiene infección de _____.	You have an infection of/in _____.
Tiene enrojecimiento de _____.	You have reddening of/in _____.
Tengo hinchazón de _____.	I have swelling of/in _____.
¿Tiene cólicos/dolores tipo regla?	Do you have menstrual cramps?
Tengo calambres.	I have cramps.

Note: In Spanish, **tener** ("to have") is also used in the following expressions, which in English use forms of "to be."

Tengo frío/calor.	I am cold/warm.	**Tengo sueño.**	I am sleepy.
Tengo sed/	I am thirsty/	**Tengo suerte.**	I am lucky.
hambre.	hungry.	**Tengo miedo.**	I am afraid.
Tengo prisa.	I am in a hurry.	**Tengo cuidado.**	I am careful.
Tengo razón.	I am right.	**Tengo 21 años.**	I am 21 years old.

Now that you've been inundated with a slew of vocabulary, it's time once again to utilize some in a dialogue. First, a few more words to be memorized; but come on . . . you're used to this by now!

VOCABULARIO | Basic interview

estar mal	to be sick
Quítese la ropa.[27]	Take off/Remove your clothing.
Desvístase, por favor.	Please get undressed.
Póngase la bata/la ropa.	Put on the gown/your clothing.
Vístase.	Get dressed.
Puede vestirse ahora.	You can get dressed now.
pues/'pos (*Mex. slang*)	well, um
siempre	always

---

[27]**la (su) ropa,** clothing; **la blusa,** blouse; **la camisa,** shirt; **el vestido,** dress; **la falda,** skirt; **bájese los pantalones,** pull down your pants/trousers; **quítese la ropa interior,** take off your underwear; **no necesita quitarse la ropa interior,** you don't need to take off your underwear; **quítese todo de la cintura hacia arriba/hacia abajo,** remove everything from the waist up/down.

ayudar, **aliviar**	to help, to alleviate
té (*m.*) **de manzanilla**	chamomile tea
¡No se preocupe!	Don't worry!
por dos días (*Mex.*)	for two days
hace dos días	two days ago (*lit.*, it makes two days)
blanco(-a)	white
estos problemas (*m. pl.*)	these problems
molestias (*f. pl.*)	problems, bothers, discomforts

▶ DIÁLOGO 3.6 | Basic interview

A basic doctor-patient interview. (*Una entrevista con una paciente.*)

DOCTOR(A) Buenos días, Señora Sánchez. Soy el (Me llamo) doctor Brown.

SEÑORA Buenos días, doctor(a). Mucho gusto.

DOCTOR(A) ¿Cómo está Ud.?

SEÑORA Estoy mal. No estoy bien, doctor(a).

DOCTOR(A) ¿Qué molestias tiene, señora? (¿Qué le duele?)

SEÑORA Me duele la cabeza, el estómago, la nariz y todo el cuerpo en general.

DOCTOR(A) ¿Por cuánto tiempo (Hace cuánto tiempo que) tiene estos problemas?

SEÑORA Hace dos días.

DOCTOR(A) ¿Toma medicina o unos remedios ahora, señora?

SEÑORA Sí, doctor(a), tomo un té y unas pastillas.

DOCTOR(A) ¿Cómo se llaman las pastillas y el té?

SEÑORA Bueno, doctor(a), es té de manzanilla y las pastillas son blancas y chicas.

DOCTOR(A) Bueno, señora, necesita llamar a la recepcionista con los nombres de las pastillas. ¿Las pastillas ayudan a Ud., señora?[28]

SEÑORA Pos (Pues), no sé.[29] Alivian las molestias un poco, pero el té siempre ayuda.

DOCTOR(A) Pues, bueno, muy bien, y ahora Ud. necesita un examen físico. Por favor, quítese la ropa y póngase la bata (necesita quitarse la ropa y ponerse la bata). Con permiso, regreso en un momento (Con permiso y ahorita regreso).

SEÑORA Sí, doctor(a).

---

[28]It is more grammatically correct to add **le**, meaning "to you": **¿Las pastillas le ayudan a Ud., señora?** More on this in Chapter 5.

[29]**no sé** I don't know

Ejercicio 30

Answer the following questions in complete sentences, according to the dialogue. *(Conteste [Favor de contestar] las preguntas con frases completas según el diálogo, por favor.)*

1. ¿Cómo se llama la señora? _____

2. ¿Cómo está la señora? _____

3. ¿Qué molestias tiene o qué le duele? _____

_____

4. ¿Desde cuándo o por cuánto tiempo le duele? _____

_____

5. ¿Qué toma la señora? _____

6. ¿Ayudan los remedios? _____

7. ¿Qué pastillas toma—de qué color y tamaño?[30] _____

_____

8. ¿Cómo se llama el té? _____

9. ¿Qué necesita la señora? _____

Now let's take a look at a very similar dialogue with some additional questions related to symptoms. First, a few more helpful vocabulary words.

 VOCABULARIO | **Basic interview (take II)**

pero	but
generalmente	generally
también	too, also
fíjese[31]	well, it's like this . . .
	(*lit.,* fix yourself on this)
como que	like, as if
em	um, uh
Con permiso.	Excuse me. (*when leaving the room*)
mi comadre	my friend, my child's godmother

_____

[30]**tamaño** size

[31]**Fíjese** is a preliminary expression to any long explanation, excuse, or juicy gossip.

[○ ○] DIÁLOGO 3.6 | Basic interview (take II)

DOCTOR(A)   ¿Qué molestias tiene? (¿Qué le duele?)

SEÑORA   Me duele la cabeza, el estómago, la nariz y todo el cuerpo en general.

DOCTOR(A)   ¿Hace cuánto tiempo que (Por cuánto tiempo) tiene los problemas?

SEÑORA   Pos (Pues), no sé, doctor(a), hace dos o tres días.

DOCTOR(A)   ¿Toma medicina o (unos) remedios ahora, señora?

SEÑORA   Sí, doctor(a), tomo un té y unas pastillas.

DOCTOR(A)   ¿Cómo se llaman las pastillas y el té?

SEÑORA   Bueno, doctor(a), es té de manzanilla y las pastillas son blancas y chicas. No sé cómo se llaman, son de mi comadre.

DOCTOR(A)   Bueno, señora, Ud. necesita llamar a la recepcionista con los nombres de las pastillas. ¿Las pastillas ayudan a Ud., señora?

SEÑORA   Pos (Pues), no sé. Alivian las molestias un poco, pero el té siempre ayuda.

DOCTOR(A)   Bueno, señora. ¿Tiene Ud. fiebre o calentura, escalofríos o cansancio?

SEÑORA   Sí, tengo fiebre y escalofríos un poco, pero no tengo mucho cansancio. Pero tengo vómitos, también.

DOCTOR(A)   Ah, pero, ¿está Ud. mareada, tiene la nariz suelta o se siente débil?

SEÑORA   Fíjese, doctor(a), pues sí, estoy mareada (tengo mareos) y me siento (estoy) débil. Fíjese, doctor(a), generalmente estoy estreñida pero ahora tengo diarrea. Me siento como que tengo el cuerpo cortado.

DOCTOR(A)   Em... ¿Tiene tos o flemas también?

SEÑORA   Tengo un poco de tos pero no tengo flemas.

DOCTOR(A)   Ah, y hace dos o tres días que Ud. tiene estas molestias. (Bueno, señora,) Ud. necesita un examen físico. Por favor, quítese la ropa y póngase la bata. Con permiso, y regreso en un momento.

SEÑORA   Sí, doctor(a).

3.7 Qualifying and quantifying pain

Because you need to *clarify, characterize symptoms,* and *quantify the pain,* you may need to, or at least want to, learn some of the following helpful phrases in Spanish:

Is there anything that alleviates the pain?	**¿Hay algo que alivia el dolor?/¿Qué alivia el dolor?**
Is there anything that makes it feel better/worse?	**¿Hay algo que le hace sentir mejor/peor?**
Does it hurt when I apply pressure?	**¿Le duele cuando pongo/aplico presión?**
Does it hurt when I remove the pressure?	**¿Le duele cuando suelto/quito la presión?**
Does it radiate to other parts of the body?	**¿Baja, sube o se mueve (el dolor) a otras partes del cuerpo?**
It just/It only . . .	**Nada más/No más/Solamente...**
What kind of pain is it?	**¿Qué tipo de dolor es?**
sharp	**agudo, punzante**
stabbing like a blade or knife (shooting pains)	**punzante como una navaja/ un cuchillo**
dull	**sordo,[32] fijo** (*Carib.*), **molesto**
constant	**constante, siempre, todo el tiempo**
pulsating/throbbing	**pulsativo**
chronic	**crónico, todo el tiempo**
intermittent, it comes and goes	**intermitente, va y viene**
a little, a little bit	**un poco**
sort of, more or less, medium	**regular, más o menos**
a lot/strong	**mucho/fuerte**

The following three questions will elicit important information about pain:

¿Es el dolor agudo o no? = Is the pain sharp or not?

¿Tiene el dolor todo el tiempo o va y viene? = Do you have (feel) the pain all the time or does it come and go?

¿Tiene el dolor un poco, más or menos, o muy fuerte? = Do you have (feel) the pain slightly, moderately or a great deal?

---

[32]**sordo** also means "deaf," and is more commonly used in this sense.

DIÁLOGO 3.7 | **Qualifying and quantifying pain**

Now let's look at a very brief dialogue about qualifying and quantifying pain. It's fairly typical in relation to the answers you are likely to receive, albeit a bit more concise and less circuitous.

DOCTORA   Señor, ¿qué tipo de dolor es? ¿Es agudo como agujas, punzante como una navaja o un cuchillo, o no?

SEÑOR   No, doctora, fíjese que nada más va y viene.

DOCTORA   ¿Es el dolor poco, regular (más o menos) o fuerte (mucho)?

SEÑOR   No, pues, doctora, fíjese, que es muy fuerte cuando viene.

CULTURAL NOTE

Rating things on a scale of 1 to 10 is not a concept common to people in Latin America, unless the patient has been more assimilated in the United States. Instead, the following terms are used: **poco** or **leve** (a little), **regular** or **más o menos** (sort of), and **mucho** or **fuerte** (a lot). The Latino patient probably would not be visiting you, the healthcare professional, however, if the pain were less than "10." Many patients would first have treated it with mom's or grandma's home remedies or a neighbor's suggestion, or gone to a pharmacy or a folk healer such as a **curandero**,[33] **yerbero**,[34] **espiritista**,[35] or **santero**[36] (depending on the patient's background); only as a last resort would they see you, not wanting to waste your valuable time unless nothing else has worked. However, mothers are likely to come in more often for their children when sick than for adults.

It is important that you ask questions using more than one example, so your patient will not merely agree out of respect and unwillingness to contradict you, the authority on health care. The patient may consider a solitary example, such as "Is it a sharp pain?," as a leading question and respond based on what he or she may believe you want

---

[33]**el curandero** is a traditional healer who tends to use herbs, rituals, and the laying on of hands.

[34]**el yerbero (hierbero)** is also a traditional healer who generally tends to use herbs and teas; **curanderos** and **yerberos** are generally found in Mexico, Central America, and South America.

[35]**el espiritista** generally summons the spirits of the dead to help in a healing, often using rituals and herbs.

[36]**el santero** generally combines African gods and Catholic saints who are each considered to possess specific powers that are often used for healing. **Santerismo**, or **Santería**, is recognized as an organized religion in many countries, including parts of the United States. **Yerberos**, **espiritistas**, and **santeros** are generally found in the Caribbean area.

to hear. Therefore, offer two or three possibilities when attempting to clarify or quantify; this allows the patient to know that it is perfectly fine to answer your question in his or her own way.

 Ejercicio 3P

Whew! It's time to lighten up a bit. Relax and try to enjoy the crossword puzzle: **un crucigrama**.

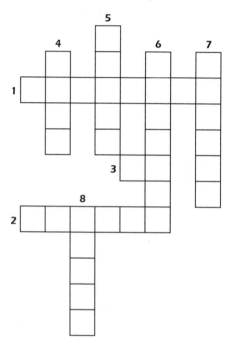

Horizontales

1   2   3

Verticales

4   5   6   7   8

Yo...   Yo...

4

What you will learn in this lesson:

- vocabulary related to linens, smoking, reading material
- to conjugate and use the verb **ser**—the other verb meaning "to be"
- to tell time
- colors and other adjectives
- the word **hay** (there is, there are, is there?, are there?)
- to conjugate and use regular -**er** verbs in the present tense
- to conjugate and use regular -**ir** verbs in the present tense
- vocabulary related to a pediatric visit
- to form, conjugate, and use the future tense
- the essentials of basic grammar/structure
- the correct use of **ser** and **estar**

The goal of this lesson is to be able to conjugate -**er** and -**ir** verbs in the present tense, and to be able to use them in sentences and questions to ask a parent or adult what brings the baby or child patient (chief complaint), to talk about what needs to be done next (talking about the future), to talk about nationality and the time of day, to describe things, and to be able to conduct a pediatric consultation.

4.1 Household items

If you work in a hospital or certain medical facilities, your patients may request some of the following items (though you would not agree to some of the items shown here!).

VOCABULARIO

la pipa

el cenicero

los cerillos
(los fósforos)

la taza

la almohada   la sábana   la cobija

la revista

el periódico

el papel

el disco compacto

el cigarro
(el cigarrillo)

el puro
(el cigarro)

4.2 "Ser"

You may have noticed that there are two verbs (**ser** and **estar**) which both mean "to be." **Ser** is often used to denote a characteristic or a more permanent state of being. It is conjugated in the following manner:

ser (to be)			
(yo) **soy**	I am	(nosotros) **somos**	we are
(tú) **eres**	you are (*familiar*)	—[1]	
(él, ella) **es**	he/she/it is	(ellos/ellas) **son**	they are
(Ud.) **es**	you are (*formal*)	(Uds.) **son**	you are

 Ejercicio 4A

Escriba (Favor de escribir) la frase con la forma correcta de **ser**. (*Write the sentence using the correct form of the verb **ser**.*)

EJEMPLO   Yo <u>soy</u> de los Estados Unidos.
          (I am from the United States.)

1. Tú _____.

2. Ellos _____.

3. Los técnicos _____.

4. Tú y yo _____.

5. El turista _____.

6. Nosotros _____.

7. Ella _____.

8. Todos[2] no _____.

9. Todo el mundo[3] no _____.

---

[1]In Spain the **vosotros** form is used here to signify the familiar, plural form of "you." Since none of the Latin American countries use this form (and most of your patients will be Latin Americans), this form has been omitted in this book. You may, however, hear the **vos** form, which is used in place of the familiar **tú** form in many Central American and some South American countries. (It is very much alive today!)

[2]**todos** all (*plural*)

[3]**todo el mundo** everyone (*singular*)

Ejercicio 4B

Responda a las preguntas con frases completas. *(Answer the questions in complete sentences. By the way, very soon we will no longer be giving the instructions to exercises in English. But not to worry—you will undoubtedly find this an easy task by now!)*

1. ¿Es ella de los Estados Unidos?

   _____

2. ¿De dónde es Ud.?

   _____

3. ¿Son los mexicanos de Brasil o de México?

   _____

4. ¿De dónde es su compadre?

   _____

5. ¿De dónde son los italianos—de Francia o de Italia?

   _____

 Telling time

Las horas	The time
¿Qué hora es?	What time is it?
¿Qué horas son?	What time is it?
temprano	early
siempre	always
tarde	late
nunca	never

Es la una.

Son las dos.

Son las cuatro y diez.

Son las diez y veinte.   Es la una y quince.[4]   Son las siete y media.

Note: **Es la una** ("It is one o'clock"). There is no word for "o'clock" in Spanish. Therefore, the feminine form (**la una**) refers to the feminine noun **la hora** ("the hour"), which is implied.

Son las dos/tres ("It is two/three o'clock" [literally, "They are the two/three," implying "hours" or o'clock]).

Fifteen after or before the hour can be expressed as **quince** ("fifteen") or **cuarto** ("quarto").

Ejercicio 4C

Favor de completar las frases.

EJEMPLO	¿Qué hora es?	Es la <u>una</u>.	1:00
1.	¿Qué hora es?	Son las _____ .	2:00
2.	¿Qué hora es?	_____.	4:15
3.	¿Qué hora es?	_____.	7:30
4.	¿Qué _____ es?	_____.	5:10
5.	¿Qué hora _____?	_____.	3:05
6.	¿Qué _____ es?	_____.	2:20
7.	¿_____ hora es?	_____.	9:07

Son las ocho y cuarenta y cinco.	It is 8:45.
Son quince para las nueve. (*Mexico*)	It is fifteen to nine.
Son las nueve menos quince.	It is nine (hours) minus fifteen
(*Spain, P.R., Cuba*)	(minutes).

---

[4]Also, **Es la una y cuarto.**

Son las diez y cincuenta.	It is 10:50.
Son diez para las once. (*Mexico*)	It is ten (minutes) to eleven.
Son las once menos diez.	It is eleven (hours) minus ten
(*Spain, P.R., Cuba*)	(minutes).

Since digital watches and clocks are so commonly used, it is very acceptable in all countries to simply say "It is ten twenty" (**Son las diez y veinte**) or "It is five forty" (**Son las cinco y cuarenta**). The only drawback, if you consider it as such, is that you must learn your numbers up to 59 (to indicate the minutes). However, you'll need to know these and more in order to be able to talk about blood pressure, cholesterol level, and so on!

Ejercicio 4D

Conteste la pregunta: ¿Qué hora es?[5]

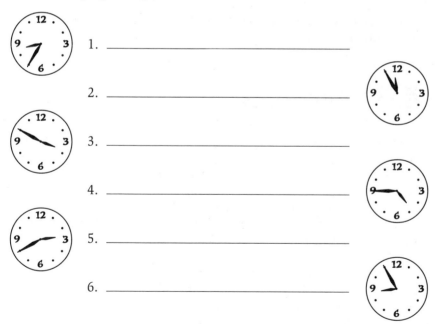

1. _____

2. _____

3. _____

4. _____

5. _____

6. _____

---

[5]**¿Qué hora es?** and **¿Qué horas son?** both mean "What time is it?"

Note: ¿Qué hora es?

pero *(but)*: ¿<u>A</u> qué hora estudias?   Estudio <u>a</u> las cinco.
                  (At) what time do you study?   I study at five o'clock.

Asking the time is straightforward, but asking about specific times requires a slightly different construction:

At what time . . . ?/What time . . . ?	**¿A qué hora...?**
What time is the appointment?	**¿A qué hora es la cita?**
The appointment is at ten.	**La cita es a las diez.**
What time do you study?	**¿A qué hora estudias?**
I study at five.	**Estudio a las cinco.**
What time do you take your pills?	**¿A qué hora toma Ud. las pastillas?**
At eight-thirty.	**A las ocho y media.**

To be more specific, you may add the following expressions:

A.M.; in the morning	**de la mañana**
P.M.; in the afternoon/evening	**de la tarde**
P.M.; at night	**de la noche**
on the dot; sharp	**en punto**

Study these examples:

Tomo café a las cinco de la mañana.
Siempre estoy en la clínica a las ocho y media en punto.
Generalmente tomo mi medicina a las nueve de la noche.

 4.4 Adjectives

Adjectives are words that describe or modify nouns or pronouns. There are two types of adjectives: quantitative and qualitative. Adjectives must agree in number and gender with the noun they describe. In Spanish the quantitative adjectives are placed before the noun; all other adjectives are generally placed after the noun.

In Spanish, where there are two or more qualitative adjectives, they can appear in any order, unlike in English. For example, in English, "two small, round white pills" is the acceptable order of adjectival placement. However, in Spanish, one can place the descriptive adjectives in any order; for example: **dos píldoras blancas, chicas y redondas**[6] is as acceptable as **dos píldoras redondas, chicas y blancas** or **dos píldoras blancas, redondas y chicas.**

---

[6]**redondo(-a)** round

Adjectives agree with the noun in gender (masculine and feminine).

Ramona toma *vino bueno y frío.* (*masculine*)
Ramón toma *medicina buena y fría.* (*feminine*)

Adjectives agree with the noun in number (singular and plural).

Nacho compra *medicinas frescas y económicas.*
  (*feminine plural*)
María necesita *medicamentos buenos y económicos.*
  (*masculine plural*)

QUANTIFYING ADJECTIVES

Quantitative adjectives are generally placed before the noun. These adjectives usually express number or amount.

• *numbers*		Tengo cinco pastillas.
		Necesito tres recetas.
• **más/suficiente**	more/enough	Necesito más medicina.
		No tengo suficientes pastillas.
• **mucho(-a)**	many, a lot of	Necesito mucha medicina.
		Tengo muchos problemas.[7]
• **poco(-a)**	few, a little	Tengo poco dinero, muchas recetas y pocas medicinas.

QUALIFYING ADJECTIVES

Los colores	Colors		
rojo(-a)	red	**blanco(-a)**	white
negro(-a)	black	**gris**	gray
naranja[8]	orange	**verde**	green
amarillo(-a)	yellow	**morado(-a)**	purple
azul	blue	**café**[10]	brown
rosa[9]	pink		

---

[7]If a noun ends with an **-a** it is generally feminine. If it ends in **-ma** it is most likely of Greek origin and is generally masculine: **el programa, el sistema, el diafragma, el diagrama**.

[8]usually expressed **de color naranja** and often as **anaranjado**
[9]usually expressed **de color rosa** and often as **rosado**
[10]usually expressed **de color café**

El ojo está[11] rojo.   La lengua está roja.
El ojo está amarillo.   La cara está amarilla.

Adjectives that end in **-o** change their ending to **-a** to agree with the feminine noun. In other words, if the noun is feminine, the color or descriptive word takes a feminine ending. Colors (adjectives) that do not end in **-o** do not change their ending in the singular: **café**, **rosa**, **gris**, **azul**. They do, however, have plural forms: **cafés**, **rosas**, **grises**, **verdes**, **azules**.

 Ejercicio 4E

Favor de completar las frases con las palabras correctas.

EJEMPLO   ¿De qué color es el libro?
           Red: El libro es rojo.

1. ¿De qué color es _____?
   Black: _____

2. ¿_____ qué _____?
   White: _____

3. ¿De _____ color _____?
   Green: _____

4. ¿De _____ la máquina?[12]
   Gray: _____

_____
[11]Remember: **está** is, it is
[12]**máquina** machine, engine

5. ¿_____ qué _____ es la _____?

   Brown: _____

6. ¿_____ color es la _____?

   Blue: _____

7. ¿De _____ es la _____?

   Brown: _____

8. ¿De qué _____?

   Yellow: _____

9. ¿_____ color _____?

   Red: _____

🖊 **Ejercicio 4F**

Favor de completar las frases con las palabras correctas.

EJEMPLO   ¿De qué color son[13] las plumas?
          White: Las plumas son blancas.

1. ¿De qué color son los libros?

   Red: _____

2. ¿De qué color _____ relojes?[14]

   White: _____

---

[13]**son** are, they are
[14]**los relojes** clocks, watches

3. ¿De qué color ——————————?

   Green: ————————————————

4. ¿De qué color ——————————?

   Black: ————————————————

5. ¿De qué color ——————————?

   Brown: ————————————————

6. ¿De qué color ——————————?

   Blue: ————————————————

7. ¿De qué color ——————————?

   Pink: ————————————————

8. ¿De qué color ——————————?

   Orange: ————————————————

9. ¿De qué color ——————————?

   Red: ————————————————

MORE QUALIFYING ADJECTIVES

alto(-a)	high, tall	**largo(-a)**	long (length)
bajo(-a)	low, short	**corto(-a)**	short (length)
rápido(-a)	fast	**rubio(-a)**	blond, light
lento(-a)	slow	**güero(-a)**	blond/light (hair
irregular	irregular	(*Mex.*)	or skin)
normal	normal, regular	**chele** (*El Salv.,*	light (hair or skin)
así así	regular, so-so,	*Nic.*)	
	moderate	**moreno(-a)**	dark skin color
gordo(-a)	fat	**claro(-a)**	light
delgado(-a)	thin, slim	**oscuro(-a)**	dark
flaco(-a)/	skinny, svelte	**pequeño(-a)/**	little, small
esbelto(-a)		**chico(-a)**	
raquítico(-a)	scrawny	**grande**	big, large

4.5 "Hay"

One of the most useful words in Spanish is **hay**, which means both "there is" and "there are," "is there?" and "are there?". You don't have to learn any endings or make any changes.

Hay	There is	**Hay una tableta.**	There is one tablet.
	There are	**Hay tres tabletas.**	There are three tablets.
¿Hay?	Is there?	**¿Hay una tableta?**	Is there a tablet?
	Are there?	**¿Hay tabletas?**	Are there tablets?

¿Cuántos sombreros hay?
Hay tres sombreros.

¿Cuánto? ¿Cuánta?	How much?
¿Cuántos? ¿Cuántas?	How many?

 Ejercicio 4G

¿Cuántos sombreros hay?

EJEMPLO   Hay dos sombreros.

1. _____

2. _____

3. _____

 4.6 Conjugation of **-er** verbs

Here is an example of a regular **-er** verb conjugation in the present tense.

comer (to eat)			
(yo) **como**	I eat	(nosotros) **comemos**	we eat
(tú) **comes**	you eat		
(él/ella) **come**	he/she eats	(ellos/ellas) **comen**	they eat
(Ud.) **come**	you eat	(Uds.) **comen**	you eat

Note: The **yo** form ends in **-o**, just as it does with the regular **-ar** verbs. The **usted/Ud.** (formal, singular) form ends with an **-e**. Once again, just drop the infinitive ending (in this case, **-er**) and add **-o**, then, **-es**, **-e**, **-emos**, and **-en**.

¡**Muy bien!** ¡**Eso es!** Very good! Now you've got it!

(**Eso es** literally means "That's it!" and is pronounced like "S.O.S." in English.)

To form the present tense of regular **-er** verbs, use these endings:

-o	**-emos**
-es	
-e	**-en**

🖉 Ejercicio 4H

Escriba (Favor de escribir) la frase con la forma correcta de **comer**.

EJEMPLO   Yo <u>como</u> muchos tacos. (I eat a lot of tacos.)

1. Tú _____.

2. Nosotros _____.

3. Él _____.

4. Ellos _____.

5. Vicente _____.

6. Octavio y Eugenia _____.

7. Tú y yo _____.

8. Todos *("All")* _____.

9. Todo el mundo *(Everyone [singular])* _____

_____.

🖉 Ejercicio 4I

Conteste las preguntas con frases completas.

1. ¿Comemos muchos tacos?

   _____

2. ¿Qué come Ud.—tacos, enchiladas,[15] pupusas[16] o tostones?[17]

   _____

3. ¿Comen Uds. enchiladas por la mañana?

   _____

4. ¿Cuándo comen Uds. enchiladas?

   _____

5. ¿Quién come chiles?

   _____

---

[15]**tacos** and **enchiladas** are typical Mexican foods.

[16]**pupusas** are a typical Salvadoran dish.

[17]**tostones** (fried round slices of banana or plantain) are typical foods in the Caribbean, referred to as such in Puerto Rico and Venezuela, as **patacones** in Colombia, and either **tostones** or **plátanos al puñetazo** in Cuba.

6. ¿Comes chiles con salsa picante?

_____

7. ¿Comen Carreras, Domingo y Pavarotti tortillas en el restaurante
o en la ópera?

_____

_____

8. ¿Come Ud. mucha grasa?[18]

_____

9. ¿A qué horas comes por la mañana, por la tarde, y por la noche?

_____

10. ¿Come el niño cereal a las siete de la mañana o a las tres
de la tarde?

_____

_____

A FEW MORE REGULAR -ER VERBS — MÁS VERBOS REGULARES QUE TERMINAN CON -ER

leer	to read	**responder**	to answer
aprender	to learn	**creer**	to believe
beber	to drink	**vender**	to sell
comprender	to understand	**ver**	to see
toser	to cough	**deber**	to owe; must/should
correr	to run		

Notes:

• Don't be thrown by the double **ee** in **leer** and **creer**: **leo, lees, lee, leemos, leen**; **creo, crees, cree, creemos, creen**. In these verb forms, the vowels that are together are pronounced separately: **leo** = lay-oh; **cree** = kray-ay.
• Technically, **ver** is irregular in the **yo** form: **veo, ves, ve, vemos, ven**. (Instead of adding just the **-o** ending, you add **-eo**.)
• When **deber** is used to mean "to owe," it is usually followed by a noun or a pronoun: **Debo dinero** ("I owe money.") When **deber** is used for "should" or "ought," it is usually followed by an infinitive: **Debo comer frutas.** ("I should eat fruit.")

_____

[18]**grasa** fat; grease

🖉 Ejercicio 4J

Conteste las preguntas con frases completas.

1. (leer) ¿Lee Ud. la revista *People* o *Geográfica Nacional* u[19] otras
   revistas? _____

2. (aprender) ¿Aprendes muy rápido el español?

   _____

3. (beber) ¿Qué bebe Ud. a las seis de la mañana?

   _____

4. (comprender) ¿Comprendemos bien el inglés?

   _____

5. (correr) ¿Corres en el parque[20] cada día?

   _____

6. (creer) ¿Cree Pedro que está enfermo?

   _____

7. (responder) ¿Respondes a todas las preguntas?

   _____

8. (vender) ¿Vendemos carros usados en el hospital?

   _____

9. (ver) ¿Qué vemos en la sala de emergencias?

   _____

10. (comer) ¿Come chiles el paciente que sufre de úlceras?

    _____

11. (correr) ¿Es difícil[21] correr si un paciente sufre de enfisema?

    _____

12. (deber) ¿Debe dinero al hospital el paciente en el cuarto #110?[22]

    _____

---

[19]**o** (or) changes to **u** when it comes before another word that begins with an "o."
[20]**el parque** the park
[21]**difícil** difficult; **fácil** easy
[22]This means "Does the patient in room 110 owe money to the hospital?"

13. (leer) ¿Es difícil leer la receta del doctor?

_____

14. (tener) ¿Tienen muchos pacientes dolor de cabeza, por[23] el estrés?[24] _____

 4.7 Conjugation of **-ir** verbs

Here is an example of a regular **-ir** verb conjugated in the present tense.

vivir (to live)			
(yo) **vivo**	I live	(nosotros) **vivimos**	we live
(tú) **vives**	you live		
(él/ella) **vive**	he/she lives	(ellos/ellas) **viven**	they live
(Ud.) **vive**	you live	(Uds.) **viven**	you live

Note: The endings are exactly the same as they are for the regular **-er** verb conjugations, except in the **nosotros** form, where the ending is **-imos**. Once again, just drop the **-ir** ending and add **-o**, then **-es**, **-e**, **-imos**, and **-en**.

¡**Muy bien**! ¡**Eso es**! (Remember: **Eso es** is literally "That's it!") Now we can become even more daring and add **Órale**, **'mano**, Mexican Spanish for "You got it, bro!"

Regular **-ir** verbs take these endings in the present tense:

-o	-imos
-es	
-e	-en

---

[23]**por** due to, because of, for
[24]**estrés**, **tensión** stress

✏️ Ejercicio 4K

Escriba (Favor de escribir) la frase con la forma correcta de **vivir**.

EJEMPLO   Yo <u>vivo</u> en los Estados Unidos.
(I live in the United States.)

1. Ellos _____.

2. Mi esposo[25] _____.

3. Los gringuitos _____.

4. Nosotros _____.

5. Julia Roberts _____.

6. Mi gato[26] y mi perro[27] _____.

7. Pilar _____.

✏️ Ejercicio 4L

¡Responda a las preguntas con frases completas!

1. ¿Dónde vive Macho Camacho? ¿Quién es Macho Camacho?

   _____

2. ¿Dónde vive Ud.? _____

3. ¿Dónde viven los norteamericanos?

   _____

4. ¿Vive Vanessa Williams en los Estados Unidos o en México, D.F.?[28]

   _____

5. ¿Quién vive en Cuba—Antonio Banderas o Fidel Castro?

   _____

6. ¿Quién vive en Francia—los franceses o los ingleses?

   _____

---

[25]**Mi esposo** My husband; **Mi esposa** My wife

[26]**gato** cat; **perro** dog

[27]**gringuito** has an **-ito** ending that softens and makes the term **gringo** sound more affectionate. Note that the **g** is followed by a **ui** instead of an **i** to keep the **g** sound hard.

[28]**México, D.F.** Mexico, Federal District—the most common way to refer to Mexico City (the capital)

7. ¿Dónde viven los italianos? _____

8. ¿Quién vive en México—Octavio Paz, Sammy Sosa o Isabel

   Allende? _____

!

Here is another regular **-ir** verb in the present tense:

abrir (to open)

abr<u>o</u>	abr<u>imos</u>
abr<u>es</u>	
abr<u>e</u>	abr<u>en</u>

✏ Ejercicio 4M

¡Escriba (Favor de escribir) la frase con la forma correcta de **abrir**!

EJEMPLO   Yo <u>abro</u> la puerta para el paciente.
                (I open the door for the patient.)

1. Tú _____.

2. El enfermero _____.

3. Nosotros _____.

4. Ellos _____.

5. Pilar _____.

✏ Ejercicio 4N

¡Favor de llenar los espacios (*fill in the blanks*) según los dibujos usando la forma correcta del verbo **abrir**!

1. Yo _____
   en el hospital.

2. Tú _____
   en la clase.

3. Uds. _____
   en la cantina.

4. Ellos _____
   en el hotel.

5. Nosotros _____
   de la casa.

6. Ramón _____ la cuenta[29]
   en el restaurante.

✎ Ejercicio 40

¡Conteste las preguntas con frases completas!

1. ¿Abren Uds. los libros de español mucho o poco?

   _____

2. ¿Dónde viven los chilenos—en Francia o en Chile?

   _____

3. ¿Abre Ud. los libros de español durante[30] "Monday Night Football"
   (fútbol americano de los lunes por la noche)?

   _____

4. ¿Cuántas personas en la clase viven en Chihuahua? ¿Cuántas
   personas en la clase tienen un chihuahua?

   _____

5. ¿Quién abre la ventana en la clase?

   _____

---

[29]**la cuenta** bill, account
[30]**durante** during

MORE -IR VERBS —
MÁS VERBOS QUE TERMINAN CON -IR

subir de peso	to gain weight	**sufrir**	to suffer
subir	to go up, to get on, to ascend	**escupir**	to spit
		cubrir	to cover
sentirse	to feel ("oneself"; -se makes it reflexive)	**escribir**	to write
		existir	to exist
		medir	to measure
asistira	to attend (an event)		

Notes:

• The verb **sentirse** is included in this list because of its frequent use. However, **sentirse** is not exactly regular—it is a reflexive verb and involves spelling changes in all forms, except the **nosotros** form: **me siento, te sientes, se siente, nos sentimos, se sienten.** You will learn about reflexive verbs in Chapter 9 and about verbs with spelling changes in Chapter 6. For the time being, the following are the most important forms for you to know:

¿Cómo se siente?   How do you/does he, she, it feel?
Me siento...   I feel . . .

• The verb **medir** requires spelling changes in the present tense: **mido, mides, mide, medimos, miden.** (See Chapter 6 for verbs with orthographic changes.)

4.8   Pediatrics
          La pediatría

 VOCABULARIO

mi hijo(-a)	my son; my daughter
¡Qué niño más fuerte!	What a strong child!
Es que...	It's that . . . , Em, um . . .
guapo(-a)	handsome, pretty
el guapo	tough guy (*Puerto Rico, Cuba*)
varonil	manly
una sonrisa	a smile
Voy a quitarle la (su) ropa.	I am going to take off his/her clothing.
No sé.	I don't know.
¿Por (Hace) cuánto tiempo?	For how long?
los nombres	names
ayudar, aliviar	to help, to relieve

estos síntomas (problemas)	these symptoms (problems)
pobrecito(-a)	poor little one
remedios caseros	home remedies
el (la) pequeñito(-a)	the little one

DIÁLOGO 4.8 | A pediatric visit

In this dialogue, we accompany Señora Sánchez and her son, José Manuel, during a visit to Dr. Brown.

DOCTOR(A) Buenos días, Señora Sánchez. Soy el doctor (la doctora) Brown.

SEÑORA Buenos días, doctor(a). Mucho gusto.

DOCTOR(A) ¿Cómo está Ud.?

SEÑORA Estoy bien, doctor(a). Es (que) mi hijo, Joselito Manuel, está enfermo.

DOCTOR(A) ¡Ay, pobrecito! ¿Qué molestias tiene el pequeñito? (¿Qué le duele?)
(El doctor toca al niño con una sonrisa.)
¡Qué niño más fuerte y varonil!

SEÑORA Gracias, doctor(a). Pues, le duele la cabeza, el estómago, la garganta y todo el cuerpo en general.

DOCTOR(A) ¿Por cuánto tiempo (Hace cuánto tiempo que) tiene estos problemas?

SEÑORA No sé, doctor(a), hace dos o tres días.

DOCTOR(A) ¿Toma medicina, té o unos remedios caseros ahora, señora?

SEÑORA Sí, doctor(a), toma un té y unas pastillas para niños.

DOCTOR(A) ¿Cómo se llaman las pastillas y el té?

SEÑORA Bueno, doctor(a), es té de manzanilla y las pastillas son blancas y chicas. No sé cómo se llaman. Son de mi comadre.

DOCTOR(A) Bueno, señora, necesita llamar a la recepcionista con los nombres de las pastillas. ¿Las pastillas ayudan a Joselito, señora?

SEÑORA Pues (Pos), no sé. Alivian las molestias un poco, pero el té siempre ayuda.

DOCTOR(A) Bueno, señora. ¿Tiene Joselito fiebre o calentura o escalofríos? ¿Come bien?

SEÑORA Sí, tiene fiebre y escalofríos, pero no tiene apetito.

DOCTOR(A) ¿Qué tan alta (Cuánto) es la fiebre, señora?

SEÑORA Pues, fíjese, doctor(a), no sé. No tengo termómetro en casa.

DOCTOR(A)   ¡No se preocupe! Vamos a tomar su temperatura ahora.
             Em... ¿Tiene tos?
SEÑORA   Sí, doctor(a), tiene un poco de tos y también tiene flema.
DOCTOR(A)   ¿De qué color es la flema?
SEÑORA   No tiene color, doctor(a), es clara (transparente).
DOCTOR(A)   Pues, bueno, ahora Joselito necesita un examen físico.
             Necesito quitarle la ropa de su hijito y examinarle.
SEÑORA   Bueno, sí, doctor(a).

 Ejercicio 4P

Favor de responder a las preguntas según el diálogo.

1. ¿Quién está enfermo? _____

2. ¿Qué molestias tiene Joselito? _____

   _____

3. ¿Qué remedios caseros toma? _____

   _____

4. ¿Tiene tos Joselito? _____

5. ¿Qué necesita hacer el doctor? _____

   _____

 **4.9   Expressing destination
              and future actions**

One of the most useful verbs to know is **ir**, which means "to go." Not
only does it express action and destination, but also it can be used to
tell what you will do in the future. This verb, however, is irregular. If
we drop **-ir**, there's nothing left! Observe the following conjugation:

ir (to go)			
(yo)	**voy**	(nosotros)	**vamos**
(tú)	**vas**		
(él, ella, Ud.)	**va**	(ellos, ellas, Uds.)	**van**

Destination: **ir** + **a** + noun (to go + to + noun)

Voy a la tienda.   I go (am going, do go) to the store.
Vas a la casa.   You go (are going, do go) to the house.

Va al laboratorio.	He/She goes (is going, does go) to the lab./ You go (are going, do go) to the lab.
Vamos a la clínica.	We go (are going, do go) to (the) clinic.
Van al hospital.	They/You go (are going, do go) to (the) hospital.
¿Adónde va Ud.?	Where are you going?
Voy al consultorio.	I'm going to the doctor's office.
¿Adónde van las enfermeras?	Where are the nurses going?
Van a la sala de emergencia.	They are going to the ER.

Notes:

- There are only two contractions in Spanish: **del** and **al**.

  de + el = del   of/from + the = of/from the
  a + el = al   to + the = to the

  El doctor camina <u>del</u> hospital <u>al</u> consultorio.
  The doctor walks from the hospital to the doctor's office.

- The question word most commonly used with questions about destination is **¿adónde?**, which means "where?" or "to where?" **¿Adónde?** implies movement. Compare:

  ¿Dónde está Ud.?   Where are you? (*no movement*)
  ¿Adónde va Ud.?   Where are you going? (*movement*)

Future action/intention: **ir** + **a** + infinitive
(to be going to + infinitive)

Voy a hablar con el paciente.	I'm going to talk with the patient.
¿Vas a tomar estas pastillas?	Are you going to take these pills?
Va a caminar a la clínica.	You are going to walk to the clinic.
¿Va a tomar más café?	Is he/she going to drink more coffee?
Vamos a trabajar en el hospital.	We are going to work in the hospital.
Van a escribir una receta.	They are going to write a prescription.

VOCABULARIO

The following are common words and phrases that signal intention or future action:

mañana	tomorrow
pasado mañana	the day after tomorrow
la semana próxima	next week
la semana siguiente	next week
la semana que viene	next week
el mes (año) próximo	next month (year)
el mes (año) siguiente	next month (year)

el mes (año) entrante	next month (year)
en una quincena	in two weeks, in fifteen days
hoy en ocho	a week from today
después	later; after
un día de estos	one of these days
Un día de estos voy a ir a París.	One of these days, I'm going to go to Paris.
Vamos a visitar la clínica de hoy en ocho.	We're going to visit the clinic a week from today.

Destination: **ir** + **a** + noun

Voy a la tienda.
Vamos al pueblo.

Future/intention: **ir** + **a** + infinitive

Ud. va a toser mucho.
Vamos a comer después.

 Ejercicio 4Q

Favor de escribir la forma correcta en el tiempo futuro: **ir a** + infinitivo.

EJEMPLO   Yo <u>voy a tomar</u> su pulso.

1. Tú _____ su pulso.

2. Petra y Pita _____ su pulso.

3. Ud. y yo _____ su pulso.

4. Los enfermeros _____ su pulso.

5. El asistente médico _____ su pulso.

6. Todos[31] _____ su pulso.

7. Todo el mundo[32] _____ su pulso.

8. El técnico _____ su pulso.

9. La doctora _____ su pulso.

🖉 Ejercicio 4R

Llene los espacios con la forma correcta del verbo **ir**.

1. (yo) _____ a recetar medicina.

2. (tú) _____ a tomar el pulso.

3. (él, ella, Ud.) _____ a estudiar español.

4. (nosotros) _____ a trabajar en la clínica.

5. (Uds., ellos, ellas) _____ a escribir la receta.

INTERROGATIVES

Emilio va a la clínica, ¿verdad?	Emilio is going to the clinic, right?
Emilio va a la clínica, ¿no?	Emilio is going to the clinic, isn't he?
¿Va Emilio a la clínica?	Is Emilio going to the clinic?

Note: To form a question, **¿verdad?** or **¿no?** can be added to the end of a statement (spoken with the appropriate questioning intonation), or the subject and verb can be inverted.

NEGATIVES

Don Diego[33] no va a vender jeringas ahora.	Don Diego is not going to sell syringes now.
María y Jaime no tienen medicinas.	María and Jaime do not have medicine.
Pilar no tiene seguro médico.	Pilar does not have medical insurance.
Nacho no va a tener dinero para comprar medicinas.	Nacho is not going to have money to buy medicine.

Note: **No** is placed before the verb; it doesn't matter what tense or person is involved. Unlike the English "I didn't, she doesn't, they don't," etc., simply place the word **no** before the conjugated verb to form the negative.

---

[31]**todos** all (*plural*)

[32]**todo el mundo** everyone (*singular*)

[33]**Don Diego.** The titles **don** for men and **doña** for women have no equivalent in English. They are used before a person's first name to express respect, affection, or social standing.

✐ Ejercicio 4S

Favor de contestar con frases completas.

1. ¿Adónde va Pedro mañana?

   _____

2. ¿Cuándo van Uds. al cine?[34]

   _____

3. ¿Qué va a comer Ud. a las 8:00 de la noche?

   _____

4. ¿Quién va a ir al hospital mañana para visitar a María?

   _____

5. ¿Cuántas personas van a la clínica para trabajar mañana?

   _____

6. ¿Vas a comer tacos de burro con mucho colesterol en la noche?

   _____

7. ¿Vamos a aprender español en la clase?

   _____

8. ¿Van a traer una cobija o una aguja si un paciente tiene frío?

   _____

9. Vas a hablar español con los pacientes mexicanos, ¿verdad?

   _____

10. Los pacientes van a mirar la televisión cuando dan sangre[35] en la Cruz Roja, ¿no?

    _____

    _____

---

[34]**al cine** to the movies

[35]**dar sangre/donar sangre** to give/donate blood; **cuando dan sangre** when they give blood

Recuerde[36]/**Acuérdese**;[37] **ir** + **a** + infinitivo = futuro

Voy a pesarle.   Vamos a tomar medicina.
Vas a inyectarle.
Va a recetar.   Van a tomar su presión.

 Ejercicio 4T

Favor de contestar con frases completas.

1. ¿Qué va a hacer[38] (Ud.) después de la clase?

2. ¿Qué va a recetar Ud. para el niño con la infección?

4.10 Emergency room
La sala de emergencias

UN BEBÉ CON DIFICULTAD AL RESPIRAR

 VOCABULARIO | **Emergency room—difficulty breathing**

todos los inviernos	every winter
cuando lo acuesto	when I put him to bed
cuando se acuesta	when he goes to bed (*lit.,* puts himself to bed)
¿Cómo suena?	What does it sound like? How does it sound?
¿Es una tos seca y ronca o con flemas?	Is it a dry and hoarse cough, or a wet cough?
Sí, es como tos de perro.	Yes, it's like a dog's cough ("a seal's bark" in English).

---

[36]**Recuerde** is the command form of **recordar** ("to remember, to recollect, to remind").

[37]**Acuérdese** is the command form of **acordarse** ("to remember, to recall, to agree").

[38]**Hacer** to do or to make. As in English, the answer to this question does not require the verb **hacer**, e.g., **Voy a estudiar el español** ("I am going to study Spanish").

¡Ah!	Oh!
¿Cuándo comenzó?	When did it begin?
hace tres días	three days ago
entonces	and so, and then, therefore
en/por la mañana	in the morning
en/por la noche	at night
tiene dificultad al respirar	he has difficulty breathing
al rato	in a little while
nada más que...	it's just that . . .

DIÁLOGO 4.10 | Emergency room—difficulty breathing

In this dialogue, we will now hear a conversation in an ER concerning a baby who is having difficulty breathing.

DOCTOR(A)   Buenos días, Señora Valdez. ¿Cómo está Ud.? ¿Y su esposo y sus otros hijos?

SEÑORA   Muy bien, doctor(a), todos estamos muy bien, excepto José Manuelito aquí. Tiene un resfriado y tos.

DOCTOR(A)   Ah, comprendo,[39] señora, entonces ahorita necesito examinar a José Manuelito. Voy a mirar los oídos, la garganta, y también voy a escuchar sus pulmones y el corazón.

SEÑORA   ¿Hay un problema, doctor(a)?

DOCTOR(A)   ¿Cuándo comenzó la tos? (¿Por cuánto tiempo[40] tiene la tos?)

SEÑORA   Pues, más o menos hace tres días.

DOCTOR(A)   ¿Es la primera vez que sufre de estos síntomas? ¿Sufre mucho de resfriados y tos?

SEÑORA   Sí, doctor(a), todos los inviernos.

DOCTOR(A)   Ah, comprendo. ¿Tose más en la mañana o por la noche?

SEÑORA   Pues, doctor(a), tose más por la noche cuando se acuesta (lo acuesto). Pero, a veces tose por la mañana también.

DOCTOR(A)   ¿Cómo es la tos? ¿Cómo suena? ¿Es una tos seca y ronca o húmeda (con flemas)?

SEÑORA   Es una tos muy fuerte, como tos de perro. Tiene mucha dificultad al respirar cuando tose también.

---

[39]**Ah, comprendo** means "Oh, I understand" in the sense of relating to or empathizing with a person or situation. **Entiendo** (from **entender**) means "I understand facts or concepts."

[40]also used: **¿Cuánto tiempo hace que...?**

DOCTOR(A)   ¿Hay otra gente enferma en su casa (hogar) ahora?
SEÑORA   Pues, todos estamos bien, nada más que todos mis hijos
            tienen gripa.[41]
DOCTOR(A)   Entonces, sí están enfermos.
SEÑORA   Pues, sí, doctor(a). ¿Pero, qué necesita mi hijo... necesita
            suero, inyecciones, amoxicilina...?
DOCTOR(A)   ¡No se preocupe, señora! Al rato, voy a recetarle me-
            dicina.

Ejercicio 4U

Preguntas sobre el diálogo:

1. ¿Cómo está José Manuelito?

   _____

2. ¿Cómo están los hermanos de José?

   _____

3. ¿Cuándo comenzó la tos y cuándo tose más José?

   _____

4. ¿Cómo es la tos? ¿Cómo suena?

   _____

DIÁLOGO 4.10 | A well-baby visit

Sorry, but there is no dialogue here! Basically, there are no well-baby
visits in Latin America. The concept simply does not translate. Why
would parents take their baby to the doctor's office if he or she is not
sick? It simply makes no sense! One suggestion for avoiding this problem is simply to schedule the "well-baby visit" around a vaccination
time. So, not to worry. We will present vocabulary and a well-baby
visit further on, once you've persuaded mom that she needs to bring
in her baby for vaccinations!

_____

[41]**gripa** (*Mex.*) = **gripe** flu

4.11 *"Ser" v. "estar"*

Here we can compare both forms of the verb "to be" (**ser** and **estar**). Note their conjugations in the examples and the differences in their usage.

Estar

Indicates temporary states or conditions

1. Position or location:
   ¿Dónde *está* la blusa?
   La blusa *está* en la silla.
2. Health (emotional and physical):
   ¿Cómo *están* Juan y María?
   ***Están* enfermos.**

Ser

Indicates constant or permanent identifiers and characteristics

1. Color:
   ¿De qué color *es* la mesa?
   ***Es* roja.**
2. Size:
   Las tazas *son* chicas.
3. Possession:
   El dinero *es* de Rockefeller.
4. Origin and nationality:
   Raúl *es* de México.
   Tú y yo *somos* mexicanos.
5. Religion:
   La familia Sánchez *es* católica.
6. Profession:
   Elisa *es* doctora.
7. Time:
   ¿Qué hora *es*?
   ***Son* las seis.**

Ejercicio 4V

Escriba la forma correcta de **ser** o **estar**!

1. Santa Claus _____ gordo.

2. Rosa _____ católica.

3. La aguja _____ en la mesa.

4. Pedro _____ enfermo.

5. Las revistas _____ chicas.

6. La bolsa _____ roja.

7. Elena _____ contenta.

8. Marcela _____ de la Argentina.

9. Yo _____ de buen humor.[42]

10. El señor Ruiz _____ médico.[43]

---

[42]**de buen (mal) humor** in a good (bad) mood
[43]**médico** doctor

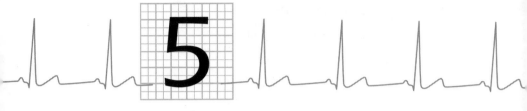

What you will learn in this lesson:

- vocabulary related to family members
- to form, conjugate, and use the present perfect tense ("Have you had . . . ?" "Have you ever had . . . ?")
- vocabulary related to medical records, patient history, review of systems, etc.
- to take a patient history
- vocabulary related to foods that are high or low in proteins, fats, salt, etc. This allows you to recommend foods for certain diets.
- to form, conjugate, and use some irregular -**er** and -**ir** verbs in the present tense

The goal of this lesson is to be able to refer to and talk about family members, take a medical history, and discuss eating habits.

5.1 | The family
| **La familia**

la mamá — **Los esposos** — el papá

la hija — **Los hermanos** — el hijo

el abuelo — **Los abuelos** — la abuela

 VOCABULARIO | **The family**

la mujer	woman	**el niño, la niña**	boy, girl
el hombre	man	**el muchacho,**	boy, girl; kid
la madre	mother	**la muchacha**	
el padre	father	**el/la joven**	young, youth
los padres	parents	**el hermano,**	brother, sister
el esposo, la esposa	husband, wife	**la hermana**	
el hijo, la hija	son, daughter	**los hermanos**	siblings
los hijos	children	**(las hermanas)**	

MONÓLOGO 5.1 | **The family**

In this series of monologues, let's meet the García family. *(Vamos a hablar [platicar] con la familia García.)*

MUJER   Me llamo Carmen Romero de García[1] y soy mujer. Soy madre y esposa también. Tengo un esposo y él se llama Carlos García.

---

[1]Women retain their maiden names and add **de** (of) + husband's surname. Carmen's maiden name is **Romero**.

HOMBRE	Me llamo Carlos García Flores[2] y soy hombre. Soy padre y esposo también. Tengo una esposa y ella se llama Carmen Romero de García.
NARRADORA	La madre y el padre son los padres. Los padres tienen dos hijos.
NIÑA	¡Hola! Soy la hija de los García. Soy una niña o muchacha joven. Me llamo Carmencita. Tengo una madre, un padre y un hermano. Mi hermano se llama Carlitos. Tiene ocho años de edad. Yo tengo diez años. Soy mayor y él es menor.[3]
NIÑO	¡Hola! Soy el hijo de los García. Soy un niño o un muchacho joven. Me llamo Carlitos. Tengo una madre, un padre y una hermana. Mi hermana se llama Carmencita. Tiene diez años de edad. Yo tengo ocho años.
NARRADORA	Carmencita y Carlitos son los hijos de los García. Los García (la señora y el señor) son los padres. Carmencita y Carlitos son hermanos.

VOCABULARIO

las madres	mothers (*in general*)
los padres de familia	fathers (*in general*)
los esposos[4]	spouses
el abuelo, la abuela[5]	grandfather, grandmother
el nieto, la nieta	grandson, granddaughter
una tía	aunt
un tío	uncle
los tíos	an aunt and uncle (*as a unit*)[6]
un sobrino, una sobrina[7]	nephew, niece

---

[2]Men usually retain their mother's maiden name, although their wives do not use this name. Men place their mother's maiden name after their father's surname. **Flores** is Carlos's mother's maiden name.

[3]**mayor** older; **menor** younger

[4]Interestingly, and perhaps rather shockingly, the feminine plural **las esposas** means "handcuffs"; this is not slang, merely an indication of how language reflects culture, and culture is reflected in the language.

[5]In some countries, **nana** is used for "grandmother," and **tata** for "grandfather." **Abue** and **abuelita(-o)** are affectionate terms.

[6]Remember, the masculine takes preference in plural situations when the unit consists of male and female members.

[7]adding an -s to any of the relations implies plural; **primos/primas** cousins; **sobrinos/sobrinas** nephews, nieces, etc.

un primo, **una prima**	cousin
un suegro	father-in-law
una suegra	mother-in-law
una nuera	daughter-in-law
un yerno	son-in-law
un cuñado, **una cuñada**	brother-in-law, sister-in-law
un novio, **una novia**	boyfriend, girlfriend
un prometido, **una prometida**	fiancé, fiancée

Ejercicio 5A

¿Cuántas personas hay en su familia? ¿Quiénes son?

EJEMPLO   En mi familia somos[8] cuatro personas: mi hija, mi hijo, mi esposo y yo.

_____

_____

Ejercicio 5B

Llene los espacios.

1. La mamá de mi mamá es mi _____.

2. El hijo de mi hermano es mi _____.

3. Mi tío es el _____ de mi papá.

4. Mi hermana es la _____ de mi tía.

5. Mi papá es el _____ de mi esposa.

6. Mi hija es la _____ de mi mamá.

7. Mi papá es el _____ de mi hijo.

8. Los hermanos de mi mamá son mis _____.

9. La esposa de mi hermano es mi _____.

10. El gran amor de mi vida es mi _____ o mi

_____.

---

[8]**Somos** ("we are") is used when the speaker is stating how many people there are in his or her family, a group, etc.

NAMES

This would be a good place to clarify how the "name thing" works in Latin America. The difference with standard practice in the United States causes many problems and confusions, which is problematic for both your records and how patients identify themselves on subsequent visits. The result is often that you are unable to find their records or the records of the rest of their family with their newly acquired, often "assigned," American names, as in the following scenario.

When a baby is born in Latin America, he or she is given one or more **nombres** ("first names"), for example, Juan Carlos—he may use one (**Juan** or **Carlos**) or both as one: **Juan Carlos**. The baby also has two **apellidos** ("surnames"), the first surname is his father's first surname, and his second is his mother's maiden name: for example, **Pérez** (paternal last name) and **García** (maternal maiden name). There are *no middle names*—the concept is completely foreign and lost on Latin Americans, and "NMI" doesn't exist either. Instead, there are only **nombres**, which translates as "first names," and there may well be three of these; for example, **Juan Carlos Manuel**.

Thus, a baby boy, **Juan Carlos Pérez García**, is born. He grows into an outstanding young man, meets a wonderful young lady, **Ana Sánchez Araiza**, courts her for an appropriate period of time, and subsequently marries her (after properly asking her father for her hand). She then becomes **Ana Sánchez de Pérez** (using her husband's paternal surname and dropping her mother's maiden name).[9]

After some time passes, Juan Carlos and Ana have two children: a boy named Juan Carlos (but everyone calls him **Carlitos**) like his father and grandfather, and a daughter named Ana María. Their names (**nombres y apellidos**)[10] are **Juan Carlos Pérez Sánchez** and **Ana María Pérez Sánchez**. Note that all children (of the same parents) have the same surnames—in this case, **Pérez Sánchez** (**Pérez**, their father's surname, and **Sánchez**, their mother's maiden name).

Our happy family is now composed of:

Juan Carlos Pérez García   the father
Ana Sánchez de Pérez   the mother

---

[9]Some younger professional women, however, are beginning to drop the **de** before the second surname.

[10]**Nombre** means "first name" only; if you want to know someone's "full name," you must ask for **nombres y apellidos**.

Juan Carlos (Carlitos) Pérez Sánchez   the son
Ana María Pérez Sánchez   the daughter

They are known as the **Pérez** family (**la familia Pérez**).

When **Mr. Pérez** comes to the clinic, he states, "My name is Juan Pérez García"; so he is promptly filed under *G* for **Garcia** as "Juan P. Garcia." (Note that the "file clerk" has eliminated the accent mark!)

When Mrs. Pérez comes to the clinic, she says, "My name is Ana Sánchez de Pérez," trying to be recognized as a member of the Pérez family. She is filed under *D* for "**de Perez**" and renamed **Ana S. DePerez** (pronounced *duh-peh-<u>rezz</u>* in English).

When Carlitos comes to the clinic, he says, "My name is Carlitos Pérez," since he has been going to school and knows that in the United States people have only one last name. Of course, he is filed under *P* for **Perez** and named **Juan C. Perez**, since his records had shown the name **Juan Carlos** and he just *must* have a "middle name."

When Mrs. Pérez brings Ana María to the clinic, she informs the receptionist that her name is "Ana María Pérez Sánchez" and, of course, the girl is filed under *S* for her new full name, **Ana Maria P. Sanchez.**

Our new "Americanized" family is now composed of

Juan P. Garcia	the father	filed under *G*
Ana S. DePerez	the mother	filed under *D*
Juan C. Perez	the son	filed under *P*
Ana Maria P. Sanchez	the daughter	filed under *S*

This is obviously a dysfunctional family, but at least they all now have middle names or initials and *no* accents!

 5.2   **More verb tenses**

THE PRESENT PERFECT

The present perfect verb tense is immeasurably useful when taking a medical history. It is the equivalent of "have you or has s/he us**ed**, suffer**ed**, shar**ed** . . ." in English. With this tense, you can now ask "Have you ever had . . . ?" (insert the name of the illness you are querying). The verb tense has the exact same meaning in English as in Spanish. It is formed by using the appropriate present-tense form of **haber** and the past participle.

haber (to have)[11]				+ past participle	
he	I have	**hemos**	we have	**tomado**	taken
has	you have			**comido**	eaten
ha	s/he has, you have	**han**	they, you all have	**sufrido**	suffered

The use of **-ado** (for **-ar** verbs) and **-ido** (for **-er**, **-ir** verbs) endings matches the use of "-ed", "-en", or "-d" endings in English.

ha tomADO/usADO...?	have you takEN/usED . . . ?
ha tenIDO...?	have you haD . . . ?
ha sufrIDO de...?	have you haD (sufferED from) . . . ?

Note that to express *ever* in Spanish, use **alguna vez** ("at any time").

¿Alguna vez ha tomado/usado...?	Have you ever taken/used . . . ?
¿Alguna vez ha tenido...?	Have you ever had . . . ?
¿Alguna vez ha sufrido de...?	Have you ever had (suffered from) . . . ?

THE PRESENT OR CONTINUOUS PROGRESSIVE

The present progressive or continuous progressive is another verb tense that can be useful when taking a medical history. It has the same meaning in Spanish as in English ("I am ____ing, you are ____ing," etc.) and can be used when inquiring if someone is eating well, taking medicine, or exercising regularly. It is formed by using the present tense of the verb **estar** with the present participle.

estar (to be)				+ present participle	
estoy	I am	**estamos**	we are	**tomando**	taking
estás	you are			**comiendo**	eating
está	s/he is, you are	**están**	they, you all are	**sufriendo**	suffering

The present participle is formed by replacing the infinitive ending with **-ando** for the "-ing" ending for **-ar** verbs and **-iendo** for the "-ing" ending for **-er** and **-ir** verbs. In Spanish, the present progressive is used to convey immediacy, in the sense of "at this time," "at this moment," or "now."

---

[11]**Haber** is almost exclusively used as an auxiliary verb, never to express possession. To express possession, **tener** is used.

¿Está tom**ando** medicina?	Are you tak**ing** any medicine (at this time)?
¿Está Ud. com**iendo** bien?	Are you eat**ing** well (lately/now)?
¿Está sufr**iendo** de vista borrosa?	Are you suffer**ing** from blurred vision (at this moment)?

5.3 Illnesses
Enfermedades

The following extensive list contains terms that you will find useful when taking a medical history (**una historia médica**). Rather than be discouraged by its length, take heart from the large number of easily recognizable cognates!

 VOCABULARIO | **Medical history**

Have you had . . . ?	**¿Ha tenido...?**
ever	**alguna vez**
Have you ever had . . . ?	**¿Alguna vez ha tenido (ha sufrido de)...?**
measles or rubella	**sarampión** (*m.*) **o rubeola** (*f.*)
mumps	**paperas** (*f. pl.*)
tonsillitis	**amigdalitis** (*f.*)
diphtheria	**difteria** (*f.*)
whooping cough, pertussis	**tosferina**(*f.*) **o tos ferina**
typhoid	**tifoidea** (*f.*)
tuberculosis, TB	**tuberculosis** (*f.*), **tisis** (*f.*)
polio	**poliomielitis** (*f.*)
smallpox	**viruela** (*f.*)
chicken pox	**viruela** (*f.*) **loca, varicela**
diabetes	**diabetes** (*f.*)
asthma	**asma**[12] (*f.*)
bronchitis	**bronquitis** (*f.*)
anemia or problems related to the blood	**anemia** (*f.*) **o problemas** (*m. pl.*) **de la sangre**
thyroid gland problems	**problemas** (*m. pl.*) **de la glándula tiroides**
other hormonal problems	**problemas** (*m. pl.*) **con otras hormonas**
hypoglycemia	**hipoglucemia** (*f.*) **(se le baja el azúcar)**
hyperglycemia	**hiperglucemia** (*f.*) **(se le sube el azúcar)**

---

[12]Although **asma** is feminine, the article **el** is used because the first syllable is stressed. You would say: **el asma crónica**.

spinal column problems	**problemas** (*m. pl.*) **de la columna vertebral**
hepatitis A, B, or C	**hepatitis** (*f.*) **tipo A, B o C**
jaundice	**ictericia** (*f.*)
pain when you urinate	**dolor** (*m.*) **cuando orina**
back problems	**problemas** (*m. pl.*) **de la espalda**
cancer or tumors	**cáncer** (*m.*) **o tumores** (*m. pl.*)
hay fever	**fiebre** (*f.*) **de heno**
scarlet fever	**fiebre** (*f.*) **de escarlatina**
rheumatic fever	**fiebre** (*f.*) **reumática**
malaria	**malaria** (*f.*), **paludismo** (*m.*)
dysentery	**disentería** (*f.*)
parasites	**parásitos** (*m. pl.*)
amoebas	**amebas** (*f. pl.*), **amibas** (*f. pl.*)
intestinal worms	**lombrices** (*f. pl.*)
tapeworm	**lombriz** (*f.*) **solitaria**
scabies	**sarna** (*f.*)
allergies	**alergias** (*f. pl.*), **coriza** (*f.*)
STDs (STIs)	**enfermedades** (*f. pl.*) **venéreas y genitales**
syphilis	**sífilis** (*f.*)
gonorrhea	**gonorrea** (*f.*)
herpes	**herpes** (*m.; f. pl.*)
pubic lice	**piojos** (*m. pl.*) **púbicos**[13]
genital warts	**verrugas** (*f. pl.*) **genitales**
chlamydia	**clamidia** (*f.*), **chlamydia** (*f.*)
AIDS	**SIDA** (*m.*)
HIV	**VIH** (*m.*)
Others	**Otras**
problems with the genitalia	**problemas** (*m. pl.*) **con (en) las partes genitales**
yeast infection	**infección** (*f.*) **por hongos**
hospitalizations	**hospitalizaciones** (*f. pl.*)
operations or surgeries	**operaciones** (*f. pl.*) **o cirugías** (*f. pl.*)

History of medicines

Historia de medicinas

Are you taking any medicine?	**¿Está tomando medicina?**
Which ones?	**¿Cuáles?**
Are you allergic to any medicine?	**¿Tiene reacción alérgica o problemas con alguna medicina?**
Do you smoke?	**¿Fuma?**
How many per day?	**¿Cuántos por día?**

---

[13]"Crabs" are **ladillas**.

Do you drink alcoholic beverages?	¿Toma bebidas alcohólicas?
Do you drink beer?	¿Toma cerveza?
Or wine?	¿O vino?[14]
Do you use illicit drugs?	¿Usa drogas?
Which ones?	¿Cuáles?
Do you share needles (straws)?	¿Comparte agujas o popotes (pajillas)?

Family history — Historia clínica de la familia

stroke or cerebral infarction	embolia (f.) o derrame (m.) cerebral
tuberculosis or lung disease	tuberculosis (f.) o enfermedades (f. pl.) pulmonares
fetal alcohol syndrome	síndrome (m.) fetal de alcohol
seizures, convulsions	convulsiones (f. pl.), ataques (m. pl.)
cataracts	cataratas (f. pl.)
glaucoma	glaucoma (f.)
high/low blood pressure	alta/baja presión (f.), presión alta/baja
hepatitis, type A, B, or C	hepatitis (f.), tipo A, B o C
goiter	bocio (m.)
Down's syndrome	síndrome (m.) de Down

Review of systems — Repaso de sistemas/Revisión sistémica

nausea	náusea (f.)
dizziness, fainting spells	mareos (m. pl.), desmayos (m. pl.)
varicose veins	várices (f. pl.), venas (f. pl.) varicosas
hemorrhoids, piles	hemorroides (f. pl.), almorranas (f. pl.)
leg cramps	calambres (m. pl.) en las piernas
hot flashes	bochornos (m. pl.), sofocos (m. pl.)
depression	depresión (f.), estar triste
sudden mood swings or changes	cambio (m.) de humor de repente
mild rash	erupción (f.) en la piel, salpullido (m.)
blurred vision	vista (f.) borrosa
headaches	dolores (m. pl.) de cabeza, jaquecas (f. pl.)
migraines	migrañas (f. pl.)
infarcts, infarctions	infartos (m. pl.)
heart attack	infarto, ataque (m.) al corazón
blood clot	coágulo (m.) de sangre
pain, pressure or tightness in the chest	dolor (m.) o presión (f.) en el pecho

---

[14]It is a good idea to ask about beer and wine separately because they are not necessarily considered to be alcohol.

palpitations	**palpitaciones** (*f. pl.*)
embolism or cerebral infarction	**embolia** (*f.*), **infarto** (*m.*)/**derrame** (*m.*) **cerebral**
shortness of breath	**falta** (*f.*) **de respiración, dificultad** (*f.*) **al respirar**
Do you pant (wheeze) when you walk a bit?	**¿Jadea cuando camina un poco?**
heart murmur	**soplo** (*m.*) **de corazón, soplo en el corazón**
to wheeze	**respirar con un silbido**
Do you wheeze?	**¿Respira con un silbido?**
blood in the stool	**sangre** (*f.*) **en el excremento**
change in frequency of urination	**cambio** (*m.*) **en frecuencia de orinar**
discharge from the penis or vagina	**desecho** (*m.*) **del pene/de la vagina**
change in color of your urine	**cambio** (*m.*) **de color de la orina**
change in stool color	**cambio** (*m.*) **de color del excremento**
tenderness in the breasts	**senos** (*m. pl.*)/**pechos** (*m. pl.*) **adoloridos**
speech or hearing difficulties	**dificultad** (*f.*) **al hablar o al oír**
to stutter	**tartamudear**

Menstruation	**Menstruación/la regla/el período**
When did you have your first period?	**¿Cuándo tuvo**[15] **la primera regla?**
Do you have irregular periods?	**¿Tiene irregularidades**[16] **o problemas con su regla o menstruación?/¿Tiene su regla cada mes o no?**
Do you bleed . . . ?	**¿Sangra...?**
slightly	**poco**
moderately	**regular**
a lot	**mucho**
When was your last period?	**¿Cuándo fue/Cuándo bajó**[17] **su última regla?**
For how many days did you bleed?	**¿Por cuántos días sangró?**
Do you have painful periods?	**¿Tiene reglas dolorosas?**
When was the first day of your last period?	**¿Cuándo fue el primer día de su última regla?**

---

[15]**tuvo** (the irregular past tense form of **tener**) you, he, she had; **¿Tuvo...?** Did you/he/she have . . . ?

[16]Since **regular** in Spanish means "sort of, more or less, moderately or so-so," it is clearer to ask about **irregularidades** (*f. pl.*).

[17]**bajó** (the regular past tense of **bajar**) to come down, as in "My period didn't come down. (I didn't get my period.)"

History of pregnancies and birth control methods	Historia de embarazos y anticonceptivos
Pregnancies and dates	**Embarazos y las fechas**
Indicate how many:	**Indique cuántos:**
miscarriages	**malpartos** (*m. pl.*), **abortos** (*m. pl.*) **naturales o abortos espontáneos**
therapeutic, induced, or elective abortions	**abortos** (*m. pl.*) **inducidos, legrados**
premature	**nacidos antes de tiempo, prematuros, sietemesinos**
stillborn	**nacidos muertos**
(full) term	**nacidos a tiempo, nacido a los nueve meses**
How many children do you have?	**¿Cuántos niños tiene?**
males	**varones**[18] (*m. pl.*), **niños**
females	**hembras**[19] (*f. pl.*), **niñas**
Did you have problems with your pregnancy?	**¿Tuvo problemas con su embarazo?**
Did you have problems with your delivery?	**¿Tuvo problemas con el parto?**
Were the deliveries:	**¿Fueron**[20] **los partos:**
vaginal	**normales**[21] **(vaginales)**
or cesarean?	**o cesáreas?**
Your due date is (more or less) . . .	**La fecha de su parto es (más o menos)...**

Birth control methods	Métodos anticonceptivos
the birth control pill	**la píldora, las pastillas**
the diaphragm	**el diafragma**
the sponge	**la esponja**
foam	**la espuma**
condoms	**los condones, los preservativos**
rubbers	**los hules**
IUD	**el espiral, el dispositivo, el aparato**
Depo®	**inyecciones** (*f. pl.*), **la Dosis, Depo**
Norplant®	**implantes** (*m. pl.*)

---

[18]**Varones** is commonly used to refer to males, sometimes to mean "manly."

[19]**Hembras** is used to refer to females in most countries, but some (like Mexico) consider it to be used only for female animals, not humans.

[20]**Fueron** (the plural of **fue**, the irregular past-tense form of **ser**) They/you were, Were you/they . . . ?

[21]**Partos normales**, which implies "vaginally," is used more frequently than **partos vaginales**.

the patch	**el parche**
cervical cap	**el capuchón cervical**
vaginal ring	**el anillo vaginal**
the rhythm method	**el método del ritmo**
withdrawal, coitus interruptus, "my husband takes care of me"[22]	**"mi esposo me cuida"**
Others	**Otros**
Did you have any problems with these methods?	**¿Tuvo problemas con estos métodos?**
Explain.	**Explique.**
Have you had a hysterectomy?	**¿Ha tenido Ud. la histerectomía?**
Have you had your tubes tied?	**¿Ha tenido Ud. ligadura de trompas?**
Have you had your tubes tied?	**¿Le amarraron[23] los tubos?**
Has your partner had a vasectomy?	**¿Ha tenido la vasectomía su pareja?**

Authorization | Autorización

I give my permission to receive medical treatment and the consulting services offered by the clinic.	**Doy mi permiso para recibir tratamiento médico y los servicios de consulta que ofrece la clínica.**
Patient's signature	**Firma** (*f.*) **del paciente**
Witness's signature	**Firma del testigo**
Date	**Fecha** (*f.*)

[cassette icon] **VOCABULARIO** | **Additional useful phrases and words**

Do you have blood loss?	**¿Tiene pérdida de sangre?**
Have you lost blood/weight?	**¿Ha perdido sangre/peso?**
What are your home activities?	**¿Qué actividades hace en la casa?**
Do you have any special problems that you would like to mention?	**¿Tiene problemas especiales que quisiera mencionar?**

---

[22]This is a common answer, referring to withdrawal or to coitus interruptus.
[23]**amarrar** to tie; **amarraron** is the past-tense form.

Would you like to speak with the social worker/ nutritionist, dietician?	¿Quisiera hablar con el trabajador social/nutriólogo (nutricionista)?
How much does the medicine cost?	¿Cuánto cuesta la medicina?
How much (What) are your fees?	¿Cuántos son sus honorarios?
I do not have insurance.	No tengo seguro[24]/aseguranza.[25]
a cyst	un quiste
a twist or sprain	una torcedura
stitches	puntos (*m. pl.*) o puntadas (*f. pl.*)
a pulled muscle or torn ligament	un desgarre
What should I do?	¿Qué debo hacer?
Do you have any change in color or texture of a mole?	¿Tiene algún cambio de color o textura en un lunar?
I am going to examine you for kidney stones.	Voy a examinarle para cálculos/piedras en los riñones.
to move one's bowels	obrar, defecar,[26] hacer caca, hacer popó

 Ejercicio 5C

Llene el formulario[27] según su propia historia médica. *(Fill out the form on pp. 118–119 according to your own medical history.)*

---

[24]**seguro** insurance in all of Latin America

[25]**aseguranza** insurance (in Southwest U.S. and parts of northern Mexico)

[26]**obrar** and **defecar** are the preferred terms; only resort to **hacer caca** or **hacer popó** for children, or if the patient looks bewildered.

[27]**Formulario** is used in some countries; whereas **la forma** or **la planilla** is used in others.

HISTORIAL O EXPEDIENTE MÉDICO
Historia del Paciente y Repaso de Sistemas

I. HISTORIA MÉDICA

Alguna vez ha sufrido de (ha tenido):
Favor de marcar los problemas que sufre
o que ha sufrido.

sarampión o rubéola ☐
paperas ☐
amigdalitis ☐
difteria ☐
tifoidea ☐
tuberculosis, tisis ☐
poliomielitis ☐
viruela ☐
viruela loca o varicela ☐
diabetes ☐
asma ☐
bronquitis ☐
anemia o problemas de la sangre ☐
problemas de la glándula Tiroides ☐
problemas con otras hormonas ☐
hipoglucemia (Se le baja el azúcar) ☐
hiperglucemia (Se le sube el azúcar) ☐
problemas de la columna vertebral ☐
hepatitis o ictericia ☐
dolor cuando orina ☐
problemas de la espalda ☐
cáncer o tumores ☐
fiebre de escarlatina ☐
fiebre reumática ☐
malaria (paludismo) ☐
disentería ☐
alergias (coriza): _____ ☐
enfermedades venéreas y genitales ☐
sífilis ☐   gonorrea ☐   herpes ☐
piojos púbicos ☐   verrugas genitales ☐
clamidia ☐   SIDA ☐   VIH ☐
Otras: _____ ☐
problemas con las partes genitales ☐
hospitalizaciones: _____ ☐
operaciones o cirugías: _____ ☐

II. REPASO DE SISTEMAS

Si sufre de algunos de estos problemas,
o ha sufrido de algunos recientemente, favor
de marcarlos y mencionar cuándo sufrió y
por cuánto tiempo duró el problema.

náusea ☐
mareos, desmayos ☐
venas varicosas (várices) ☐
almorranas o hemorroides ☐
calambres en las piernas ☐
bochornos ☐
depresión ☐
erupción en la piel, o salpullido ☐
cambio de humor de repente ☐
vista borrosa ☐
dolores de cabeza ☐
infartos ☐
dolor o presión en el pecho ☐
palpitaciones ☐
embolia, infarto (derrame) cerebral ☐
falta de respiración o dificultad al respirar ☐
jadea cuando camina un poco ☐
soplo de corazón ☐
respira con un silbido ☐
sangre en el excremento ☐
cambio en frecuencia de orinar ☐
desecho del pene o de la vagina ☐
cambio de color de la orina ☐
cambio de color del excremento ☐
senos (pechos) adoloridos ☐
infección por hongos ☐
sarna ☐

III. HISTORIA DE MEDICINAS   Sí

¿Está tomando medicina? ☐
Cuál(es): _____
¿Tiene reacción alérgica o problemas
con alguna medicina? _____ ☐
¿Fuma? Cuántos por día: _____ ☐
¿Toma bebidas alcohólicas? ☐
¿Toma cerveza ☐   o vino ☐?*
¿Usa drogas? Cuáles: _____ ☐
¿Comparte agujas o popotes (pajillas)? ☐

IV. HISTORIA CLÍNICA DE LA FAMILIA

Incluye a sus padres, abuelos y hermanos.

enfermedades del corazón ☐
retardación (retraso o atraso) mental ☐
diabetes ☐
cáncer ☐
problemas (p)siquiátricos ☐
embolia o derrame cerebral ☐
tuberculosis o enfermedades
    pulmonares ☐
síndrome fetal de alcohol ☐

convulsiones ☐
cataratas ☐
glaucoma ☐
alta/baja presión ☐
hepatitis, tipo A, B, C ☐
bocio ☐
síndrome de Down ☐
Otros: _____ ☐

V. MENSTRUACIÓN

¿Cuándo tuvo (bajó) su primera regla? _____

¿Tiene irregularidades o problemas con su regla? _____

¿Sangra?   Poco ☐   Regular ☐   Mucho ☐

¿Cuándo fue (bajó) su última regla? _____

¿Por cuántos días sangró? _____

¿Tiene reglas dolorosas? _____

¿Cuándo fue el primer día de su última regla? _____

VI. HISTORIA DE EMBARAZOS Y ANTICONCEPTIVOS

Embarazos y las fechas _____

Indique cuántos: malpartos (abortos naturales o espontáneos)   _____

abortos inducidos, legrados   _____

nacidos antes de tiempo, prematuros   _____

nacidos muertos   _____

nacidos a tiempo (a los nueve meses)   _____

¿Cuántos niños tiene? _____   varones (niños) _____   hembras (niñas) _____

¿Tuvo problemas con el embarazo?   sí ☐   no ☐   _____

¿Tuvo problemas con el parto?   sí ☐   no ☐   _____

¿Fueron los partos: normales** (vaginales) _____ o cesáreas _____?

La fecha de su parto es (más o menos): _____

Métodos anticonceptivos	¿Usando ahora?	¿Qué ha usado?
la píldora (las pastillas)	☐	☐
el diafragma	☐	☐
la esponja	☐	☐
la espuma	☐	☐
los condones, preservativos, hules	☐	☐
el espiral, dispositivo, aparato	☐	☐
inyecciones (La Dosis)	☐	☐
implantes (Norplant)	☐	☐
el método del ritmo	☐	☐
"Mi esposo me cuida"	☐	☐
Otros: _____	☐	☐

¿Tuvo problemas con estos métodos? Explique: _____

_____

¿Ha tenido Ud. la histerectomía?   sí ☐   no ☐

¿Ha tenido Ud. ligadura de trompas? (¿Le amarraron*** los tubos?)   sí ☐   no ☐

¿Ha tenido la vasectomía su pareja?   sí ☐   no ☐

AUTORIZACIÓN

Doy mi permiso para recibir tratamiento médico y los servicios de consulta que ofrece la clínica.

_____	_____	_____
Firma del paciente	Fecha	Firma del testigo

---

*It's a good idea to ask about beer and wine separately as they are not always considered to be alcohol.

****partos normales** implies vaginally and is used more frequently than **partos vaginales**.

*****amarrar** to tie

5.4   Types of food
Tipos de comidas

We are going to assume you did extremely well on the last exercise and are now ready to forge ahead by learning some names of foods. This, of course, will allow you to determine the type of diet your patient has and what you may want to suggest for creating healthier eating habits.

BASIC FOODS — COMIDAS BÁSICAS

la sal   la pimienta   el pan   la tortilla

la mantequilla   los huevos,   la sopa, el caldo   el queso
                   los blanquillos
                   (Northern Mex.)

bajo[28] en colesterol   low in cholesterol
bajo en sodio   low in sodium
alto en potasio   high in potassium
bajo en azúcar   low in sugar
bajo en grasas   low in fats
alto en fibra   high in fiber
alto en proteínas   high in proteins
alto en calcio   high in calcium
bajo en carbohidratos   low in carbohydrates
mucha acidez   a lot of acidity
muchas vitaminas   many vitamins
cuidado con...   careful with . . .

---

[28]**bajo** or **alto** can change to be feminine or plural depending on the noun.

**La comida en latas (enlatadas), en paquetes (empaquetadas)
o congelados contiene muchos preservativos y sal.**
Canned, packaged, or frozen foods contain a great many preservatives
and salt.

FRUITS — **LAS FRUTAS**

la piña,	la pera	la fresa	el plátano (Mex.),
el ananás (Arg.)			la banana, el banano,
			el guineo (C. Am.,
			Carib.)

la naranja, **la china** (*P.R.*)	orange
la manzana	apple
la sandía	watermelon
el limón	lemon
el plátano macho (*Mex.*),	plantain
el plátano (*C. Am., Carib.*)	
la toronja, **el pomelo** (*Arg., Spain*)	grapefruit
las uvas	grapes
el durazno, **el melocotón**	peach
la lima	lime

MEXICAN FOOD — **COMIDAS MEXICANAS**

la torta	la quesadilla	la enchilada	el chile, el ají
	y el taco		(Carib.)

el arroz	rice
los frijoles, **las habas**,	beans
las habichuelas (*P.R.*)	
la salsa picante	hot sauce

la cebolla	onion
el ajo	garlic
el mole (*Mex.*)	dark brown sauce prepared with chocolate, peanuts, and chiles
los cacahuates, el maní (*Carib.*)	peanuts
el jugo, el zumo	fruit juice

VEGETABLES — **LOS VEGETALES, LAS VERDURAS, LAS LEGUMBRES**

el tomate, el jitomate[29]	las papas	la calabaza	el maíz, el elote (Mex.), la mazorca

los ejotes (*Mex.*), las judías verdes (*Spain*), las habichuelas verdes (*Cuba*)	string beans
la coliflor	cauliflower
las espinacas	spinach
la lechuga	lettuce
los chícharos, los petit pois (*Carib., C. Am.*), los guisantes, las arvejas	peas
la zanahoria	carrot

MEAT — **LA CARNE**

el puerco	pork	la hamburguesa	hamburger
la chuleta	chop (pork chop)	el bistec	steak, minute steak
el lomo	loin (pork loin)	las costillas	ribs
el jamón	ham	la milanesa	breaded veal
el tocino	bacon	el guisado	stew

---

[29]**jitomate** = red tomato, from Mexico City southward (in Mexico). **Tomate** (in Mexico City) = **tomatillo** or small green tomatoes in northern Mexico and other Latin American countries.

POULTRY — **AVES**

el pollo, la gallina	chicken
el pavo, el guajolote (*Mex.*), **el guanajo** (*Cuba*)	turkey
el pato	duck

BEVERAGES — **BEBIDAS**

la soda, el refresco, los frescos (*C. Am.*)	soft drink
las aguas frescas	natural fruit drinks made with water
el jugo	juice
la leche	milk
el licuado (*Mex.*), **la batida** (*Carib.*), **el batido** (*C. Am.*)	a smoothie (natural fruit drinks made with milk)
el té	tea (teas are generally used for medicinal purposes)

SHELLFISH AND FISH — **MARISCOS Y PESCADOS**

las almejas	clams
las ostras, los ostiones	oysters
la langosta	lobster
los camarones	shrimp
el pulpo	octopus
el tiburón	shark
el huachinango, **el pargo**	red snapper
el ceviche	raw fish cocktail in a tomato base, "cooked" in lime juice in the sun
el lenguado	sole fish

DESSERTS — **LOS POSTRES**

la gelatina

el pay (Mex.), la tarta

las galletas

el pan dulce

el flan	custard-like dessert
el arroz con leche	rice pudding
el pastel (*Mex.*), el bizcocho, la torta, el queque (*Carib.*)	cake
el helado, la nieve (*Mex.*), el mantecado (*Carib.*)	ice cream, sherbet

TABLEWARE — LOS CUBIERTOS

la cuchara	el tenedor	el cuchillo	la cuenta

la taza	cup	el tazón	bowl
la servilleta	napkin	el mantel	tablecloth
el plato	plate	la propina	tip

 Ejercicio 5D

¡Conteste con frases completas!

1. ¿Qué usamos para tomar sopa? _____

_____

2. ¿Qué cubiertos usamos para cortar la carne? _____

_____

3. ¿Comemos chícharos con un cuchillo? _____

_____

4. ¿Tomas café en un plato o en una taza? _____

_____

5. ¿A quién dejas una propina—a un mesero[30] o a un doctor?

_____

---

[30]**un mesero(-a)** waiter, server; **una mesera** waitress, server

6. ¿A qué hora tomamos el almuerzo?[31] _____

_____

7. ¿El tenedor va al lado derecho o izquierdo[32] del plato?

_____

8. ¿Le gusta[33] cuándo su hijo limpia su boca con la mano o la ser-

villeta? _____

MÁS VOCABULARIO

es rico(-a)[34]	it's delicious	**es o está seco(-a)**	it's dry or stale
es sabroso(-a)	it's delicious	**está (un poco)**	it's (a little) raw
es delicioso(-a)	it's delicious	**crudo(-a)**	
es dulce	it's sweet	**está maduro(-a)**	it's ripe
es amargo(-a)	it's bitter	**está quemado(-a)**	it's burned
es agrio(-a)	it's sour	**traigo**	I bring
es fresco(-a)	it's fresh	**lo siento mucho**	I'm very sorry

5.5 Diet
La dieta

VOCABULARIO

los resultados	results	**cuidar**	to take care of
las pruebas	tests	**la dieta**	diet
evitar	to avoid	**puede**	you (he, she, it) can
los análisis	analyses	**controlar**	to control
indicar	to indicate	**a continuación**	following
cierto(-a)	certain	**según**	according to

---

[31]**almuerzo** lunch

[32]**derecho(-a)** right; **izquierdo(-a)** left; **lado** side

[33]**¿Le gusta?** Do you like? (Is it pleasing to you?)

[34]In this and some of the following expressions **es** and **está** can be used inter-changeably.

Ejercicio 5E

Favor de llenar el siguiente párrafo[35] con una enfermedad que requiere una dieta especial y de llenar los espacios según esa dieta.

DOCTOR(A)   Los resultados de sus pruebas (análisis) indican que tiene

_____. Necesita evitar ciertas comidas.

Si cuida su dieta, puede controlar el problema.

Necesita evitar comidas con _____.

Trate de evitar las siguientes comidas: _____,

_____, _____, _____,

_____, _____, _____.

Pero las siguientes comidas son muy buenas para esta

dieta: _____, _____, _____,

_____.

 # 5.6 Indirect object pronouns

After an extensive section on foods, one more simple concept is required: **gustar**, "to like." With this verb, you can discuss your likes and dislikes of certain foods and also invite your Latino friends over for dinner . . . or at least go out to a good Latino restaurant.

First, let's quickly review the constructions with **doler** (see Chapter 1, section 1.8, "Chief complaint").

¿Le duele?   Does it hurt you? Is it painful to you?
Me duele.   It hurts me. It is painful to me.

Gustar follows the same principles as **doler**.

doler (ue) (to hurt, to be painful)		**gustar** (to like, to be pleasing)	
me duele(n)	nos duele(n)	me gusta(n)	nos gusta(n)
te duele(n)		te gusta(n)	
le duele(n)	les duele(n)	le gusta(n)	les gusta(n)

---

[35]**párrafo** = paragraph

Study the following statements with **gustar** and their English equivalents.

1	2	3		3	2	1
Me	gusta	el pastel	=	The cake	is pleasing	to me
Me	gusta	la fruta	=	Fruit	is pleasing	to me
No me	gusta	la iguana	=	The iguana	is not pleasing	to me

!

We do not conjugate **gustar** like other verbs. Think of it as:
"It is pleasing to me." = *I like.*

Now look at these statements in the plural form.

1	2	3		3	2	1
Me	gust<u>an</u>	<u>los</u> dulces	=	Sweets	<u>are</u> pleasing	to me
No me	gust<u>an</u>	<u>las</u> uv<u>as</u>	=	Grapes	<u>are</u> not pleasing	to me

 Ejercicio 5F

¡Conteste con frases completas!

1. ¿Le gusta el pastel? Sí, _____ el pastel.

2. ¿Le gusta el pollo? Sí, _____ el pollo.

3. ¿Le gusta el flan con chiles? No, no _____.

4. ¿Le gustan las almejas? _____

5. ¿Le gustan las uvas? _____

6. ¿Le gustan las zanahorias? _____

7. ¿Qué comidas le gustan que son saludables (*healthy*)?

_____

8. ¿Qué comidas le gustan que son dañinas (*harmful*) o que no son saludables? _____

_____

Ejercicio 5G

¡Conteste con frases completas! (In this exercise, note the use of **Le gusta**, singular form, when followed by the infinitive of a verb. It does not matter if the things referred to after the infinitive are plural form.)

1. ¿Le gusta comer los frijoles? _____

_____

2. ¿Dónde le gusta comer, en la casa o en el restaurante?

_____

3. ¿Le gusta tomar sopa caliente y picante en el desierto?

_____

4. ¿Qué le gusta comer en la mañana? _____

_____

5. ¿Le gusta beber cervezas mexicanas? _____

_____

6. ¿Le gusta comer chícharos con las manos? _____

_____

Just as you would not say, "My eyes are painful to I," you do not say, **Los ojos yo duelen**. You need a different pronoun. Verbs such as **gustar** and **doler** use indirect object pronouns to express "to me, to you, to him, to her," etc. Examine the following indirect object pronouns:

Singular		Plural	
me	to me	**nos**	to us
te	to you (*familiar*)		
le	to him, to her	**les**	to them
le	to you (*formal*)	**les**	to you (*formal*)

¿**Le gusta...?**	Do you like . . . ? (Is . . . pleasing *to you?*)
¿**Te gustan...?**	Do you like . . . ? (Are . . . pleasing *to you?*)
Me gusta la salsa picante.	I like the hot sauce. (The hot sauce is pleasing *to me.*)
Nos gusta caminar.	We like to walk. (Walking is pleasing *to us.*)
Le duelen los oídos.	His ears hurt. (His ears are painful *to him.*)

5.7 Irregular -er and -ir verbs

THREE IRREGULAR VERBS: **TENER, VENIR, PONER**

You've already been using the verb **tener**, so it will be quite easy to learn the conjugation of **venir**. You've seen **poner** in its command form; **Póngase la bata, Póngase su ropa**, as well as **¿Le duele cuando pongo presión?** Now, here they are in full in the present tense.

tener (to have)		**venir** (to come)		**poner** (to put)	
tengo	tenemos	vengo	venimos	pongo	ponemos
tienes		vienes		pones	
tiene	tienen	viene	vienen	pone	ponen

If you have noticed a puzzling change in the stem of these verbs and feel you really need to know the reason, check the footnotes.[36] However, it is not necessary at this point. Just concentrate on the **yo** and **usted** forms.

 Ejercicio 5H

Escriba (Favor de escribir) la frase con la forma correcta de **tener**.

EJEMPLO   Yo <u>tengo</u> una aguja grande.

1. Tú _____.

2. La enfermera _____.

3. Ud. _____.

4. El paciente _____.

5. Nosotros _____.

6. Ella y Ud. _____.

7. Elián y yo _____.

8. Ella _____.

---

[36]All three verbs end in -**go** in the **yo** form: **tengo, vengo, pongo**.

Both **tener** and **venir** change the **e** to **ie** in their stem in the **tú, él, ella, Ud., ellos, Uds.,** forms.

Except for the **yo** form, **poner** is conjugated like a regular -**er** verb.

Ejercicio 5I

¡Conteste (Favor de contestar) con frases completas!

1. ¿Tiene Ud. una aguja grande?

_____

2. ¿Quién tiene la aguja grande?

_____

3. ¿Tiene Ud. dos Tylenol™?

_____

4. ¿Dónde tiene Ud. el Valium™?

_____

5. ¿Tenemos anestesia para el dolor hoy?

_____

6. ¿Tienen los pacientes náusea a veces?[37]

_____

7. ¿Tiene el doctor alta presión?

_____

Ejercicio 5J

¡Complete usando la forma correcta del verbo **tener**!

EJEMPLO   Yo <u>tengo</u> frío y náusea.

1. Tú _____.

2. Ella _____.

3. El paciente _____.

4. Nosotros _____.

5. Ellos _____.

6. Uds. _____.

7. Elena y Juana _____.

---

[37]**a veces** at times, sometimes

✏️ Ejercicio 5K

Complete la frase con la forma correcta de **venir** y **poner**.

EJEMPLO   Nosotros <u>venimos</u> aquí al hospital y <u>ponemos</u> las almohadas en la cama.

1. Los enfermeros _____ y _____.

2. Usted _____ y _____.

3. Tú y yo _____ y _____.

4. Javier y Margarita _____ y _____.

5. Yo _____ y _____.

6. Tú _____ y _____.

7. Ustedes _____ y _____.

✏️ Ejercicio 5L

Conteste (Favor de contestar) con la forma correcta de **tener**.

1. ¿Tiene Ud. frío? _____

2. ¿Dónde tiene Ud. comezón? _____

3. ¿Quién tiene calambres? _____

4. ¿Tienen Uds. miedo de las agujas? _____

_____

5. ¿Le duele el brazo después de dar tantas[38] inyecciones?

_____

6. ¿Tiene náuseas después de comer tripas?[39] _____

_____

7. ¿Tiene la medicina que está tomando (que toma)? _____

_____

8. ¿Tiene algo para la náusea? _____

_____

---

[38]**tantas** so many
[39]**tripas** tripe or stuffed intestine casings

Ejercicio 5M

UN CRUCIGRAMA

This crossword provides an opportunity to test how well you remember basic parts of the body in Spanish.

Horizontales

1   2   3   4   5   6   7

Verticales

8   9   10   11   12   13   14   15

6

What you will learn in this lesson:

- to conjugate and use more irregular verbs in the present tense
- days, months, and dates
- to form the imperative (command forms)
- vocabulary related to a physical exam
- to conduct a physical exam in Spanish
- vocabulary related to a neurological exam (in the ER)
- to conduct a neurological exam in Spanish

The goal of this lesson is to be able to use the command form and thus give instructions and conduct a general physical and neurological exam.

6.1 **Irregular verbs in the present tense**

Before learning the fairly simple principles that enable you to form commands (called the imperative mood), let's just be totally certain that the stems, roots, or bases of the regular verbs in the present tense are deeply ingrained in your **cerebro**. From there, we will move on to the irregular verbs in the present tense, which will, in turn, directly lead to the formation of the imperative. From this, you will be able to instruct your patients with ease during any physical exam.

Recuerden *(Remember)*: regular verb endings in the present tense

tomar (to drink, to take)		**comer** (to eat)		**vivir** (to live)	
tom**o**	tom**amos**	com**o**	com**emos**	viv**o**	viv**imos**
tom**as**		com**es**		viv**es**	
tom**a**	tom**an**	com**e**	com**en**	viv**e**	viv**en**

Now let's review two commonly used irregular verbs:

estar (to be)		**ser** (to be)	
estoy	estamos	soy	somos
estás		eres	
está	están	es	son

Estar

Location
La mesa <u>está</u> en el piso.
Juan <u>está</u> en Arizona.

Temporary state or condition
José <u>está</u> enfermo.
Yo <u>estoy</u> contenta.
La sopa <u>está</u> caliente.

Ser

Permanent condition, characteristic, or identifier
Yo <u>soy</u> doctor.
Santa Claus <u>es</u> gordo.
Ella <u>es</u> americana.
José <u>es</u> de México.

There are some irregular verbs that are quite simple: they only change in the **yo** form. The conjugation is actually quite regular within its irregularity. Just note the letter "**g**" in the **yo** conjugation. Fortunately, the rest of the verb is conjugated exactly as if it were regular (except in **oír** and **decir**, **tener** and **venir**, which are only slightly different). Note the following infinitives and their first-person singular or **yo** forms.

Also, once you have learned the forms of some basic irregular verbs, you actually have learned many other verbs as well (for example, **poner: componer, reponer, suponer; decir: contradecir, malde-cir; traer: contraer, distraer**). Examine the following infinitives and their irregularities in the present tense, especially in the **yo** or first-person singular form.

hacer (to make, to do)		**poner** (to put)		**salir** (to exit, to leave)	
hago	hacemos	pongo	ponemos	salgo	salimos
haces		pones		sales	
hace	hacen	pone	ponen	sale	salen

tener (to have)		**venir** (to come)	
tengo	tenemos	vengo	venimos
tienes		vienes	
tiene	tienen	viene	vienen

traer (to bring)		**caer** (to fall)	
traigo	traemos	caigo	caemos
traes		caes	
trae	traen	cae	caen

decir (to say, to tell)		**oír** (to hear)	
digo	decimos	oigo	oímos
dices		oyes	
dice	dicen	oye	oyen

ir (to go)		**dar** (to give)	
voy	vamos	doy	damos
vas		das	
va	van	da	dan

Ejercicio 6A

Complete las frases con la forma correcta de **poner, hacer** y **salir**.

1. Yo (poner) _____ la loción en la cara; (hacer) _____ la cama y (salir) _____ de la casa.

2. Tú _____
_____ .

3. Su esposo _____

_____.

4. Los niños _____

_____.

5. La enfermera _____

_____.

6. Ud. _____

_____.

✐ Ejercicio 6B

Complete las frases con la forma correcta de **traer** y **caer**.

1. Yo (traer) _____ la receta a la farmacia, pero (caer)

   _____ porque no camino bien con las muletas.[1]

2. Pepe _____

_____.

3. Tú _____

_____.

4. Los accidentados _____

_____.

5. El enfermo _____

_____.

6. Ud. _____

_____.

7. Yo y tú _____

_____.

8. Ellos _____

_____.

_____

[1]**las muletas** crutches

9. María y Rosita _____

_____ .

10. Uds. _____

_____ .

✎ Ejercicio 6C

Complete las frases con la forma correcta de **ir** y **dar**.

1. Yo (ir) _____ al hospital y yo (dar) _____
el regalo[2] al paciente.

2. El personal[3] del hospital _____

_____ .

3. La familia _____

_____ .

4. Ud. _____

_____ .

5. Los abuelos _____

_____ .

6. Uds. _____

_____ .

7. Nosotros _____

_____ .

8. Los doctores _____

_____ .

9. Emilio _____

_____ .

10. La enfermera _____

_____ .

---

[2]**el regalo** gift
[3]**el personal** personnel, staff

STEM-CHANGING VERBS

The stem of a verb is what is left after the infinitive ending has been removed. You have already discovered that some verbs (**tener, venir, doler [duele]**) have changes in their stems in the present tense. Many verbs have a consistent pattern of changes and are often referred to as "shoe" or "boot" verbs. You will see why soon.

The most common changes are from an **o** in the stem to **ue** or from an **e** in the stem to **ie** in all forms, except the **nosotros** form. When a line is drawn around the forms with stem changes, it forms a shoe or boot, hence its name. And fortunately, "to boot," the **nosotros** form keeps the same vowel as in the infinitive form!

¡Ay, Dios mío, me duele la cabeza! Enough of this, I have a headache! Just examine the following verbs, and the patterns will make sense. Then, if need be, refer back to this explanation.

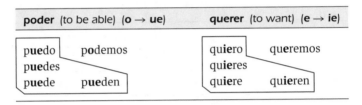

poder (to be able) (o → ue)		**querer** (to want) (e → ie)	
puedo	podemos	quiero	queremos
puedes		quieres	
puede	pueden	quiere	quieren

Other **o → ue** verbs		Other **e → ie** verbs	
probar	to try on, to test	**cerrar**	to close
mover	to move	**pensar**	to think
dormir	to sleep	**perder**	to lose
contar	to count, to tell	**encender**	to light, to turn on
doler[4]	to hurt	**extender**	to extend
encontrar	to find	**sentarse**	to sit down
volver	to return	**sentirse**	to feel

Note: **Sentarse** and **sentirse** are reflexive verbs, which means that the action of the verb reflects back to the individual. Reflexive verbs are discussed in Chapter 9, but for the time being, the following **yo** and **Ud.** forms are useful:

sentarse	**me siento** (I sit, am sitting, do sit)
	se sienta (you sit/he, she sits, etc.)
sentirse	**me siento** (I feel, am feeling, do feel)
	se siente (you feel/he, she feels, etc.)

---

[4]**me duele** it is painful to me, it hurts (from **doler**); **el dolor** is the noun meaning "pain."

✎ Ejercicio 6D

Llene los espacios con la forma correcta de **querer**.

1. El Señor Gómez _____ tomar su temperatura.

2. El paciente _____ tomar dos Tylenol™.

3. Yo no _____ pesarme.[5]

4. Ud. _____ sentarse.

5. Las pacientes _____ desconectarse de la máquina.[6]

6. Ellas _____ comer el lonche.[7]

✎ Ejercicio 6E

¡Complete las frases usando la forma correcta del verbo **querer**!

EJEMPLO   Yo <u>quiero</u> comer…

1. Tú _____.

2. Ella _____.

3. Nosotros _____.

4. Los pacientes _____.

5. Ud. _____.

✎ Ejercicio 6F

Llene los espacios con la forma correcta del verbo **poder**.

EJEMPLO   ¿Dónde (yo) <u>puedo</u> comprar medicinas?

1. ¿Dónde (yo) _____ tomar el peso?

2. ¿Dónde (él) _____ tomar su temperatura?

3. ¿Dónde (nosotros) _____ tomar raspados?

4. ¿Cuándo (yo) _____ desconectar la máquina?

5. ¿Cuándo (ellos) _____ escuchar el pulso?

---

[5]**pesarme** to weigh myself; **pesarse** to weigh oneself (a reflexive verb)
[6]**desconectarse de la máquina** to disconnect themselves from the machine
[7]**lonche** lunch (slang expression)

Ejercicio 6G

Conteste las preguntas con la forma correcta de **poder**.

1. ¿Qué puede hacer el paciente?

_____

2. ¿Dónde puedes comprar tacos y enchiladas?

_____

3. ¿Cuándo pueden venir Uds. a la clínica?

_____

4. ¿Quién puede hablar español?

_____

5. ¿Adónde podemos ir mañana?

_____

OTHER EXAMPLES

Let's look at some of the other verbs that follow the same pattern. Remember that stem changes occur in all forms, except the **nosotros** form.

e → ie

cerrar (to close)		**pensar** (to think)	
cierro	cerramos	pienso	pensamos
cierras		piensas	
cierra	cierran	piensa	piensan

o → ue

volver (to return)		**dormir** (to sleep)	
vuelvo	volvemos	duermo	dormimos
vuelves		duermes	
vuelve	vuelven	duerme	duermen

📝 Ejercicio 6H

Complete las frases con la forma correcta de **volver, cerrar** y **dormir**.

1. Yo (volver) _____ al hospital, (cerrar)

    _____ la puerta y (dormir) _____ .

2. El paciente _____

    _____ .

3. Los doctores _____

    _____ .

4. El enfermero _____

    _____ .

5. Las enfermeras _____

    _____ .

6. El lesionado _____

    _____ .

COMMON -ER VERBS (REGULAR AND IRREGULAR)

Present	
-o	-emos
-es	
-e	-en

aprender	to learn	**leer**	to read
caer (g)	to fall (*yo caigo*)	**padecer (zc)**	to suffer from
comer	to eat		(*yo padezco*)
comprender	to understand	**parecer (zc)**	to appear, to seem
correr	to run		(*yo parezco*)
creer	to believe	**perder**	to lose
deber	to owe, should	**poner (g)**	to put (*yo pongo*)
doler (ue)	to hurt	**prender**	to pin, to turn on
	(*me duele*)	**proteger (j)**	to protect
extender (ie)	to extend		(*yo protejo*)
	(*yo extiendo*)	**querer (ie)**	to want (*yo quiero*)
entender (ie)	to understand	**responder**	to respond
	(*yo entiendo*)	**saber**	to know (*yo sé*)

ser	to be (*yo soy*)	**torcer (ue)(z)**	to twist, turn
hacer (g)	to make, to do		(*yo tuerzo*)
	(*yo hago*)	**vender**	to sell
tener (ie)(g)	to have (*yo tengo*)	**ver**	to see

Notes:

- Some verbs have spelling changes in the **yo** form, but their other forms are conjugated the same as regular verbs or the same as stem-changing verbs.

(**zc**)

padecer: pade**zc**o, padeces, padece, padecemos, padecen

parecer: pare**zc**o, pareces, parece, parecemos, parecen

(**j**)

proteger: prote**j**o, proteges, protege, protegemos, protegen

(**z**)

torcer: tuer**z**o, tuerces, tuerce, torcemos, tuercen

- **Saber** has an irregular **yo** form in the present tense but the other forms are conjugated like a regular -**er** verb: **sé, sabes, sabe, sabemos, saben**.
- Recall that **ver** is very slightly irregular: **veo, ves, ve, vemos, ven**.

COMMON -IR VERBS (REGULAR AND IRREGULAR)

Present	
-o	-imos
-es	
-e	-en

abrir	to open	**morir (ue)**	to die (*yo muero*)
dormir (ue)	to sleep	**producir (zc)**	to produce
	(*yo duermo*)		(*yo produzco*)
escribir	to write	**subir**	to go up, ascend;
insistir	to insist		get on
introducir (zc)	to introduce	**sufrir**	to suffer
	(*yo introduzco*)	**venir (ie)(g)**	to come (*yo vengo*)
ir	to go (*yo voy*)	**vivir**	to live
medir (i)	to measure		
	(*yo mido*)		

Notes:

- Some verbs have spelling changes in the **yo** form, but their other forms are conjugated the same as regular verbs.

  (zc)

  introducir: introduzco, introduces, introduce, introducimos, introducen
  producir: produzco, produces, produce, producimos, producen

- **Medir** is an **e → i** stem-changing verb: **mido, mides, mide, medimos, miden**.

Now let's take a look at these irregular present tense verbs in action with examples:

tener (to have)	
tengo	tenemos
tienes	
tiene	tienen

Tengo muchos amigos.
Tengo frío, calor, etc.

tener que + infinitive   *to have to*

Tengo que comer.   I have to eat.
Tiene que descansar.   You have to rest.

Remember: **hacer, poner, salir, venir, traer, oír, decir** are conjugated like the verb **tener**.

ir (to go)	
voy	vamos
vas	
va	van

ir + **a** + noun   *destination*
Voy a la clínica.   I'm going to the clinic.

ir + **a** + infinitive   *the future tense*
Voy a tomar 2 aspirinas.   I'm going to take 2 aspirins.

Remember: **dar** is conjugated like **ir**.

STEM-CHANGING VERBS WITH SAMPLE SENTENCES

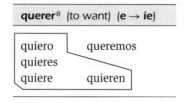

querer[8] (to want) (e → ie)

quiero	queremos
quieres	
quiere	quieren

querer + noun

Quiero mucho arroz.	I want a lot of rice.
Quiero más información.	I want more information.
Quiero una muestra de orina.	I want a urine sample.

querer + infinitive   to want + infinitive

| Quiero comer. | I want to eat. |
| Quiero descansar. | I want to rest. |

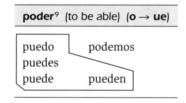

poder[9] (to be able) (o → ue)

puedo	podemos
puedes	
puede	pueden

| puedo | I can |
| no puedo | I can't |

poder + infinitive   to be able + infinitive

Puedo comer.	I can (am able to) eat.
Puedo mover el brazo.	I can (am able to) move my arm.
No puede respirar.	He can't (is not able to) breathe.

6.2   Days of the week
Los días de la semana

You have mastered how to courteously greet a Latino patient in Spanish; determine his or her chief complaint; qualify, quantify, and char-

---

[8]Other **e → ie** verbs: **pensar, perder, extender, entender, encender, sentarse, sentirse**.

[9]Other **o → ue** verbs: **dormir, volver, recordar, mostrar, torcer, encontrar, contar**.

acterize the pain or symptoms; and take a patient history. Now it's time to learn the days of the week and months so you can specify exactly which days your patient should take the medicine or when to return for another office visit.

Please also remember that in Spanish, the date is listed first, then the month, followed by the year. For example: 4/3/2005 in most of the world indicates March 4, 2005, while in the United States it is seen as April 3, 2005. Thus, unless you are familiar with this system, it may be best to write out the actual month: **el 3 de abril**.

lunes	martes	miércoles	jueves	viernes	sábado	domingo
	1	2	3	4	5	6
7	8	9	10	11	12	13
14	15	16	17	18	19	20
21	22	23	24	25	26	27
28	29	30	31			

Important points to remember about days in Spanish:

- Days of the week are never capitalized.
- The days of the week are masculine words.
- **El lunes** is the first day of the week.
- Always use **el** or **los** before the day except with **Hoy es…** and **Mañana es…**

Examine the following sentences with days of the week:

Hoy es lunes.	Today is Monday.
Mañana es martes.	Tomorrow is Tuesday.
Pasado mañana es miércoles.	The day after tomorrow is Wednesday.
Ayer fue domingo.	Yesterday was Sunday.
Antier fue sábado.	The day before yesterday was Saturday.
Voy el lunes.	I'm going on Monday.
Salgo el martes.	I leave on Tuesday.
Regreso el jueves.	I return on Thursday.
Trabajo los viernes.	I work Fridays (on Fridays).
No canto los domingos.	I don't sing on Sundays.

Notes:

- When the name of the day ends in **s**, the word does not change from singular to plural: **el jueves, los jueves**.
- Whereas in English we say, "I run on Wednesdays," in Spanish we say **Corro los miércoles**, with no equivalent for the word *on*.

 **Ejercicio 61**

Favor de contestar con frases completas.

1. ¿Qué día es hoy?

   _____

2. ¿Qué día es mañana?

   _____

3. ¿Qué día es pasado mañana?

   _____

4. Hoy es lunes. ¿Qué día es mañana?

   _____

5. Hoy es lunes. ¿Qué día es pasado mañana?

   _____

6. Hoy es jueves. ¿Qué día es mañana?

   _____

7. Hoy es jueves. ¿Qué día es pasado mañana?

   _____

8. ¿En qué día hay clases de español?

   _____

9. ¿En qué días hay trabajo?

   _____

10. ¿Cuándo vamos a la iglesia?[10]

    _____

---

[10]**iglesia** church

antes de/después de

Las 7:00 de la mañana es antes de las 8:00.
El número uno es antes del número dos.
El lunes es antes del martes.

Las 10:00 de la noche es después de las 9:00.
El número 4 es después del número 3.
El domingo es después del sábado.

 Ejercicio 6J

Favor de contestar con frases completas.

1. ¿Qué día es después del sábado?

   _____

2. ¿Qué día es antes del sábado?

   _____

3. ¿Qué día es después del domingo?

   _____

4. ¿Qué día es antes del domingo?

   _____

5. ¿Qué número es después del número 95?

   _____

6. ¿Qué número es antes del número 101?

   _____

7. ¿Qué horas son después de las tres de la tarde?

   _____

8. ¿Qué horas son antes de las dos de la tarde?

   _____

6.3
Months of the year
Los meses del año

enero	abril	julio	octubre
febrero	mayo	agosto	noviembre
marzo	junio	septiembre	diciembre

- Months are never capitalized in Spanish.
- Occasionally, you may find **septiembre** spelled as **setiembre**.

 Ejercicio 6K

Favor de contestar con frases completas.

1. ¿Qué mes es antes de febrero? _____

2. ¿Qué mes es antes de mayo? _____

3. ¿Qué mes es antes de agosto? _____

4. ¿Qué mes es antes de noviembre? _____

5. ¿Qué mes es antes de abril? _____

6. ¿Qué mes es antes de julio? _____

7. ¿Qué mes es antes de octubre? _____

8. ¿Qué mes es antes de enero? _____

El cumpleaños[11] de Abrahán Lincoln es el 12 de febrero.
El cumpleaños de Benito Juárez es el 21 de marzo.
Mi cumpleaños es el 17 de octubre.

 Ejercicio 6L

Favor de contestar con frases completas.

1. ¿Cuándo es su[12] cumpleaños?

_____

---

[11]**el cumpleaños** birthday
[12]**su** your

2. ¿Cuándo es el cumpleaños de su madre?

_____

3. ¿Cuándo es el cumpleaños de su padre?

_____

4. ¿En qué mes es el Día de las Madres?

_____

5. ¿En qué mes es el Día de los Padres?

_____

6. ¿En qué mes es el Día de la Independencia de los Estados Unidos?

_____

7. ¿En qué mes es el Día de la Independencia mexicana?

_____

8. ¿En qué mes es el Día de Dar Gracias?[13]

_____

9. ¿En qué mes es el Día de los Novios?[14]

_____

10. ¿En qué mes es el Día de la Raza?[15]

_____

11. ¿En qué mes es el Día de los Muertos?[16]

_____

12. ¿En qué mes es Navidad? _____

!

El mes:	Mi cumpleaños es en mayo.
La fecha:	Mi cumpleaños es el 17 de mayo.
Fecha de nacimiento:	Nací el 17 de mayo de 1975.
	_or_ 17/5/75

---

[13]In Puerto Rico, Thanksgiving is known as **El Día de Acción (de Dar) Gracias**.
[14]**Día de los Novios** Valentine's Day (literally, the Day of the Sweethearts)
[15]**Día de la Raza** Columbus Day (literally, the Day of the Race)
[16]**Día de los Muertos** All Souls' Day (literally, the Day of the Dead)

6.4 Authority figures and home remedies

In Latin America, generally speaking, priests, doctors, teachers, and other professionals are looked upon as authority figures. From the time one is young, a Latino is taught *not* to question authority, because this is rude and impertinent. This concept often extends into other aspects of life. In Latin America, the doctor still tends to make the decisions that he or she feels are best for the patient, and the patient would rarely presume to ask too many questions, if any. From the doctor's standpoint, such questions would be seen as disrespectful and even as a brazen challenge ("I'm the doctor, who are you to question my superior knowledge?"). Thus, the concept of including patients in on their course of treatment, which is encouraged in the United States, is bewildering to many Latin Americans. If a healthcare professional asks a Spanish-speaking patient, "What do you feel about . . . ?" or "What would you rather do about . . . ?", the patient is likely to smile politely, look a bit quizzical, and think to himself, "Well, you're the doctor, that's why I'm here. You tell me." However, the patient may well say aloud, **Lo que Ud. diga, doctor(a)** ("Whatever you say, doctor"). Note that in some Latin American countries with a large indigenous population, prolonged eye contact may be considered rude or challenging, particularly when directed toward authority figures.

Many times Latin American patients may have already tried several "remedies" on their own; therefore, asking them to participate will cause them to think "I tried everything I knew already, why are you asking me?" A probable sequence of home remedies could be as follows:

- Call mom or grandma. She probably will recommend **té de manzanilla** (chamomile tea) or **té de yerbabuena** (mint tea), or a variety of other teas. These teas are nearly always staples in the home.
- Try something from the medicine cabinet left over from last time one had similar symptoms (and don't be surprised if it's those leftover **antibióticos**).
- Try something from the neighbor's, cousin's, or other helpful person's medicine cabinet.
- Go to the drugstore and ask the pharmacist, "What are people taking for these symptoms?"
- Start a series of antibiotic injections or pills.

- See an herbalist (**un yerbero**)[17] and drink different teas consisting of herbs or roots one does not always have in the home.
- See a **curandero** or **santero**.

If nothing has worked thus far, the patient may now go to the clinic or the doctor's office.

A notable exception to this course of events is if the patient is a child. With children, Latinos do not like to take chances and seem to go for the "whole enchilada" right away. This process seems to hold true for all socioeconomic levels. As an aside, it is worth mentioning that in Latin America there is little discrimination in regard to color or country of origin; however, there is a definite separation between the socioeconomic classes.

 # 6.5 The imperative mood or command form

It's time to take a look at (or better yet to learn) the imperative or command form. The imperative mood is a helpful tool for giving instructions, whether for exams, follow-up explanations, or prescriptions, giving directions, or simply informing your patient what you want him or her to do.

In English the same form of the verb is used in the present tense as is used in the command form. For example:

Present tense	*Command*
I **walk** on my heels.	**Walk** on your heels!
I **take** pills every day.	**Take** your pills!

In Spanish, for regular verbs, the last letter is different in the present tense **yo** form and in the command form. (There are a few other letter changes in irregular verbs and the **g**-changing verbs in the **yo** form that you will see a bit later; but, for now, not to worry!)

Study the pictures and the command forms on the next page.

---

[17]**yerbero**, also spelled **hierbero**

COMMANDS — *EL IMPERATIVO O LOS MANDATOS*

Tomar

¡Tome Ud.!   ¡Tomen Uds.!   ¡No tome Ud.!   ¡No tomen Uds.!

Comer

¡Coma Ud.!   ¡Coman Uds.!   ¡No coma Ud.!   ¡No coman Uds.!

Abrir

¡Abra Ud.!   ¡Abran Uds.!   ¡No abra Ud.!   ¡No abran Uds.!

To make a command

If a verb ends in **-ar**	drop **-ar** and add **e**	hab<u>lar</u>	hab<u>le</u> Ud.
If a verb ends in **-er**	drop **-er** and add **a**	com<u>er</u>	com<u>a</u> Ud.
If a verb ends in **-ir**	drop **-ir** and add **a**	abr<u>ir</u>	abr<u>a</u> Ud.

Remember, in the command form:

- **-ar** verbs end in **-e** (*singular*) or **-en** (*plural*)
- **-er** and **-ir** verbs end in **-a** (*singular*) or **-an** (*plural*)

Verbos de **-ar**

Infinitive	Command (**Ud.**) Add -**e**	Command (**Uds.**) Add -**en**
tomar	tom**e**	tom**en**
caminar	camin**e**	camin**en**
fumar	fum**e**	fum**en**
exhalar	exhal**e**	exhal**en**
inyectar	inyect**e**	inyect**en**
examinar	examin**e**	examin**en**

Verbos de **-er** e **-ir**

Infinitive	Command (**Ud.**) Add -**a**	Command (**Uds.**) Add -**an**
comer	com**a**	com**an**
abrir	abr**a**	abr**an**
beber	beb**a**	beb**an**
toser	tos**a**	tos**an**
vivir	viv**a**	viv**an**
escupir	escup**a**	escup**an**

 Ejercicio 6M

Escriba un mandato según el dibujo[18] usando **Ud.** y **Uds.**

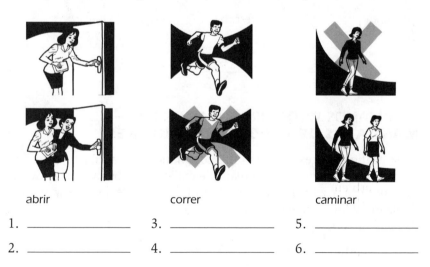

abrir   correr   caminar

1. _____   3. _____   5. _____

2. _____   4. _____   6. _____

---

[18]**dibujo** drawing

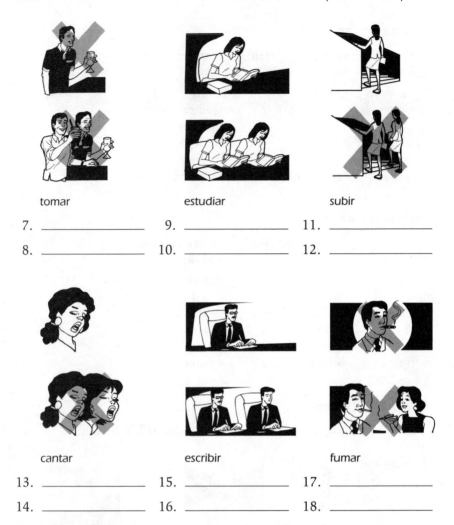

tomar   estudiar   subir

7. _____   9. _____   11. _____

8. _____   10. _____   12. _____

cantar   escribir   fumar

13. _____ 15. _____ 17. _____

14. _____ 16. _____ 18. _____

COMMANDS WITH IRREGULAR VERBS —
MANDATOS DE VERBOS IRREGULARES

Look at the pictures and read the commands below. Try to determine a pattern, and then go on to read the explanation below the drawings. In many cases with languages, that old axiom, "A picture is worth a thousand words" actually makes a great deal of sense.

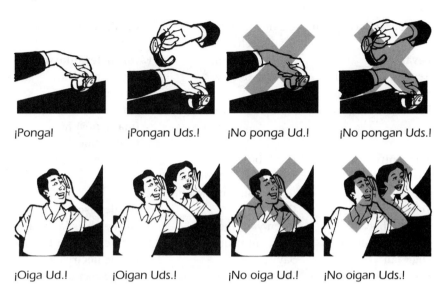

¡Ponga!　　　　¡Pongan Uds.!　　　¡No ponga Ud.!　　¡No pongan Uds.!

¡Oiga Ud.!　　　¡Oigan Uds.!　　　¡No oiga Ud.!　　¡No oigan Uds.!

How to make a command with an irregular verb:

1. Find the **yo** form.　　　　EJEMPLO: decir　(yo) digo
2. Remove the -**o** ending.　　EJEMPLO: dig
3. Add the correct ending.　　EJEMPLO: dig + a → Diga Ud.

Note: With these verbs, as with regular verbs, add -**e**, -**en** to -**ar** verbs and add -**a**, -**an** to -**er** and -**ir** verbs.

COMMON COMMANDS

The following is a list of typical commands or structures that you will use frequently. We highly suggest memorizing the ones in the left-hand column that you use repeatedly. You may find the ones in the right-hand column (**Favor de** + infinitive—the shortcut!) to be easier to use, particularly if you draw a blank or if you only refer to them from time to time. Memorize the ones that you handle with the most ease. But, at least now, you can understand how they are formed and can deduce how to do so with other verbs not included here.

Siéntese	Sit down, sit up	**Favor de sentarse**
Relájese/aflójese	Relax	**Favor de relajarse/ aflojarse**
Acuéstese	Lie down	**Favor de acostarse**
Acuéstese boca arriba	Lie down on your back	**Favor de acostarse boca arriba**

Acuéstese boca abajo	Lie down on your stomach	**Favor de acostarse boca abajo**
Levántese	Stand up/get up	**Favor de levantarse**
Respire profundo	Breathe deeply	**Favor de respirar profundo**
Detenga la respiración	Hold your breath	**Favor de detener (mantener) la respiración**
No respire	Don't breathe	**Favor de no respirar**
Ya[19]	Okay, That's enough, You can breathe now[20]	
Tosa	Cough	**Favor de toser**
Abra la boca	Open your mouth	**Favor de abrir la boca**
Saque[21] **la lengua**	Stick out your tongue	**Favor de sacar la lengua**
Diga "ah"	Say "ah"	**Favor de decir "ah"**
Escupa	Spit	**Favor de escupir**
Extienda el brazo	Extend your arm	**Favor de extender el brazo**
Doble el brazo	Bend your arm	**Favor de doblar el brazo**
Cierre los ojos	Close your eyes	**Favor de cerrar los ojos**
Haga un puño	Make a fist	**Favor de hacer un puño**
Lávese las manos	Wash your hands	**Favor de lavarse las manos**
Muévase/No se mueva[22]	Move/Don't move, Hold still	**Favor de moverse/ no moverse**
Póngase en cuclillas	Squat down	**Favor de ponerse en cuclillas**
Agáchese	Bend over/Duck down[23]	**Favor de agacharse**
Tome dos pastillas	Take two pills	**Favor de tomar dos pastillas**
Descanse	Rest	**Favor de descansar**
Observe la reacción	Observe the reaction	**Favor de observar la reacción**
Venga aquí	Come here	**Favor de venir aquí**

---

[19]**Ya** has many meanings: "all right already," "that's fine," "that's enough," "that's all," "okay" . . . **¡Ya!**

[20]You can also say **Respire normal** ("Breathe normally now").

[21]Verbs that end in **-car** have a spelling change in the command form in order to retain the hard **c** sound. In the **Ud./Uds.** commands, the **c** changes to **qu**: sacar—saque, saquen; indicar—indique, indiquen; tocar—toque, toquen.

[22]from **moverse**; note the spelling change

[23]You can also say **Doble la cintura** ("Bend over").

Regrese mañana	Come back tomorrow	Favor de regresar mañana
Traiga la muestra	Bring the sample	Favor de traer la muestra
No tema	Don't be afraid	Favor de no temer
No tenga miedo	Don't be afraid	Favor de no tener miedo
¡Indique (señale) dónde le duele!	Indicate where it hurts!	¡Favor de indicar (señalar) dónde le duele!
¡Indique cuándo le duele!	Indicate when it hurts!	¡Favor de indicar (señalar) cuándo le duele!

In addition, the following simple phrase can be used frequently, as you demonstrate something for the patient to imitate:

¡Haga esto!	Do this!	¡Favor de hacer esto!

6.6 A physical exam
Un examen físico

Let's see how well you do using the imperative form while ordering your patient about in the following physical exam.

VOCABULARIO | A physical exam

saque la lengua	stick out your tongue
trague/pase saliva, por favor	swallow, please
tosa, por favor	cough, please
acuéstese, por favor	lie down, please
por favor, doble...	please bend . . .
aflójese, por favor	relax/loosen up
mire este punto	look at this dot/point
mire esta luz	look at this light
otra vez	again
póngase la ropa	put your clothes on
puede vestirse ahora,[24] puede ponerse la ropa	you can get dressed now
abra	open
diga	say (command)
palpar	to palpate

---

[24]This form is gentler and less harsh, especially when used by a male to a female.

☷ MONÓLOGO 6.6 | A physical exam

In this monologue, listen to how the doctor uses the imperative form
to give the patient instruction during a physical exam.

DOCTORA   Buenas tardes, señora… Hoy necesito examinarle. ¿Okey?
            Primero, voy a examinar sus ojos.[25] Por favor, mire la luz
                (este punto).
            Bueno, saque la lengua, por favor.
            Gracias. Por favor, abra la boca y diga "Ah."
            Pase saliva, por favor. (Trague, por favor.)
            Gracias. Ahora, quiero escuchar sus pulmones.
            Respire profundo por la boca, por favor.
            Otra vez… otra vez.
            Tosa, por favor.
            ¡Acuéstese!
            Doble las rodillas, por favor.
            Relájese, necesito palpar (examinar) su estómago.
            Gracias. Siéntese otra vez.
            Afloje la pierna… gracias.
            Bueno, es todo.
            Puede vestirse ahora (Puede ponerse la ropa), y regreso en
                un momento (ahorita regreso).

 Ejercicio 6N

Favor de contestar las siguientes preguntas con frases completas.

1. ¿Qué va a examinar el doctor primero?

_____

2. ¿Qué dice el doctor de la luz?

_____

3. Favor de escribir cinco cosas[26] que el doctor dice al paciente.

_____

_____

---

[25]**Examinar sus ojos** may be used in Spanish, but the Royal Academy of Spain
would prefer **examinarle los ojos**. The words **mi(s)** and **su(s)** are considered unneces-
sary with body parts. **El, los, la,** or **las** is generally used, but it is easier to use **mi(s)**
and **su(s)** when one is just learning Spanish and thinking from English to Spanish.
[26]**cosas** things

___

 6.7 A neurological exam
Un examen neurológico

At times a neurological exam may follow or be more appropriate for your needs, so here is a sample of one. Remember, you each have your own routine, so just note the structures and replace the order with your own. If you need to add instructions not included here, you now have enough knowledge and background to be able to do so.

 VOCABULARIO | **A neurological exam**

hacerle un examen	to examine you	**las cejas**	eyebrows
		cierre	close
examinarle[27]	to examine you	**abra**	open
haga esto	do this	**toque**	touch (from *tocar*)
mire	look	**las puntas del pie**	tiptoes
así	like this	**muerda**	bite (from *morder* [o → ue])
empuje contra	push against		
jale (hale)	pull (from *jalar*)	**infle**	inflate
empuje	push (from *empujar*)	**suba**	shrug, lift, go up (from *subir*)
resista	resist (from *resistir*)	**una sonrisa**	a smile
siga[28]	follow (from *seguir*)	**¿Siente más aquí o acá?**	Do you feel more here or here?
¿Puede oír esto?	Can you hear this?	**dé vuelta**[29]	turn (from *dar*)
¿Oye esto?	Do you hear this?	**extienda las manos**	hold out your hands
apriete	squeeze (from *apretar* [e → ie])	**palmas hacia arriba/abajo**	palms up/down
levante	raise, lift		

___

[27]**Necesito examinarle** is a little easier to remember and say than **Necesito hacerle un examen**.

[28]**Siga** comes from **seguir**, an **e → i** stem-changing verb: **sigo, sigues, sigue, seguimos, siguen**.

[29]**Dar vuelta** is an idiomatic expression that means "to turn." The **Ud.** command form of **dar** is **dé**; the **Uds.** command form is **den**.

MONÓLOGO 6.7 | A neurological exam

At times a neurological exam may be necessary, and this monologue provides an example.

DOCTORA Buenas tardes… Pase, por favor… Siéntese aquí.
Voy a hacerle un examen neurológico. (Necesito examinarle.)
Por favor, mire aquí.
Siga mi dedo con los ojos, pero no mueva la cabeza.
¿Oye esto? (¿Puede oír esto?)
Levante las cejas. Baje las cejas.
Cierre los ojos. Abra los ojos.
Una sonrisa grande, por favor.
Haga esto. Infle las mejillas (los cachetes).
Empuje contra mi mano con su cabeza. (Resista.)
Ahora contra la otra mano. (Resista.)
Muerda muy fuerte. Así. Suba los hombros.
Apriete mis dedos—fuerte.
Empuje contra mis manos. (Resista.) Jale mis manos. (Resista.)
¡Levántese! Cierre los ojos. Abra los ojos. Camine derecho.
Dé vuelta y camine en los talones.
Dé vuelta y camine en las puntas de los pies.
Toque mi dedo con su dedo. Toque su nariz con su dedo. Otra vez. Otra vez.
Levante los brazos enfrente de Ud., palmas hacia arriba. Ahora, palmas hacia abajo, palmas hacia arriba, palmas hacia abajo,… más rápido, muy bien. Gracias.
Siéntese, por favor, y extienda las piernas (los pies). ¿Siente esto?
¿Siente más aquí o acá?
Muchas gracias. Espere aquí, un momento.

 Ejercicio 60

Write all of the command forms you find in the preceding dialogue and also list the infinitive form of their verbs.

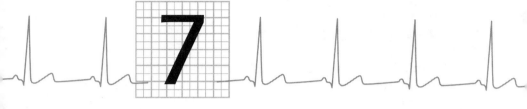

What you will learn in this lesson:

- to use the "key power verbs" with infinitives
- to use key power verbs in sentences concerning treatment instructions and procedures
- to give prescription and follow-up instructions
- to give directions for how to get to the laboratory, restroom, etc.
- vocabulary related to a pelvic exam and a pap smear
- to conduct a culturally sensitive pap smear
- to form, conjugate, and use the present progressive (continuous) tense
- to perform and run lab tests

The goal of this lesson is to be able to use a shortcut for forming grammatically correct questions and answers in their simplest possible form; give follow-up and prescription instructions, and directions; conduct a culturally sensitive pelvic exam and pap smear; and perform and run lab tests in Spanish.

7.1 **Key power verbs**

The following "key power verbs" or conjugated basic verbs can be used with any infinitive to form a statement, a question, or a command. If you use only **necesito** or **necesita** *with any infinitive,* you will be able to express the majority of what you need to convey—and the best aspect is that the structures will be easy to form and grammatically correct. Just remember to keep it simple!

The verbs in bold letters in the middle column are your power verbs. You may wish to interchange them for variety; for example, **Necesito tomar su pulso**, **Voy a tomar su pulso**, or **Quiero tomar su pulso**.

Also, remember that the **él/ella/Ud.** form (called the third-person singular) will help you cover a lot of ground:

El técnico va a sacarle sangre.	The lab tech is going to draw your blood.
Su hijo necesita antibióticos.	Your son needs antibiotics.

Therefore, in the power-verb column, you'll find the "power persons": first-person singular (**yo**) and third-person singular (**él**, **ella**, **Ud.**), which are the most important forms in the health profession.

The left-hand column consists of "question words" that are placed before a verb to form a question: *¿Cuándo* **necesito** (**yo**) **tomar las pastillas, doctor?**, or *¿Qué* **quiere** (**Ud.**) **tomar—pastillas o cápsulas?**

In the right-hand column, the **-le** connected to the end of the infinitive means "(to) you, (to) her, (to) him." For example:

Necesito inyectarle.	I need to inject you./I need to give a shot to you.

To indicate "(to) me," connect **-me** to the infinitive. For example:

¿Va a inyectarme?	Are you going to give me a shot/to give a shot to me?

HOW TO USE THE CHART

You may choose any power verb followed by any infinitive to form a sentence:

Necesito inyectarle.	I need to inject you.

or you may choose any question word followed by any power verb + any infinitive to pose a question:

Qué necesita tomar?	What do you need to take?

or, to be more specific, you may insert an appropriate noun:

¿Qué medicina necesita tomar?	What medicine do you need to take?

Question words	Power verbs	Infinitive
¿Quién? (Who?)	**Necesito**[1] (I need) **Necesita**[1] (You need, he/she needs)	inyectarle tomar
¿Qué? (What?)		enyesar[2]
¿Cuándo? (When?)	**Quiero** (I want) **Quiere** (You want) **Quisiera** (I would like, you would like, would you like?)	pesarle examinarle sacar sangre
¿Cuánto(-a)? (How much?)		sacar rayos X
¿Cuántos(-as)? (How many?)	**Voy a** (I am going [to]) **Va a** (You are going [to])	ponerle o aplicarle un suero
¿Dónde? (Where?)	**Favor de** (Please)	traerme sus medicinas
¿Cómo? (How?)	**Puedo** (I am able [to]) **Puede** (You are able [to])	decir "ah" extender el brazo
¿Por qué? (Why?)	**Es necesario** (It is necessary)	hacer una cita medirle
¿Cuál?/¿Cuáles? (Which?)	**Permítame** (Allow me) **¿Me permite...?** (May I . . . ?)	comer frutas lavarse las manos
¿Cada cuándo? (How often?)		consultar
¿Cuántas veces? (How many times?)	**Tengo que** (I have to) **Tiene que** (You have to) **Debo** (I must) **Debe** (You must)	descansar mucho hacer ejercicio hacerle una prueba

Using the structures in the chart, you can say nearly everything you require while interviewing patients, taking histories, conducting exams, and giving instructions. If you need an infinitive not listed here, just remember that the dictionary is your friend.

The following phrases can also be used with the infinitive. They enable you to avoid the use of the subjunctive, which greatly simplifies matters.

Antes de (Before)   **Al** (Upon)
Después de (After)   **Hasta** (Until)

---

[1]**Necesito** and **Necesita** are the most important and versatile power verbs, particularly if you need to limit your selection. They can be used for nearly everything and are truly the main key power verbs.

Necesito can replace **quiero, quisiera, voy a, puedo, es necesario, tengo que,** and **debo.**

Necesita can replace **quiere, quisiera, va a, favor de, puede, es necesario, tiene que,** and **debe.**

[2]**enyesarle** to put your . . . in a plaster cast

Ejercicio 7A

Favor de escribir diez frases o preguntas que Ud. utiliza con los *"power verbs."*

TREATMENT PROCEDURES — PROCEDIMIENTOS CURATIVOS

Some phrases for describing treatment procedures use key power verbs and the infinitive. Others use a key power verb followed by a thing (noun): **Quisiera una bolsa de hielo.** ("I would like an ice-pack.")

Necesito	**desinfectar** (to disinfect)
Quiero	**curar** (to cure)
Favor de	**aislar** (to isolate)
Voy a	**bajar** (to lower)
Puedo	**operar** (to operate)
Quisiera[3]	**inmunizar** (to immunize)
(etc.)	**lavar** (to wash)
	limpiar (to clean)
Necesita	**observar** (to observe)
Quiere	**preparar** (to prepare)
Tiene que	**entablillar** (to put on a splint)
Va a	**enyesar** (to put in/on a cast)
Debe	**poner** (to put)
Puede	**secar** (to dry)
Quisiera[3]	**mover** (to move)
(etc.)	**tomar** (to drink, to take)
	descansar (to rest)
	frotar/sobar (to rub, massage)
	guardar (estar en) cama (to be/stay in bed)
	ingresarse/internarse (to admit/to hospitalize)
	consultar con un especialista (to visit a specialist)
	alimentación intravenosa, suero (intravenous feeding)
	baño de asiento (sitz bath)
	bolsa de agua caliente (hot water bottle)
	bolsa de hielo (ice pack)
	duchas/lavados (douches)

---

[3]Since **quisiera** is derived from the verb **querer**, but is a different tense, the endings are unlike those of the present tense. It is actually easier to use, since the endings in first- and third-person singular are the same, and it is also more polite. However, there are occasions when you need to be firmer with your patient and **necesita** or **debe** work better.

enemas/lavativas (enemas)
fomentos de agua caliente (hot water compresses)
rayos X/radiografías/placas (X rays)
quimioterapia (chemotherapy)
radiaciones (radiation treatment)
receta médica (medical prescription)
sonda/catéter (catheter)
terapia (therapy)
transfusión de sangre (blood transfusion)
tratamiento hormonal (hormone treatment)
mucho descanso/muchos líquidos (plenty of rest/fluids)

7.2 Prescription and diet instructions

In order to give specific instructions to your patients regarding prescriptions and dosages, the following list will be of great help. To form an instruction, begin with the command form of the verb and the type of medication. Much, but not all, of the medicine is taken internally; thus, the instruction should start with **Tome** ("Drink" or "Take," in the command form). The next part is to specify "what." Most medications taken internally come in the following formats:

la píldora	pill	**la cápsula**	capsule
la tableta	tablet	**el jarabe**	syrup
la pastilla	pill	**el líquido**	liquid
el trocito	lozenge	**la medicina**	medicine
la gragea	coated pill	**el medicamento**	medication

You learned earlier that nearly all qualitative adjectives follow the noun, for example, **la píldora azul** ("the blue pill"); while all quantitative adjectives precede the noun, for example, **dos píldoras azules** ("two blue pills"). Again, remember that the nouns and adjectives must agree in number and gender.

Tome <u>dos</u> píldoras azul<u>es</u>.   Take two blue pills.
Tome <u>una</u> pastilla blanc<u>a</u>.   Take one white pill.

On the subject of quantities, the metric system is most commonly used in Latin America, and you can be reasonably sure that your patients are familiar with **mililitros**, **gramos**, and so on.

SPOONS

A common measurement for liquid medicine is "spoons." In Spanish a spoon is **una cuchara**.

- A tablespoon for measuring is **una cucharada**.
- A teaspoon is referred to in the diminutive as **una cucharadita** or **una cucharita**.

Notes:

- "Tablespoonful" adds the -**ada** ending to **cucharada** "spoon"; a "teaspoonful" adds the -**ita** ending, giving **cucharadita** or **cucharita**.
- To avoid potential confusion, it may be helpful to simply specify **una cuchara grande** or **una cuchara chica**.

Tome dos cucharadas del jarabe para la tos.
Take two tablespoonsful of the cough syrup.

Tome una cucharadita del líquido.
Take a teaspoonful of the liquid.

INSERTION AND APPLICATION

There are other methods of using medicine besides taking it internally. The following list consists of some of the formats and appropriate verbs that may be used:

For inserting[3] into a body cavity, use the verb:

introduzca (from *introducir*)   insert

Things that may be inserted include:

el supositorio	the suppository
el aplicador	the applicator
el dedo	the/your finger

Avoid using verbs such as **ponga** (from **poner**) or **meta** (from **meter**) because they have a harsh connotation, similar to "stick in" or "stuff in" in English.

---

[3]The verb **insertar** in Spanish is less harsh than **poner** or **meter**, but not as "polite" as **introducir**.

Introduzca el supositorio con cuidado.
Insert the suppository carefully.

Introduzca el aplicador en la vagina.
Insert the applicator in the vagina.

For medication applied topically, use:

frote (from *frotar*)	rub
sobe (from *sobar*)	massage
ponga (from *poner*)	put
aplique (from *aplicar*)	apply

Things that are applied topically are:

la loción	lotion	**el ungüento**[4]	ointment
la crema	cream	**la solución**	solution
la pomada	ointment, salve		

Frote la pomada...	Rub the salve/ointment . . .
Sobe la crema...	Massage the cream . . .
Ponga el ungüento en...	Put the ointment on . . .
Aplique la solución...	Apply the solution . . .
Ponga (Aplique) las gotas en los ojos/oídos.	Put/Apply the drops in the eyes/ears.

Other methods and the appropriate verbs are listed below.
    For **trocitos** (lozenges), use the following verbs as applicable:

tome (from *tomar*)	take
mastique (from *masticar*)	chew
masque (from *mascar*)	chew
chupe (from *chupar*)	suck

For an **inhalador** (inhaler), use:

inhale (from *inhalar*)	inhale
dé (from *dar*) **dos bombazos**[5]	take two puffs

---

[4]Whenever you see **ü**, the umlaut signals that the **u** (*oo*) sound is pronounced.
[5]The noun **bombazo** comes from **bombear**, "to pump, bomb, burst."

For **espray** (spray), use:

rocíe (from *rociar*)   spray

For **parches** (patches), use:

aplique (from *aplicar*)   apply
ponga (from *poner*)   put

FREQUENCY

The next part of the instruction focuses on when and how often the medicine is used:

3 veces al (por) día	3 times a day
cada 8 horas	every 8 hours
al levantarse	upon getting up
al acostarse	when or upon going to bed
con comida	with food
sin comida	without food
en ayunas	fasting, without eating in the morning
antes de[6]...	before . . .
después de...	after . . .

Occasionally the instruction is to take the medicine "every other day." A literal translation of this would be **cada otro día**, which could be misunderstood for "every day." Latin Americans count the first and the last day. In many countries the saying **Hay ocho días en una semana** is taught. The week begins with **el lunes** as day one and ends with **el lunes** again as day eight. If you count today, then tomorrow is the other day.

Most Latin American doctors would instruct the patient to take the medicine **cada tercer día**, or "every third day." (Today, **lunes**, is the first day; tomorrow, **martes**, is the second day; and the day after tomorrow, **miércoles**, is the third day. Thus, the patient would take the medicine on **lunes**, but start counting **miércoles** again as day one, or in other words, on Monday and Wednesday, or every other day.) To resolve the dilemma, use the following: **un día sí**, **un día no**. This is understood by everyone, everywhere.

---

[6]**antes de, después de, al,** and **hasta** can be followed by an infinitive (**antes de comer, después de levantarse, al comer, hasta terminar toda la medicina**) or a noun (**después de la cena** [after dinner]).

Tome 2 pastillas 3 veces por día con comida.
Take 2 pills 3 times a day with food.

**Introduzca el supositorio en el recto cada noche antes
de acostarse.**
Insert the suppository each night before going to bed.

Ponga un parche en el brazo cada día al levantarse.
Put a patch on the arm every day upon getting up.

DURATION

The last part of the instruction deals with how long the medicine should be taken.

por 10 días	for 10 days
por un período de una semana	for a period of one week
por el resto de su vida	for the rest of your life
como sea necesario	as needed

Note: **P.R.N.** is the same abbreviation in Spanish, since it is derived from Latin. The closest translation is **cuando sea necesario**, which literally means, "whenever it may be necessary." Perhaps the concept of "if one is good, two or four are even better" is cross-cultural. But just to be sure, it's best to qualify instructions in Spanish by stating something to the effect of:

Tome entre 1 y 2 pastillas cada 4 a 6 horas, pero sólo si le duele (arde, pica, molesta) mucho, pero no más de 8 pastillas al día.[7]

 Ejercicio 7B

Escriba estas instrucciones en inglés.

1. Tome dos pastillas tres veces al día por diez días, hasta terminar

   todas las pastillas. _____

   _____

---

[7]"Take 1 to 2 pills every 4 to 6 hours, but only if it hurts (burns, itches, bothers you) a lot, but no more than 8 pills per day."

2. Introduzca el supositorio en el recto cada noche antes de acostarse por un período de dos semanas. _____

_____

3. Aplique la crema en las llagas[8] tres veces al día, por una semana.

_____

 Ejercicio 7C

Favor de escribir dos conjuntos de instrucciones típicas que Ud. dice muy a menudo a sus pacientes. Seleccione dos síntomas o enfermedades diferentes. *(Write two different sets of instructions that you often give to patients. Choose two different symptoms or illnesses.)*

 7.3 Pap smear

El examen de papanicolau

Bueno, su paciente se presenta en su consultorio para su examen pélvico o de Papanicolau. You may want to ask your patient if she would like you to explain what you're doing as you go along, or before the exam, or if she would rather you just perform it and see if she has any questions afterward. **¿Prefiere una explicación durante el examen, o no?** After the exam, you may ask, **¿Tiene preguntas, Señora López?** "Do you have any questions, Mrs. López?"

Asking beforehand is thoughtful because some women are quite embarrassed about the genitalia, discussing it, or even thinking about it. Others, obviously, are more outspoken. At the risk of generalizing, the indigenous women of Mexico and Central America are often embarrassed, do not necessarily want to hear much explanation, and would rather just "get it over with." Some older women may feel the same. The Caribbean women living in the United States are often more open about the body and ask quite a few questions. Younger women and teenagers may also do so.

Once again, the degree of comfort or discomfort with the subject may depend on the education level, age, socioeconomic level, and/or the patient's level of assimilation into the U.S. culture. Many **latinoamericanas**, perhaps with less education, those from rural areas, or those who are taught not to question authority (in this case, the doctor) may even have had a hysterectomy, but not know exactly what

---

[8]**llagas** oozing wounds, bedsores

organs were removed. They may have had an IUD inserted by a doctor in their native country and not even be aware of it. Some of you have undoubtedly encountered situations such as these, while others may read this in disbelief. It all depends on your patient populations.

The following monologue is an example of what you may want to say while performing a pap smear. We recommend that you learn and adapt the structures to your own routine and order for conducting exams. The sentence structure and the key expressions (such as "Move down, move down") are what should be focused on.

 VOCABULARIO | **Pap smear**

hacia	toward
desde el/del cuello hacia abajo	from the neck on down
la glándula tiroides	thyroid gland
¿Nota...?	Do you notice . . . ? (from *notar*)
vestirse	to dress yourself
Muévase más hacia mí./Favor de moverse más hacia mí.	Move more toward me. (*loosely,* Move down, move down.)
Muévase más para aquí/acá.	Move more toward here. Move down, move down.[9]
Favor de moverse hasta la orilla de la mesa.	Please move down to the edge of the table.
Adelante, avance, por favor./ Favor de avanzar.	Please move forward. (*implying down*)
Muévase hacia atrás.	Move back.
introducir el espéculo/el pato	to insert the speculum
algunos	some
Separe las rodillas, por favor./ Favor de separar las rodillas.	Please separate your knees.

MONÓLOGO 7.3 | **Pap smear**

This monologue contains phrases for use with conducting a pap smear or pelvic exam.

DOCTORA   ¿Es su primer examen de papanicolau?
          Voy a examinarle en general y a examinar sus pechos (senos) y partes genitales también.

---

[9]To make it even easier, just **más acá**, **más acá** will probably be sufficient. However, do not use **abajo** ("down, below") or **bajar** ("to lower or get off [out]"). **Bajarse de** is used for getting out of a car, or getting off a train, bus, bike, or horse. "Down" literally means "down" and your patient just may get off the exam table. Indeed, many questions or statements are taken more literally in Spanish than in English (see the cultural explanation in Section 7.4 of this chapter).

Necesito examinar su glándula tiroides. Voy a escuchar el (su)[10] corazón.

Voy a escuchar los (sus) pulmones. Por favor, respire profundo por la boca.

Acuéstese, por favor. (Favor de acostarse.)

Ponga los pies aquí.[11]

Voy a escuchar su corazón otra vez—y ahora su estómago.

Ahora necesito examinar los senos. ¿Examina Ud. sus senos en casa? ¿Nota Ud. algo que le preocupa?

Ahora voy a poner presión en su estómago. ¿Le duele?

Muévase más hacia mí, por favor. (Favor de moverse más para acá.)

Son mis manos... Son mis dedos.

Ahora, voy a introducir el espéculo (pato). Va a sentir un poco de presión ahora.

Aquí están los cultivos y la muestra del examen de papanicolau.

Y ahora, voy a introducir(le) mis dedos para examinarle.

Es todo. Puede moverse más hacia atrás y sentarse ahora. (Muévase más hacia atrás y siéntese, por favor.)

En un momento la enfermera va a llevar las muestras al laboratorio. Después, regreso con algunos de los resultados, y vamos a hablar más.

Ahora Ud. puede vestirse.[12] (Favor de vestirse.)

 Ejercicio 7D

Favor de contestar las siguientes preguntas.

1. ¿Cómo se dice[13] en español "Move down, move down"?

_____

2. What is the politest way to say, "I am going to insert the speculum"?

_____

3. What is the politest way to say, "You can get dressed now"?

_____

---

[10]Remember to use either **el/la** or **su** with body parts, but not both.

[11]The word **estribos** means "stirrups (for a horse's saddle)." There is no specific word for stirrups on an exam table. It is easier to point to the stirrups and use **aquí** ("here").

[12]**Ahora Ud. puede vestirse** is more polite, less harsh, and less threatening.

[13]**¿Cómo se dice...?** How do you say . . . ? (literally, How is . . . said?)

7.4   Beware of direct translations

A word of caution is due. As you may have noticed, at times the translation from English to Spanish is not literal. Very often, a native English speaker may use an expression that other English speakers have no problem understanding; however, in Spanish the expression would be interpreted quite differently—often almost literally!

Many English expressions can cause misunderstandings if they are translated directly. For example, if you ask someone in English, "Can you spell your name?", he or she will start spelling the name for you. If you ask someone in Spanish, **¿Puede deletrear su nombre?**, he or she would answer **Sí** and wonder why you asked such a question, because the patient has been writing his or her name correctly from a very early age. Or you may ask your patient, "What brought you here today?", inquiring about symptoms. Asking the literal translation, **¿Qué lo trajo aquí hoy?** might get you the answer **el bus** or **mi tía**.

Whereas English is composed of a great many expressions, especially when asking questions, Spanish is much more literal. One interprets the meaning exactly as it is expressed. Be careful to ask the question for which you want an answer before you make a literal translation.

Following are a few more common English expressions that do not translate literally into Spanish (the answers, of course, are not generally stated aloud, but certainly are often thought):

Can I have your name?   ANSWER: No. What is wrong with your own name?

Do you have a phone?   ANSWER: Yes, I have three phones.

I'll give you a ring tomorrow.   ANSWER: Wow, are we getting engaged tomorrow?

Smoke-free building.   ANSWER: Am I free to smoke in this building?

Watch your head!   ANSWER: That is impossible!

There are no makeup exams.   ANSWER: (Male) Why would I wear makeup? That's for women! (Female) Darn, and I can apply makeup in 10 minutes every morning, I've got it down to a science, not to mention that I'm really good at it!

7.5 Giving directions
Las instrucciones y direcciones

Often after a physical exam, it is necessary to "run some tests."[14] Of course, you must be able to direct your patient to the lab, restroom, or clinic. The following will help you give accurate directions.

Siga (Camine)   Dé vuelta (Doble)   Dé vuelta (Doble)
Ud. derecho.   a la izquierda.   a la derecha.

VOCABULARIO

Siga (Camine) Ud.	Continue (Walk)	**Dé**	Give (command
derecho	straight ahead		form of *dar*)
adelante	forward	**Dé vuelta.**	Turn.
a la derecha	to the right	**una vuelta**	a turn
Dé vuelta (doble)	Turn	**Doble**	Turn (command
a la izquierda	to the left		form of *doblar*)
una cuadra	one block	**Vire**	Turn (command
la calle	the street		form of *virar*)
Siga	Continue, Follow	**cruzar**	to cross
	(command form		
	of *seguir*)		

 Ejercicio 7E

Ud. quiere mandar (*to send*) a un paciente a la clínica, al consultorio de dentistas, a la Cruz Roja, etc. Use el mapa para dar instrucciones.

EJEMPLO   **Pregunta**: Está en el hospital. ¿Dónde está el laboratorio?
           Respuesta: Necesita salir (Salga) de la puerta del hospital y dé vuelta a la derecha. Camine derecho por tres cuadras y dé vuelta a la izquierda. Camine derecho por una cuadra. Necesita cruzar la calle y allí está el laboratorio.

---

[14]The phrase *run some tests* is a great example of an expression that would create confusion if it were translated literally.

la glorieta

Está en el hospital. ¿Dónde está…?

1. (la clínica) _____

   _____

   _____

2. (el consultorio de dentistas) _____

   _____

   _____

3. (la Cruz Roja) _____

   _____

   _____

4. (el baile) _____

   _____

   _____

5. (el banco) _____

   _____

   _____

Notes:

- When standing, walking, or driving, use **a la derecha** ("to the right"), **a la izquierda** ("to the left"), and **derecho** "straight ahead."
- However, if *right* and *left* are used as adjectives (descriptive words) to modify a noun (thing), then they must agree in number and gender with that noun.

el brazo derecho	**la pierna derecha**
el brazo izquierdo	**la pierna izquierda**

7.6 Present progressive tense

In Chapter 5, we introduced you to an extremely easy tense to form and use—the "present progressive" or the "continuous progressive" tense. In Spanish this tense can often be interchanged with the present tense, but it signals that the action is being done "as we speak," or that it started a while ago but is still being carried out. For example:

Do you take medicine?	**¿Toma medicina?**
Are you taking any medicine?	**¿Toma medicina?** *or* **¿Está tomando medicina?**

Let's take a closer look at the present progressive tense.

Ahora/en este momento/ahorita

Estoy tomando vino tinto.   Estoy hablando español.   Estoy tocando[15] las maracas.

---

[15]from **tocar** to touch; to play (a musical instrument)

Estamos bailando.

Beto y Alicia están comprando[16] boletos.

Los novios están besándose.[17]

Los verbos de -**ar**:   **estar** + verb stem + -**ando**

hablar (to speak)
estoy + habl + ando (I am + speak + ing)
Estoy hablando.

estoy hablando	estamos hablando
estás hablando	
está hablando	están hablando

Ahora/en este momento/ahorita

Estoy comiendo un taco con salsa picante.

Estás escribiendo una receta.

Está bebiendo vitamina C disuelta[18] en agua.

---

[16]from **comprar** to buy, to purchase
[17]from **besar** to kiss; **besarse** to kiss each other
[18]**disuelto(-a)** (from **disolver**) dissolved

Está poniendo unas   Estoy vendiendo las sillas.   Estamos abriendo la
píldoras en mi bolsa.   maleta en el hospital.

Los verbos de **-er** e **-ir**:   **estar** + stem + **-iendo**

Estoy comiendo.   I am eating.
Estoy viviendo.   I am living.

estoy com**iendo**	estamos com**iendo**	estoy viv**iendo**	estamos viv**iendo**
estás com**iendo**		estás viv**iendo**	
está com**iendo**	están com**iendo**	está viv**iendo**	están viv**iendo**

 Ejercicio 7F

Complete las frases con la forma correcta de **tomar**.

EJEMPLO   Ahora yo <u>estoy tomando</u> las cápsulas.

1. Tú _____.

2. Mario _____.

3. Los viajeros[19] _____.

4. Mi esposo y yo _____.

5. El paciente _____.

---

[19]**viajeros** travelers

Ejercicio 7G

Complete las frases con la forma correcta de **comer**.

EJEMPLO   En este momento yo <u>estoy comiendo</u> un tamal lleno
de colesterol y sal.

1. _____ tú _____

_____.

2. _____ Carmen _____

_____.

3. _____ sus hermanos _____

_____.

4. _____ tú y yo _____

_____.

5. _____ el tío Tomás _____

_____.

UNAS IRREGULARIDADES

The following are present participles of some irregular stem-changing verbs. Remember that in many situations, the present tense works just as well as the present or continuous progressive. Therefore, don't stress over this tense, just be able to recognize it.

ser	→	siendo	poder	→ pudiendo
pedir	→	pidiendo	sentir	→ sintiendo
decir	→	diciendo	ir	→ yendo
venir	→	viniendo	leer	→ leyendo
seguir	→	siguiendo	caer	→ cayendo
medir	→	midiendo	creer	→ creyendo
ver	→	viendo	huir	→ huyendo

Notes:

• For the sake of pronunciation, a **y** is added between two vowels in this form of **ir**, **leer**, **caer**, **creer**, and **huir**.
• **Huir** means "to flee, run away." Its conjugation in the present tense is **huyo, huyes, huye, huímos, huyen**.

¡**Bueno!** Enough grammar! Let's have a look at some lab test instructions.

7.7   Blood test
Muestra—análisis de sangre

LAB TESTS AND DIAGNOSTIC RESULTS — PRUEBAS DEL LABORATORIO Y LOS RESULTADOS DIAGNÓSTICOS

 VOCABULARIO | Blood test

Permítame	Allow me
Quiero obtener	I want to obtain/get
una muestra	a sample
Favor de extender/	Please extend
Extienda, por favor	
Favor de mantener/	Please hold
Mantenga, por favor	
Favor de no moverse/	Please don't move
No se mueva, por favor	
Favor de poner/Ponga, por favor	Please put
Favor de cerrar/Cierre, por favor	Please close
No tenga miedo	Don't be afraid

 MONÓLOGO 7.7 | Blood test

El paciente llega al laboratorio y la técnica necesita hacerle unas pruebas.

TÉCNICA   Señora, permítame el brazo derecho. Quiero obtener una muestra de sangre.

Extienda (Favor de extender) el brazo y favor de mantenerlo[20] (manténgalo) derecho. No lo doble. (Favor de no doblarlo.)

No se mueva, por favor. (Favor de no moverse.) Voy a poner el torniquete.

Haga un puño, por favor. (Favor de hacer un puño.)

Primero la aguja duele un poco, pero no por mucho tiempo. No tenga miedo. Es rápido.

Ahora, sí, abra la mano y ponga presión (favor de abrir la mano y poner presión) en el brazo para mantener el algodón.

---

[20]In **mantenerlo** and **manténgalo** (the command form), **lo** means "it," referring to the arm.

Ejercicio 7H

Responda a las siguientes preguntas según el monólogo.

1. ¿Qué quiere obtener la técnica del brazo derecho de la paciente (la señora)? _____

2. ¿Qué tiene que (necesita) hacer con el brazo derecho la señora?

_____

3. ¿Qué va a poner la técnica? _____

_____

4. ¿Necesita la paciente cerrar la mano o los ojos? _____

_____

5. ¿Duele un poco o mucho la aguja? _____

_____

6. ¿Qué tiene que hacer la señora para mantener el algodón?

_____

 7.8 Urine test
La muestra de la orina

 VOCABULARIO | **Urine test**

la toalla	the towel
desechable	disposable
separar	to separate
de frente	from the front
hacia atrás	toward the back
alrededor	around
la tapadera	the cover
deje	leave
el excusado, el inodoro	the toilet
después	after
el frasco	jar, container
repisa (f.)	shelf
gabinete (m.)	cabinet
ventanilla (f.)	little window

🔊 MONÓLOGO 7.8 | **Urine test**

EL ENFERMERO　　Ahora necesito una prueba (muestra) de su orina.

(*para las mujeres*)
Tome (Favor de tomar) las toallas desechables con Ud.
al baño y lávese (y lavarse) las manos. Separe (Necesita separar) los labios vaginales con las toallas
desechables. Luego, necesita limpiarse cada labio
de frente hacia atrás y entre[21] los labios vaginales.
Comience[22] a orinar (Puede orinar) en el excusado,
después orine en el frasco y termine de orinar en
el excusado. Ponga (Favor de poner) la tapadera y
deje (favor de dejar) el frasco en la ventanilla (la
repisa, el gabinete). Y lávese las manos después.

(*para los hombres*)
Necesita limpiarse alrededor del pene.
Comience a orinar (Puede orinar) en el excusado,
después orine en el frasco y termine de orinar en
el excusado. Ponga (Favor de poner) la tapadera y
deje (favor de dejar) el frasco en la repisa (el gabinete, la ventanilla). Y lávese las manos después.

✏️ Ejercicio 7 I

Conteste (Favor de contestar) con frases completas, por favor.

1. ¿Qué necesita el enfermero? _____

2. ¿Qué necesita llevar al baño la señora? _____

_____

3. ¿Qué tiene que lavar la señora? _____

_____

4. ¿Dónde tiene que orinar? _____

5. ¿Dónde necesita dejar el frasco la paciente? _____

_____

---

[21]**entre** between
[22]**comience** (command form) start, begin; **comenzar** to start, begin

7.9 Sputum test
La muestra de esputo

 VOCABULARIO | **Sputum test**

mañana por la mañana	tomorrow morning
lo (*m.*)	it
la (*f.*)	it
tosa, favor de toser	please cough
escupa, favor de escupir	please spit
vez	time
veces	times (*series*)
tráigalo, favor de traerlo	please bring it

 MONÓLOGO 7.9 | **Sputum test**

DOCTOR Tome (Favor de tomar) este frasco y llévelo (favor de lle-
varlo) a casa. Mañana por la mañana tosa (favor de toser) profundamente dos o tres veces.
Escupa (favor de escupir) la flema en el frasco.
Después, tráigalo (favor de traerlo) al laboratorio, por favor.

7.10 Skin tests
Pruebas de la piel

 VOCABULARIO | **Skin tests**

la piel	skin
la fiebre del valle	valley fever
(coccidioidomicosis)	(coccidioidomycosis)
hinchazón (*f.*)	swelling
enrojecimiento (*m.*)	redness
algún/alguna	any
estas reacciones (*f. pl.*)	these reactions
regresar	to return
el consultorio	doctor's office
verle	to see you
pasado mañana	day after tomorrow

MONÓLOGO 7.10 | Skin tests

DOCTORA   Favor de extender (Extienda, por favor) el brazo y no se
mueva (favor de no moverse). El técnico va a sacar
unas pruebas de la piel. Una es la tuberculina y la otra
es para la fiebre del valle.[23]
La primera está en el brazo derecho. La segunda está en el
brazo izquierdo.
Favor de observar (Observe, por favor) la reacción de la
piel por hinchazón o enrojecimiento.
Favor de no rascar el área.
Si tiene alguna de estas reacciones después de veinte y
cuatro[24] horas, regrese (favor de regresar) al consultorio. Quiero verle en mi consultorio pasado mañana.

Ejercicio 7J

Conteste (Favor de contestar) con frases completas.

1. ¿Para qué son las pruebas de la piel? _____

_____

2. ¿Sacan las pruebas en las piernas? Si no, ¿dónde? _____

_____

3. ¿Qué reacciones necesita observar o buscar?[25] _____

_____

4. ¿Qué tiene que hacer la paciente si observa algunas de estas re-

acciones? _____

5. ¿Cuándo quiere la doctora ver a la paciente en el consultorio?

_____

---

[23]**la fiebre del valle** valley fever (coccidioidomycosis)
[24]more commonly spelled **veinticuatro**
[25]**buscar** to look for, search for

7.11   Taking X rays
Las radiografías

 VOCABULARIO | **Taking X rays**

venga	come
entonces	then, and so
sacar	to take out; to take (*as in X rays*)
en ayunas, sin comer	fasting
tragar, pasar	to swallow
nos permite	permit us, allow us

 MONÓLOGO 7.11 | **Taking X rays**

DOCTORA   El técnico necesita sacar radiografías (rayos x).
Entonces, venga mañana a las ocho de la mañana. Puede lavarse la boca o los dientes, sin pasar agua.
Después, Ud. necesita tomar un líquido para poder ver[26] sus órganos internos.

7.12   Results and diagnosis
Resultados y diagnósticos

 VOCABULARIO | **Results and diagnosis**

pequeña variante	a little variation
muestran	they show
yo sé	I know
principios (*m. pl.*)	beginnings
tanto	so much
descanso (*m.*)	rest
mejorar	to better (improve), to get better
faltar	to miss
aliviar	to alleviate
mostrar	to show
por lo menos	at least
sugerir	to suggest

---

[26]**para poder ver** *literally,* "in order to be able to see"

DIÁLOGO 7.12 | **Results and diagnosis**

DOCTORA   Bueno, señor, la sangre, su orina y esputo están normales. Pero el examen de la piel y la radiografía muestran una pequeña variante en el pulmón derecho. Esto indica que Ud. tiene los principios de una enfermedad muy común en esta área y clima que se llama fiebre del valle.

SEÑOR   ¿Qué debo hacer, doctora?

DOCTORA   ¡No se preocupe! Con una dieta alta en proteínas y con mucho descanso, Ud. va a aliviarse (mejorar) en tres meses.

SEÑOR   Por lo menos sé qué (sé lo que) tengo. Me siento un poco más tranquilo. Pero no puedo faltar tanto al trabajo.

DOCTORA   Bueno, señor, Ud. necesita mejorarse. Voy a recetarle unas vitaminas y continúe (siga) con esta dieta por dos meses.

Ejercicio 7K

Conteste (Favor de contestar) con frases completas.

1. ¿Cómo están la sangre, la orina y el esputo del señor?

   _____

2. ¿Qué muestran las pruebas de la piel y la radiografía?

   _____

3. ¿Qué enfermedad indican estos resultados? _____

   _____

4. ¿Qué sugiere la doctora? _____

5. ¿Qué da la doctora al señor? _____

8

What you will learn in this lesson:

- to form and use possessive adjectives: *my, your, his, her, its, our, their*
- to form and use the impersonal **se**
- to form and use demonstrative adjectives: *this, that, these, those*
- to form, conjugate, and use regular verbs in the past tense
- to form, conjugate, and use irregular verbs in the past tense
- vocabulary related to a well-baby visit
- to conduct a return pediatric visit for failed treatment
- to treat an asthma attack in the ER

The goal of this lesson is to be able to discuss and understand medical situations in the past tense, to conduct a pediatric visit for failed treatment, and to treat an emergency adult asthma attack.

8.1 Possessive adjectives

mi(s)	my	**nuestro(s), nuestra(s)**	our
tu(s)	your (*familiar*)		
su(s)	his, her, your (*formal*)	**su(s)**	their, your (*formal*)

mi bolsa (f.)

tu bolsa (f.)

mi rebozo (m.)

tu rebozo (m.)

la bolsa   purse, handbag, bag, sack, and sometimes pocket
                (Pocket is also known as **bolsillo**.)

el rebozo   colorful Mexican-style shawl often used by indigenous women
                to carry their infants. **Rebozos** are also sold in markets to
                tourists for whatever use they deem interesting.

The possessive adjectives **mi**, **tu**, and **su** do not change, regardless of whether the noun is masculine or feminine.

mis bolsas (f.)

tus bolsas (f.)

mis rebozos (m.)

tus rebozos (m.)

Mi, tu, and su change to mis, tus, and sus to agree with a plural noun.

Ejercicio 8A

Llene los espacios con la forma correcta de **mi/mis** o **tu/tus**.

EJEMPLOS   **mi** medicina—**mis** medicinas
            tu receta—**tus** recetas

1. (mi/mis)   _____ pulsos   _____ depresor

               _____ tío   _____ nueras[1]

2. (tu/tus)   _____ suegra[2]   _____ martillos

               _____ gasa   _____ doctora

---

[1]**nuera** daughter-in-law
[2]**suegra** mother-in-law

3. (mi/mis)   _____ vendas   _____ primos

               _____ llave   _____ pacientes

4. (tu/tus)   _____ otoscopio   _____ cliente

               _____ cuñados³   _____ estetoscopio

nuestra bolsa (f.)

nuestras bolsas (f.)

nuestro rebozo (m.)

nuestros rebozos (m.)

- If the noun is feminine singular, use **nuestra**.
- If the noun is masculine singular, use **nuestro**.
- If the noun is feminine plural, use **nuestras**.
- If the noun is masculine plural, use **nuestros**.

🖊 Ejercicio 8B

Llene los espacios con la forma correcta de **nuestro**.

1. _____ almohada   _____ venda

   _____ inyección   _____ pastillas

---
³**cuñados** brothers-in-law; brothers- and sisters-in-law

2. _____ otoscopios   _____ martillos

   _____ aguja   _____ lavabo⁴

3. _____ jeringa   _____ cuchara

   _____ curitas   _____ gasa

4. _____ clínicas   _____ goteros

   _____ depresor   _____ termómetros

Remember that **su** ("his, her, their, your [formal]") only has two forms: **su** and **sus**. The important thing is the number of the noun it modifies, regardless of whether it means "his," "her," "your," or "their."

If there is just one: use **su**.

If there are two or more: use **sus**.

el doctor de Ana	→	su doctor
los doctores de Ana	→	sus doctores
la gasa de Tomás	→	su gasa
los goteros de Tomás	→	sus goteros
el paciente de Ud.	→	su paciente
los pacientes de Ud.	→	sus pacientes
la gasa de José y Juana	→	su gasa
las curitas de José y Juana	→	sus curitas
la prueba de Uds.	→	su prueba
los exámenes de Uds.	→	sus exámenes

✎ Ejercicio 8C

Cambie la forma a **su** o **sus**.

1. el pato de Mario   _____

2. la bata de Juana   _____

3. las jeringas de Juan   _____

4. el martillo de José y Juan   _____

5. las píldoras de María   _____

6. los goteros de las clínicas   _____

7. el estetoscopio del doctor   _____

8. los otoscopios del hospital   _____

---

⁴**lavabo** bathroom or restroom sink (Often **el lavamanos** is used for bathroom sink or washbasin.)

9. la aguja de las enfermeras _____

10. la receta de las clínicas _____

11. las vendas de los pacientes _____

12. los libros de Juana y Yolanda _____

8.2 "Se impersonal"

Most of you have seen signs that state, **"Se habla español aquí."** This is literally translated as "One speaks Spanish here." However, in English it is loosely translated as "Spanish is spoken here." This structure in Spanish is the equivalent of the passive voice in English, where the person is not specified. Please note the following examples:

Singular

Plural

<u>Se habla</u> español aquí.

<u>Se hablan</u> español e inglés aquí.

<u>Se toma</u> whisky en los EE.UU.[5]

<u>Se toman</u> tequila y vino en México.

_____

[5]**EE.UU.** = Estados Unidos

Se come la hamburguesa en casa aquí.

Se comen los tacos en el restaurante aquí.

Se toca la guitarra eléctrica para la música de "roc."

Se tocan los bongoes para la música de "salsa."

Singular

Se come pescado cerca del mar.

One eats fish close to the sea.
Fish is eaten close to the sea.

Plural

Se comen frijoles allí también.

One eats beans there also.
Beans are eaten there also.

 Ejercicio 8D

Cambie la frase para emplear **se**.

1. Aquí fuman pipas. _____

2. Aquí fuman tabaco. _____

3. Aquí preparan la comida mexicana. _____

_____

4. Aquí preparan platos franceses. _____

_____

5. Aquí dan las inyecciones. _____

6. Aquí dan la vacuna. _____

7. Aquí enyesan el brazo. _____

8. Aquí enyesan los dedos. _____

9. Aquí venden aspirina. _____

10. Aquí venden gasa. _____

✏ Ejercicio 8E

Escriba estas frases en español.

1. One speaks Spanish here. _____

2. Medicine is sold here. _____

3. One reads in the doctor's waiting room. _____

_____

4. One buys medicine in the drugstore. _____

_____

5. Bandages are sold here. _____

6. Drugs are sold in the street. _____

7. The clinic opens at 8:00. _____

8. One wears guayaberas[6] there too. _____

_____

---

[6]**guayaberas** tropical-style shirt

8.3   Demonstrative adjectives

| **esta enfermera** | **esa enfermera** | **estas enfermeras** | **esas enfermeras** |
| this | that | these | those |

| **esta aguja** | this needle | **esa aguja** | that needle |
| **estas vendas** | these bandages | **esas vendas** | those bandages |

 Ejercicio 8F

Llene los espacios con la forma correcta de **esta, estas, esa** o **esas**.

1. (that) _____ medicina es para la tos.

2. (these) _____ pastillas son fáciles de tragar (pasar).

3. (those) _____ enfermeras son muy eficientes.

4. (this) _____ aguja es grande.

5. (that) _____ puerta está cerrada.

| **este doctor** | **ese doctor** | **estos doctores** | **esos doctores** |
| this | that | these | those |

| **este vaso** | this glass | **ese vaso** | that glass |
| **estos goteros** | these droppers | **esos goteros** | those droppers |

Feminine singular		Masculine singular	
esta	this	este	this
esa	that	ese	that
Feminine plural		**Masculine plural**	
estas	these	estos	these
esas	those	esos	those

 Ejercicio 8G

Llene los espacios con la forma correcta de **este, estos, ese** o **esos**.

1. (these) _____ termómetros son buenos.

2. (those) _____ depresores son usados.

3. (that) _____ libro es muy interesante.

4. (this) _____ martillo es grande.

5. (that) _____ microscopio no funciona.

 The preterit tense

You are now ready to embark upon the past tense. Yes, when your patient waxes eloquent about his or her life's story, you will now have the ability to grasp the essence, if not the entire **novela**. The following are some words and phrases that alert you to the oncoming usage of the preterit (past tense), or of an action that has taken place and is now finished.

VOCABULARIO

ayer	yesterday	**anteayer (antier)**	the day before yesterday
anoche	last night	**antenoche**	the night before last
antes	before	**la semana pasada**	last week
el otro día[7]	the other day	**hace dos días**	two days ago

---

[7]**el otro día** the other day. This is commonly used to refer to any time from two days ago to five years ago or even more.

THE PRETERIT TENSE OF REGULAR VERBS

-ar tomar		-er comer		-ir abrir	
tom<u>é</u>	tom<u>amos</u>	com<u>í</u>	com<u>imos</u>	abr<u>í</u>	abr<u>imos</u>
tom<u>aste</u>		com<u>iste</u>		abr<u>iste</u>	
tom<u>ó</u>	tom<u>aron</u>	com<u>ió</u>	com<u>ieron</u>	abr<u>ió</u>	abr<u>ieron</u>

The preterit endings

-ar		-er and -ir	
-é	-amos	-í	-imos
-aste		-iste	
-ó	-aron	-ió	-ieron

!

¡Cuidado!

habl<u>o</u>	I speak	**habl<u>ó</u>**	he/she/you spoke
habl<u>e</u>	speak!	**habl<u>é</u>**	I spoke

Ejercicio 8H

Complete las frases con la forma correcta de **tomar** en el pretérito.

EJEMPLO   (Yo) <u>tomé</u> un vaso de vino ayer.

1. Tú _____.

2. Ana y yo _____.

3. Ud. _____.

4. Los turistas _____.

5. El hombre guapo _____.

6. Nosotros _____.

7. Martín y Graciela _____.

8. Tú y Jorge _____.

Ejercicio 8I

Conteste, por favor.

1. ¿Cuándo tomaron tú y Jorge el vaso de vino? _____

_____

2. ¿Tomó Juan el agua en México? _____

_____

3. ¿Qué tomaron ellos en la fiesta anoche? _____

_____

4. ¿Cuántas tazas de café tomaron Uds. la mañana después de la

fiesta? _____

5. ¿Quién tomó la limonada en la cantina antier (anteayer)?

_____

6. ¿Tomaron los turistas mucha agua en el desierto? _____

_____

Ejercicio 8J

Complete las frases con la forma correcta de comer en el pretérito.

EJEMPLO   Yo comí armadillo anoche.

1. Javier _____.

2. Tú _____.

3. Nosotros _____.

4. Lucía _____.

5. Los viajeros _____.

6. La azafata[8] _____.

7. El banquero y yo _____.

8. El maestro y tú _____.

---

[8]**azafata** airline stewardess, flight attendant (Other terms include **la aeromoza, el aeromozo, el sobrecargo.**)

🖉 Ejercicio 8K

Llene los espacios con la forma correcta de **comer** en el pretérito.

1. Anoche el maestro y tú _____ chiles verdes.

2. Ayer él _____ tres platos de arroz con pollo.

3. Antier tú _____ demasiado[9] y necesitaste tomar Alka Seltzer™.

4. La semana pasada nosotros _____ mayonesa en la playa y regresamos enfermos.

5. Anoche ellos _____ iguana en salsa roja.

6. El mes pasado yo no _____ por tres días como protesta.

7. El año pasado los turistas _____ en el mismo restaurante cada noche.

🖉 Ejercicio 8L

Llene los espacios con la forma correcta de **abrir** en el pretérito.

1. Anoche Jesús y Celia _____ todas las botellas de medicina.

2. Ayer ella _____ la puerta del cuarto de baño de los caballeros por error.

3. Antenoche tú _____ la ventana y entró mucha nieve.[10]

4. Esta mañana la enfermera _____ la puerta del baño para el paciente.

5. Anoche el paciente _____ la botella de pastillas.

6. Ayer yo _____ mi libro de español pero no estudié nada porque me atacó la flojera.[11]

---

[9]**demasiado** too much
[10]**la nieve** snow
[11]**me atacó la flojera** I had an attack of laziness (literally, laziness attacked me).

Ejercicio 8M

Cambie el verbo al pretérito y escriba la frase.

EJEMPLO   (yo/escribir/receta/ayer) Yo escribí una receta ayer.

1. (tú/recibir/visita/ayer)

   _____

2. (ella/comprar/termómetros/ayer)

   _____

3. (Uds./vender/otoscopios/ayer)

   _____

4. (nosotros/necesitar/vendas/ayer)

   _____

5. (Juan y María/correr/kilómetro/ayer)

   _____

6. (yo/caminar/cuadra/ayer)

   _____

7. (Ud./aprender/verbos/ayer)

   _____

8. (tú/escribir/instrucciones/ayer)

   _____

9. (mis hermanos/limpiar/cuartos/ayer)

   _____

10. (Uds./visitar/el hospital/ayer)

   _____

THE PRETERIT TENSE OF STEM-CHANGING AND OTHER VERBS

The good news is that many verbs that have changes in the stem in the present tense are completely regular in the preterit. Compare the following stem-changing verbs:

encontrar (o → **ue**) (to find, encounter)			
Present tense		Preterit tense	
encuentro	encontramos	encontré	encontramos
encuentras		encontraste	
encuentra	encuentran	encontró	encontraron

perder (e → **ie**) (to lose)			
Present tense		Preterit tense	
pierdo	perdemos	perdí	perdimos
pierdes		perdiste	
pierde	pierden	perdió	perdieron

However, -**ir** verbs that have stem changes in the present tense also have stem changes in the preterit. Study the following examples:

dormir (o → **ue**) (to sleep)			
Present tense		Preterit tense	
duermo	dormimos	dormí	dormimos
duermes		dormiste	
duerme	duermen	durmió*	durmieron*

*The **o** in the stem changes to **u** in the third-person singular and plural.

preferir (e → **ie**) (to prefer)			
Present tense		Preterit tense	
prefiero	preferimos	preferí	preferimos
prefieres		preferiste	
prefiere	prefieren	prefirió*	prefirieron*

*The **e** in the stem changes to **i** in the third-person singular and plural.

medir (e → **i**) (to measure)			
Present tense		Preterit tense	
mido	medimos	medí	medimos
mides		mediste	
mide	miden	midió*	midieron*

*The **e** in the stem changes to **i** in the third-person singular and plural.

When a verb ends in **-er** or **-ir** and has a vowel that immediately precedes the preterit ending, the third-person singular ending changes from **-ió** to **-yó**, and the third-person plural ending changes from **-ieron** to **-yeron**. An accent mark is added to the **i** in all the other forms. Compare the following:

leer (to read)		caer (to fall)		oír (to hear; to listen)	
leí	leímos	caí	caímos	oí	oímos
leíste		caíste		oíste	
leyó	leyeron	cayó	cayeron	oyó	oyeron

Notes:

- Exceptions to this rule are **traer**, which is completely irregular in the preterit tense, and all verbs that end in **-guir** (for example, **distinguir**, **extinguir**).
- Verbs that end in **-uir** follow this rule; however, the only accent added to the **i** in the preterit endings is in the first-person singular: **huir: huí, huiste, huyó, huimos, huyeron**.

Verbs that end in **-car**, **-gar**, and **-zar** have a spelling change in the first-person singular of the preterit tense:

$$c \rightarrow qu \qquad g \rightarrow gu \qquad z \rightarrow c$$

Study the following examples:

buscar (to look for)		llegar (to arrive)		comenzar (to begin, start)	
bus**qué**	buscamos	lle**gué**	llegamos	comen**cé**	comenzamos
buscaste		llegaste		comenzaste	
buscó	buscaron	llegó	llegaron	comenzó	comenzaron

 Ejercicio 8N

Escriba las siguientes frases en el pretérito.

EJEMPLO   Yo llego al hospital, leo una revista y comienzo a trabajar.
           Yo llegué al hospital, leí una revista y comencé a trabajar.

1. El técnico pierde la jeringa y no saca muestras de la sangre.

   _____

2. Uds. oyen la música y duermen profundamente.

   _____

3. Yo muestro y explico los resultados a los pacientes.

_____

4. Los niños salen de la clínica pero no cierran la puerta.

_____

5. Yo no alcanzo[12] la repisa alta y pido ayuda.[13]

_____

6. Los farmacéuticos leen la receta pero no entienden las instruccio-

nes. _____

_____

7. La doctora Ríos cae en la nieve y muerde la lengua.

_____

8. Indico dónde me duele, pero la enfermera no comprende.

_____

9. Yo oigo las noticias[14] y despierto a mis hijos.

_____

10. Yo toco la guitarra y mis hermanos huyen del cuarto.

_____

8.5   Irregular verbs in the preterit

Now that you have absorbed the preterit tense of regular and stem-changing verbs, you will obviously have little problem with irregular verbs! (We are jesting, of course. Simply try to remember what you can of these verbs.) The most commonly used irregular past-tense verbs in medical settings are the following:

hacer	¿Qué **hizo** or pasó?
decir	¿Qué **dijo** el doctor?
ser	¿Cuándo **fue** su primera/última regla?
tener	¿Cuándo **tuvo** Ud. el primer síntoma/la primera regla/ el problema por primera vez?

_____

[12]from **alcanzar** to reach
[13]from **pedir ayuda** to ask for help
[14]**las noticias** the news

First, let's tackle the verbs **hacer**, **decir**, **ir**, and **ser**.[15]

hacer		decir		ir/ser	
hice	hicimos	dije	dijimos	fui	fuimos
hiciste		dijiste		fuiste	
hizo	hicieron	dijo	dijeron	fue	fueron

🖉 Ejercicio 8O

Complete las frases, usando la forma correcta de **hacer** en el pretérito.

EJEMPLO   Yo <u>hice</u> la cama en el cuarto del hospital.

1. Él _____.

2. Ud. _____.

3. Tú _____.

4. Nosotros _____.

5. Cheo y yo _____.

6. Elena y Tadeo _____.

7. Yo _____.

🖉 Ejercicio 8P

Llene los espacios con la forma correcta de **hacer** en el pretérito.

EJEMPLO   Ayer yo <u>hice</u> la comida.

1. (Tú) _____ la piña colada.

2. (Mario) _____ una cama.

3. (Ella) _____ una mesa.

4. (Nosotros) _____ un yoyo.

5. (Javier y Alejandro) _____ una silla.

6. (Uds.) _____ un error.

7. (Tú) _____ una blusa.

8. (Yo) _____ una guayabera blanca.

---

[15]Strangely, the preterit forms of the verbs **ir** ("to go") and **ser** ("to be") are the same. There is usually no confusion because the verbs are used in different contexts.

✎ Ejercicio 8Q

¿Qué hizo Ud. ayer? (Use **hacer, decir** e **ir** cuando sea posible.)[16]

_____

_____

_____

✎ Ejercicio 8R

Complete las frases con la forma correcta de **ir** en el pretérito.

EJEMPLO   Yo <u>fui</u> al hospital anoche.

1. Tú _____.

2. Elena _____.

3. Marco y yo _____.

4. Rodolfo y Tadeo _____.

5. Armando _____.

6. Nosotros _____.

Now let's examine two important verbs that are similar in their preterit forms.

tener		estar	
tuve	tuvimos	estuve	estuvimos
tuviste		estuviste	
tuvo	tuvieron	estuvo	estuvieron

✎ Ejercicio 8S

Complete las frases con la forma correcta de **tener** en el pretérito.

EJEMPLO   Yo <u>tuve</u> dolor de cabeza.

1. Mi primo _____.

2. Tú _____.

3. Carmen _____.

_____

[16]**cuando sea posible** whenever it's possible

4. Tamara y Dolores ——————————————————.

5. Marco y yo ——————————————.

6. Alejandro y Rafael ——————————————.

7. Uds. ——————————————.

8. Yo ——————————————.

✏️ Ejercicio 8T

Use la forma correcta de **tener** e **ir** para completar las frases.

EJEMPLO   Yo <u>tuve</u> mareos cuando <u>fui</u> al consultorio.

1. Laura ——————————————.

2. Felipe y yo ——————————————.

3. Tú ——————————————.

4. Los chamacos[17] ——————————————.

5. Mi tía ——————————————.

6. Mis cuñados ——————————————.

7. Uds. ——————————————.

8. Yo ——————————————.

✏️ Ejercicio 8U

Complete las frases con la forma correcta de **estar** en el pretérito.

EJEMPLO   La atención médica <u>estuvo</u> bien.

1. La fiesta ——————————.

2. Las clases ——————————.

3. Ellos ——————————.

4. Yo ——————————.

5. Tú ——————————.

6. Nosotros ——————————.

---

[17]**chamacos** kids

Ejercicio 8V

Conteste, por favor, con frases completas.

1. ¿Estuvimos bien ayer en la clínica?

_____

2. ¿Estuvieron enfermos durante el examen?

_____

3. ¿Estuvimos contentos en la fiesta?

_____

4. ¿Estuvo bonito el baile[18] folklórico?

_____

5. ¿Estuviste cansado[19] al esperar[20] en el hospital?

_____

 Well-baby visit

VOCABULARIO

to give	**dar**	to turn over	**voltear(se)**
to breast-feed	**dar pecho**	to begin to	**empezar a**
food	**el alimento**	to crawl	**gatear**
to feed	**alimentar**	to sit	**sentar**
to sleep	**dormir**	to stand	**parar(se)**
he/she sleeps,	**duerme**	for the first time	**por primera vez**
you sleep		a walker	**una andadera**
on one's back	**boca arriba**	pacifier	**un chupón**
on one's stomach	**boca abajo**		**(bobo)**
on one's side	**de lado**	he/she/you said	**dijo**
to wean	**destetar**	Did he/she/you	**¿Dijo...?**
At what age?	**¿A qué edad?**	say . . . ?	
to begin to	**comenzar a**		

---

[18]**el baile** dance

[19]**cansado(-a)** tired

[20]**al esperar** upon waiting/while waiting (Remember: the infinitive can be used after **al**.)

Can he/she stand by himself/herself?	¿Puede pararse solo(-a)?
Did he say any words before . . . months?	¿Dijo alguna palabra antes de los... meses?
Does he/she coo/babble?	¿Balbucea?
When did he say "mama" or "papa" for the first time?	¿Cuándo dijo "mamá" o "papá" por primera vez?
Is she talking well?	¿Habla bien o tiene problemas?
Is he teething?	¿Le están saliendo los dientes?
Does she sleep well? Does she take naps?	¿Duerme bien? ¿Toma siestas?
Does she sleep on her back/stomach?	¿Duerme boca arriba/abajo?
Does she sleep all night?	¿Duerme toda la noche?
When did she begin to crawl?	¿Cuándo comenzó (empezó) a gatear?
Does he turn over by himself?	¿Se voltea solo?
Do you use a car seat?	¿Usa un asiento de carro para niños?
What does he eat? Does he drink milk? What kind?	¿Qué come? ¿Toma leche? ¿Qué tipo?
How often does he drink milk/eat?	¿Cada cuándo toma leche/come?
What does she eat?	¿Qué come? ¿Qué tipo de alimentos come?
Does she eat well? Does she eat table food?	¿Come bien? ¿Come comida normal?
Does she have behavioral problems?	¿Tiene problemas con su comportamiento?
When was the first time that . . . ?	¿Cuándo fue la primera vez que...?
Did he/she have difficulty with . . . ?	¿Tuvo dificultad al... (+ infinitive)?

Remember: A well-baby visit works best when scheduled around vaccination times.

8.7 Emergency room visit: ear infection
La sala de emergencia: una infección del oído

 VOCABULARIO | **An emergency room visit for a failed treatment of an ear infection**

podría	he/she/you could	¿Me explico?	Do you understand? Am I being clear?
¡Ajá!	Aha!		
entiendo	I understand	Por eso	That's why, Due to that

con razón	no wonder (*lit.,* with reason)	en voz alta	out loud
		me parece	it seems to me
pensando a solas	thinking to oneself	se me hace	it seems to me
		¡Qué pena!	How embarrassing!

DIÁLOGO 8.7 | An emergency room visit for a failed treatment of an ear infection

DOCTOR   Buenos días, Señora Soto. ¿Cómo le va? ¿Cómo sigue Jaimito de la infección del oído?

SEÑORA   Bueno, doctor, yo estoy muy bien, pero mi hijo sigue mal. No se ha mejorado. (No está mejor.) Sigue con calentura y gripa (resfriado, catarro).

DOCTOR   ¿Le dio a (Tomó) Jaimito los antibióticos que le receté su última visita?

SEÑORA   Sí, doctor(a), pero se me hace (parece) que la medicina no le sirvió.

DOCTOR   A ver, señora, ¿cómo le dio la medicina? ¿Cuánto y cuántas veces al día le dio los antibióticos?

SEÑORA   Pues, le di una cucharadita una vez por día, doctor.

DOCTOR   *(Pensando a solas)* Por eso, con razón... no me escuchó. Podría evitar esta consulta, pero no siguió mis instrucciones la primera vez.

    (En voz alta) Ajá, bueno, señora, una cucharadita está bien, pero necesita tomar la medicina tres veces al día, por diez días. Es muy importante tomar la dosis exacta.

SEÑORA   ¡Ay! ¡Qué pena, doctor! ¿Qué debo hacer?

DOCTOR   Bueno, Señora Soto, voy a recetarle antibióticos otra vez, pero necesita tener mucho cuidado con las instrucciones. Esta vez *(porque es la segunda vez)*, tiene que darle a Jaimito una cucharadita, pero dos veces por día por un período de una semana. ¿Me explico?

SEÑORA   Sí, doctor, ahora entiendo... una cucharadita dos veces cada día y por toda una semana. Pero, ¿puedo darle Tylenol™ o está bien darle Motrin™ también con la medicina que me recetó?

DOCTOR   Sí, señora, el antibiótico sirve con o Tylenol™ o Motrin™, para quitarle el dolor y la fiebre. Está bien, pero sólo el antibiótico con Tylenol o el antibiótico con Motrin, no debe tomar las tres medicinas juntas.[21] ¿Me explico?

---

[21]**juntas** together

SEÑORA   Sí, doctor.
DOCTOR   ¿Tiene otra pregunta o preocupación?
SEÑORA   No, doctor, creo que es todo.
DOCTOR   Bueno, Señora Soto, llámeme si tiene preguntas o dudas, y
         cuídese (a Ud.) y cuide mucho a Jaimito. ¡Que le vaya bien!
SEÑORA   Igualmente, doctor, gracias.

Ejercicio 8W

Conteste las preguntas sobre el diálogo.

1. ¿Cómo sigue Jaimito? _____

2. ¿Sirvió la medicina que recetó el doctor? _____

   _____

3. ¿Cuánto y cuántas veces al día la mamá dio los antibióticos a Jaimito? _____

4. ¿Qué dijo el doctor? ¿Cuál fue o debe ser la dosis exacta?

   _____

5. ¿Qué más[22] preguntó la señora al doctor? _____

   _____

6. ¿Qué contestó el doctor a la señora? _____

   _____

8.8 Emergency room visit: an asthma attack
La sala de emergencia: un ataque de asma

Vamos a ver otro diálogo que utiliza el pretérito. Este diálogo es de un
señor en la sala de emergencia con un ataque de asma.

 VOCABULARIO | **An asthma attack in the emergency room**

dificultad (*f.*) **al respirar**	difficulty breathing	**Ya sé**	I know
falta de respiración	shortness of breath	**ya no**	no longer
		nebulizador (*m.*)	nebulizer
		tubito	small tube

---

[22]**¿Qué más** What else

respirar con silbidos	to wheeze	**ya**	now, no longer
		de repente	suddenly
el peor ataque	the worst attack	**estuve pintando**	I was painting
que sufrí	that I had	**estuve trabajando**	I was working
que he sufrido	that I have had	**agarrar**	to grab
comenzó, empezó	he/she/it/you began	**agarré**	I grabbed
		¡Qué bueno!	That's good!
comencé, empecé	I began		
familiares (*m., f., pl.*)	family members		

DIÁLOGO 8.8 | An asthma attack in the emergency room

La sala de emergencia: un adulto con un ataque de asma.

DOCTORA   Buenas noches, señor. Sé que tiene dificultad al respirar. Trate de[23] no hablar, por favor, y respire profundo en este nebulizador (tubito). Muy bien, Señor López. Después, voy a hablar con Ud. de su historia médica y voy a examinarle en general. Pero ahorita necesito escuchar su corazón y pulmones.
(Después de diez minutos)

DOCTORA   ¿Se siente mejor ahora? Veo que Ud. ya no respira con silbidos.

SEÑOR   Sí, doctora, ya puedo respirar (respiro) bien. Me siento mejor, gracias. Hace veinte años que sufro de asma, pero éste es el peor ataque que he sufrido en toda la vida.

DOCTORA   Ah, pues, ¿qué pasó esta vez, Señor López?

SEÑOR   Pues, este ataque comenzó de repente.[24] Estuve en mi casa, estuve trabajando y pintando y comencé a toser. Luego, empecé a respirar con un silbido. Agarré mi inhalador y me di dos bombazos, pero no me ayudó. Después de media hora de sufrir, por fin mi esposa me llevó al hospital.

DOCTORA   ¡Qué bueno! Aparte del asma, ¿sufre de otras enfermedades?

SEÑOR   Sí, doctora, sufro de alta presión y tomo Vasotec.

DOCTORA   ¿Tiene problemas o reacciones alérgicas a algunas medicinas?

SEÑOR   Pues, cuando tomé penicilina una vez, me salieron ronchas.

---

[23]command form—**tratar de** to try to
[24]**de repente** suddenly

DOCTORA	¿Tiene familiares que sufren o que han sufrido de diabetes o problemas del corazón?
SEÑOR	Sí, de diabetes, pero gracias a Dios, yo no, todavía.
DOCTORA	Bueno, Señor López, el técnico va a sacar unas radiografías de sus pulmones y luego voy a examinarle completamente.
SEÑOR	Está bien, doctora. Muchas gracias.
DOCTORA	Bueno, ahorita regreso.[25]

🖉 Ejercicio 8X

Conteste las preguntas sobre el diálogo.

1. ¿Primero, la doctora pregunta mucho al paciente o la doctora da explicaciones al paciente? _____

2. ¿Qué preguntó la doctora al paciente primero? _____

   _____

3. ¿De qué enfermedades sufre el paciente y qué medicina toma?

   _____

4. ¿Fue el peor ataque que ha tenido el paciente en toda su vida?

   _____

5. ¿Qué pasó? _____

6. ¿Tiene familiares que han sufrido de diabetes o problemas de corazón? _____

7. ¿Qué va a hacer el técnico? _____

   _____

8. ¿Qué va a hacer la doctora después? _____

   _____

---

[25]In Mexico, **ahora** means "now"; **ahorita**, "right now"; **ahora mismo**, "right away." However, in some other countries, such as Puerto Rico, **ahorita** means "now" and **ahora** "right now."

What you will learn in this lesson:

- when to use and how to form reflexive verbs
- what is and how to use the "personal **a**"
- when and how to form and use direct object pronouns (it, them)
- to explain in Spanish how to do a breast self-exam at home
- to understand one single dialogue which encompasses all basic grammar structures and tenses to which you have been exposed up to this point
- to create your own dialogue tailored to your own specific field and needs
- vocabulary related to a dental exam
- to perform a dental exam in Spanish
- vocabulary related to an ophthalmologic exam
- to perform an eye exam in Spanish
- vocabulary related to dermatology

The goal of this lesson is to be able to understand a dialogue using all tenses and structures (including the reflexive verb and direct object pronouns) taught thus far wherein the patient presents abdominal pain, and to then create your own specialized dialogue, as well as to be able to perform a dental, eye, and dermatological exam in Spanish.

9.1 Reflexive verbs

We are now ready at last to reveal in detail the concept that you have been so diligently questioning (or, perhaps, the concept by which you have been so frustratingly confused) for much of this book—the reflexive verb! You may have noticed that many reflexive verbs deal with actions of daily routine and personal hygiene. Think of a reflexive verb as a situation in which a person is doing something to him or herself. Study the differences between the following paired examples. The expressions on the left side are not reflexive; those on the right side are reflexive.

Yo lavo la ropa.
(**lavo** I wash)

Yo me lavo la cara.
(**me lavo** I wash myself)

Tú levantas los platos de la mesa.

Tú te levantas.

Él pone los vasos en la mesa.

Él se pone el sombrero.

Ella despierta a su hijo.   El hijo se despierta.

Notes:

- In the first example, the subject **yo** is doing something to something else, **la ropa** ("clothes"), so the verb is not reflexive; in the paired example, the subject **yo** is doing something to the doer's own face, **la cara**, so the verb is reflexive.
- Observe that there are no changes in the conjugations of the verbs. Regular **-ar**, **-er**, and **-ir** verbs, stem-changing verbs, and irregular verbs are conjugated as they would be in the present tense. The only difference is the addition of a reflexive pronoun (**me**, **te**, **se**, etc.) to each verb form.

Study the conjugations of two regular, reflexive **-ar** verbs:

llamarse (to call [oneself])		lavarse (to wash [oneself])	
me llamo	nos llamamos	me lavo	nos lavamos
te llamas		te lavas	
se llama	se llaman	se lava	se lavan

	Me llamo Carla.	**Me lavo las manos.**
	I call myself Carla.	I wash my hands.
pero:	**Llamo a la niña.**	**Lavo las manos de mi hija.**
	I call the child.	I wash my daughter's hands.

 Ejercicio 9A

Llene los espacios con la forma correcta de **lavar** o **lavarse**.

1. Yo _____ la ropa de los chamacos.

2. Yo _____ el pelo.

3. Tú _____ los vasos de cristal.

4. Tú _____ las manos del bebé.

5. Ella _____ la cara.

6. Ella _____ el carro sucio.[1]

7. Nosotros _____ los brazos.

8. Nosotros _____ las mesas en el restaurante.

9. Uds. _____ la pared[2] en la sala.[3]

10. Uds. _____ la boca después de comer.

ponerse (to put on [oneself]; to get/become)	
me pongo	nos ponemos
te pones	
se pone	se ponen

✏️ Ejercicio 9B

Llene los espacios con la forma correcta de **poner** o **ponerse**.

1. Yo _____ la medicina en la silla.

2. Yo _____ el anillo de plata[4] en el dedo chico.

3. El enfermero _____ la comida en la mesa.

4. Tú _____ la blusa de color rosa que te queda grande.[5]

5. Los doctores _____ las vendas en las heridas.

6. Ellas _____ los pantalones por la mañana al levantarse. [6]

7. Los niños _____ los pies en el sofá y la mamá _____ enojada.

8. Tú _____ los dulces en la mesa sin un plato. (¡Qué descuidado!)[7]

---

[1]**sucio** dirty
[2]**la pared** wall
[3]**la sala** living room
[4]**el anillo de plata** the silver ring
[5]**que te queda grande** that's big on you
[6]**al** upon; **al levantarse** upon getting up
[7]**qué descuidado** how careless

9. Nosotros _____ los sombreros en la cabeza.

10. El doctor _____ el yeso en la pierna del niño.

When you look up a verb in the dictionary, you will find the main entry (for example, **lavar**, "to wash") and you may also find a category for the reflexive form (for example, **lavarse**, "to wash oneself"). The reflexive infinitive form is a signal that you conjugate the verb as you normally would, but you add the reflexive pronouns:

me	myself	**nos**	ourselves
te	yourself		
se	himself, herself, itself, yourself	**se**	themselves, yourselves

Ejemplos:

lavar	**Yo me lavo la cara.**	**María se lava la cara.**
	I wash my face.	María washes her face.
sentirse	**¿Cómo se siente?**	**Me siento bien.**
	How are you feeling?	I feel fine.
ponerse	**Yo me pongo la bata.**	**Ricardo se pone la bata.**
	I put on the robe.	Ricardo puts on the robe.

POWER VERBS AND REFLEXIVE INFINITIVES

Recall from Chapter 7 that you can use the key power verbs with any infinitive—including reflexive infinitives! All you have to do is attach the appropriate reflexive pronoun to the infinitive, and you're off and running! Observe the following examples:

Necesito acostar**me**	Necesit**amos** acostar**nos**
Necesit**as** acostar**te**	
Necesit**a** acostar**se**	Necesit**an** acostar**se**

Quiero desvestirme, bañarme y acostarme temprano.	I want to get undressed, bathe, and go to bed early.
¡Ay, Paco! Debes afeitarte con más cuidado.	Oh, Paco! You should shave more carefully.
Ud. puede vestirse ahora.	You can get dressed now.
Su hijo puede ponerse la camiseta ahora.	Your son can put on his T-shirt now.
Vamos a lavarnos las manos e[8] irnos.	We're going to wash our hands and leave.

---

[8]**y** changes to **e** when preceding a word that begins with "i."

Ellos tienen que cuidarse y mejorarse.	They have to take care of themselves and get better.
Favor de sentarse aquí y quitarse los zapatos.	Please sit here and take off your shoes.

COMMON REFLEXIVE VERBS

acostarse	to lie down; to go to bed	**lavarse**	to wash (oneself)
afeitarse	to shave (oneself)	**levantarse**	to get up; to stand (oneself) up
bajarse	to get down/off; to lose (weight)	**llamarse**	to call oneself
		moverse	to move
bañarse	to bathe (oneself), to take a bath	**relajarse**	to relax
		sentarse	to sit down/sit up
contagiarse	to become infected	**subirse**	to get up (on); to gain (weight)
desmayarse	to faint		
embarazarse	to get pregnant	**vestirse**	to dress oneself
enfermarse	to become sick		

✐ Ejercicio 9C

Llene los espacios con la forma correcta del infinitivo reflexivo.

EJEMPLO　(lavarse) Debes <u>lavarte</u> bien las manos.

1. (irse) Tenemos que ＿＿＿＿＿＿＿＿＿ mañana por la mañana.

2. (ingresarse) El doctor dijo que debo ＿＿＿＿＿＿＿＿＿ en el hospital.

3. (vestirse) Los niños pueden ＿＿＿＿＿＿＿＿＿ solos.[9]

4. (sentarse) Estamos cansados y sólo[10] queremos ＿＿＿＿＿＿＿＿＿ en el sofá.

5. (levantarse) Necesito ＿＿＿＿＿＿＿＿＿ muy temprano mañana.

6. (bajarse) Señor Glotón, Ud. necesita ＿＿＿＿＿＿＿＿＿ de peso.

---

[9]**solos** by themselves, on their own
[10]**sólo** only, just

7. (llamarse) No es verdad que quiero _____ el rey del mundo.[11]

8. (moverse) Pepito, tienes que _____ más para acá.

9. (bañarse) ¡Niños, no me molesten![12] Yo voy a _____ ahora mismo.

10. (limpiarse) Después de comer tacos con chiles, ajo y cebollas, necesito _____ los dientes.

!

Reflexive v. nonreflexive verbs

Reflexivo

Él <u>se</u> despierta a las 6:00.	He wakes (himself) up at 6:00./ He gets up at 6:00.

No reflexivo

Él despierta a su hija.	He wakes his daughter (up).

Power verbs and reflexive infinitives

Necesit<u>o</u> poner<u>me</u> la ropa.	I need to put on my clothes.
Ud. deb<u>e</u> subir<u>se</u> de peso.	You ought to gain weight.
¡Los niños tien<u>en</u> que levantar<u>se</u> ya!	The children have to get up now!

 Ejercicio 9D

Escriba 15 frases usando los verbos de esta sección. Escriba 5 frases reflexivas, 5 frases que no son reflexivas, y 5 frases con *power verbs* e infinitivos reflexivos.

---

[11]**el rey del mundo** the king of the world
[12]**¡no me molesten!** don't bother me!

PERSONAL "A"

It's time to explain a quirky aspect of the Spanish language—the personal **a**. There is no equivalent translation for this in English; you simply have to internalize it. In Spanish, you need to add the preposition **a** after a verb and before a person or persons (direct object). However, don't insert the **a** after a verb and before a thing. Study the following examples:

Yo veo la puerta.	*but*	Yo veo a la doctora.
Yo miro la televisión.		Yo miro al[13] hombre guapo.
Yo oigo la música.		Yo oigo a las enfermeras.

Note: The personal **a** is *not* used after the verb **tener**.

Tengo dos tíos y cinco tías.   Tenemos muchos pacientes.

 Ejercicio 9E

Llene los espacios con **la**, **a la**, **el** o **al**.

1. Miran _____ libro.

2. Mire _____ Señora Fernández de Ríos.

3. Oigo _____ corazón.

4. Oigo _____ doctor.

5. Vemos _____ receta.

6. Vemos _____ enfermera.

7. Escuchas _____ corazón.

8. Escuchas _____ paciente.

9.2 Direct object pronouns
Pronombres de complemento directo

Singular, feminine

Tengo la receta.	→	<u>La</u> (*it*) tengo.
Tengo la venda.	→	<u>La</u> tengo.
Veo la jeringa.	→	<u>La</u> veo.
Veo a la doctora.	→	<u>La</u> veo.

---

[13]Remember that **al** is the contraction of **a** and **el**.

La precedes the verb; the verb remains the same.[14]

Singular, masculine

Tengo el estetoscopio. → <u>Lo</u> (*it*) tengo.
Tengo el martillo.　　→ <u>Lo</u> tengo.
Veo el dedo.　　　　→ <u>Lo</u> veo.
Veo al doctor.　　　→ <u>Lo</u> veo.

Lo precedes the verb; the verb remains the same.[15]

 ## Ejercicio 9F

Escriba las frases usando **lo** o **la** como complemento directo.

EJEMPLO　Compro la piñata. → La compro.

1. Compra la receta. _____

2. Hacemos la cita. _____

3. Busco el termómetro. _____

4. Toman la medicina. _____

5. Vemos al paciente en la mañana. _____

6. Venden la venda en el mercado. _____

7. Escribe el resultado de la prueba. _____

8. El doctor receta un antibiótico. _____

9. Miro a la enfermera. _____

10. Veo al técnico en la calle. _____

Plural, feminine

Tengo las recetas.　→ <u>Las</u> (*them*) tengo.
Tengo las vendas.　→ <u>Las</u> tengo.
Veo las jeringas.　　→ <u>Las</u> veo.
Veo a las doctoras.　→ <u>Las</u> veo.

Las ("them, you") precedes the verb; the verb remains the same.

---

[14]**La** her, it. In some countries **la** can also mean "you" when speaking to a female.
[15]**Lo** him, it. In some countries **lo** can also mean "you" when speaking to a male. In other countries the word **le** can mean both "you, him, her" as well as "to you, to him, to her" (an indirect object pronoun for males or females).

Plural, masculine

Tengo los estetoscopios. → <u>Los</u> (*them*) tengo.
Tengo los martillos.   → <u>Los</u> tengo.
Veo los dedos.   → <u>Los</u> veo.
Veo a los doctores.   → <u>Los</u> veo.

Los ("them, you") precedes the verb; the verb remains the same.

 ### Ejercicio 9G

Escriba las frases usando **los** o **las** como complemento directo.

EJEMPLO   Compro las jeringas. → Las compro.

1. Llevo los instrumentos. _____

2. Mira las rodillas. _____

3. Tocan los tobillos. _____

4. Comen frutas y verduras. _____

5. Toman el té y el tequila por la tarde. _____

_____

6. Compramos las sillas de ruedas en la tienda. _____

_____

7. Ves las cucarachas en el baño. _____

8. Llamo a los enfermeros. _____

9. Empacan[16] los instrumentos en la maleta. _____

_____

10. Miras a las mujeres en la playa. _____

_____

[16]from **empacar** to pack

Direct object pronouns

me	nos
te	
la, lo	**las, los**

The direct object pronoun is placed before the verb.

¿Ves al doctor y a la enfermera?	Sí, **los** veo.
¿Compraste las medicinas?	No, no **las** compré.
¿Cuándo escuchas la música?	**La** escucho por las tardes.
¿Comiste el bistec?	No, no **lo** comí.

Monthly breast self-examination
9.3 Autoexamen (Autoexploración) mensual de los senos

DIÁLOGO 9.3 | **Monthly breast self-examination**

ENFERMERA   ¿Ud. se examina los senos en casa cada mes?

PACIENTE   Pues, fíjese que no. ¿Necesito yo examinarme? No sé cómo hacerlo.[17] ¿Puede Ud. explicarme cómo examinarlos?[18]

ENFERMERA   Claro que sí. Hay tres pasos muy fáciles. Primero, examínese los senos al bañarse. Es más fácil sentir bolitas o bultos con la piel mojada. Después de bañarse, mírese en un espejo[19] y examínese los senos otra vez.

    Después, acuéstese y ponga la mano derecha detrás de la cabeza, así.[20] Use la mano opuesta, o sea,[21] la mano izquierda, para tocarse el seno derecho. Use las yemas[22] de los dedos para buscar bolitas o bultos. Mueva las yemas de los dedos alrededor[23] del seno. Luego,[24] use la

---

[17]**hacerlo** to do it (**lo** "it" refers to the exam)
[18]**examinarlos** to examine them (**los** "them" refers to the breasts)
[19]**un espejo** mirror
[20]**así** like this
[21]**o sea** or in other words
[22]**yemas** tips (fleshy part of the fingertip, finger pads)
[23]**alrededor** around
[24]**luego** then (*in a series*), later

	mano derecha para examinarse el seno izquierdo... así. Luego, apriétese los pezones, suavemente, para ver si hay una secreción o desecho.
PACIENTE	¿Cada cuándo debo examinarme los pechos?
ENFERMERA	Debe examinarse después de su regla, no antes.
PACIENTE	¿Y si ya no baja la regla por el cambio de vida...?
ENFERMERA	Si ha tenido la histerectomía o está en la menopausia, debe hacerlo el primero de cada mes.
PACIENTE	Y si encuentro algo, ¿qué hago?
ENFERMERA	Llámenos[25] para hacer una consulta. Su doctora va a examinarle más detalladamente.
PACIENTE	Gracias, señorita. Creo que entiendo ahora. Voy a co- menzar a examinarme cada mes. Muchas gracias y hasta pronto.
ENFERMERA	Por nada, señora, cuídese mucho y que le vaya muy bien.

 Ejercicio 9H

1. Escriba cada verbo reflexivo y su definición en este diálogo.

2. Escriba cada mandato y su definición en este diálogo.

3. All healthcare professionals describe procedures in their own way. Change or add to the above dialogue (in Spanish), as you would explain things to your own patients.

 9.4 Abdominal pain
Dolor abdominal

Now you have covered the basic grammar and tenses necessary to make yourself understood. The following dialogue synthesizes and utilizes many of the structures in one single dialogue. Please note how everything learned up to this point can be used to express what you need to relate to your patient in a simple, yet grammatically correct form.

---

[25]**Llámenos** Call us (The direct object pronoun **nos** is attached to the command.)

🔲 **DIÁLOGO 9.4** | **A patient with abdominal pain**

DOCTORA Buenos días, Señor Gómez. Pase (Pásele, Adelante, Entre) y siéntese, por favor. Soy la doctora Martínez.

PACIENTE Gracias, doctora. Mucho gusto.

DOCTORA Muy bien. ¿Prefiere Rafael o Señor Gómez?

PACIENTE Prefiero Rafael, por favor.

DOCTORA Entonces, Rafael, dígame, ¿qué molestias tiene?

PACIENTE Bueno, doctora, es que me duele la barriga.

DOCTORA ¿Desde cuándo (¿Por cuánto tiempo or ¿Hace cuánto tiempo) le duele, Rafael?

PACIENTE Bueno, pues, doctora, es que el dolor comenzó hace dos o tres días, más o menos.

DOCTORA ¿Cómo es el dolor? ¿Es punzante, fijo o va y viene?

PACIENTE Bueno, doctora, va y viene (viene y se va), pero cuando tengo el dolor, es muy fuerte.

DOCTORA Entonces, ¿es como retortijones?

PACIENTE Sí, doctora. Así es... como retorcijones.

DOCTORA Bueno. ¿Tiene otros síntomas como diarreas, vómitos o fiebre?

PACIENTE Hace más o menos dos o tres días que tuve fiebre y diarrea. Nunca he tenido vómitos, pero no tengo nada de estos síntomas ahora, y por eso me preocupa este dolor, doctora.

DOCTORA No se preocupe, Rafael. Dígame, ¿cómo comenzó el dolor: después de comer, espontáneamente o después de un esfuerzo físico?

PACIENTE ¡Ay, doctora! La verdad es que todo pasó hace unos días en el cumpleaños de mi hija. Yo creo que comí demasiado y en la noche el dolor comenzó muy fuerte con diarrea. Después en la mañana tuve fiebre, pero con unas aspirinas se me quitó y no he tenido más diarrea desde ayer.

DOCTORA Bien, Rafael, no se angustie. Necesito examinar su abdomen. Por favor, acuéstese aquí. Rafael, señale con el dedo dónde le duele. Dígame si le duele cuando pongo presión (profundizo).

PACIENTE Es ahí, doctora, ahí mismo cuando Ud. pone presión. ¡Ay, me duele!

DOCTORA Ya pasó, Rafael. Levántese, pero primero siéntese y después puede levantarse, para evitar mareos. Parece que su dolor va a aliviarse con este medicamento, pero también, el técnico necesita hacer unos análisis.

PACIENTE Bueno, doctora, y ¿cómo tomo la medicina?

DOCTORA	Ahora le explico. Tome una tableta cada ocho horas por cinco días. ¿Me explico? (¿Entendió?)[26] O sea, tres veces al día, antes del desayuno, del almuerzo y de la comida.
PACIENTE	Comprendo y, ¿cuándo necesito ir para los análisis?
DOCTORA	Haga la cita para mañana y regrese aquí dentro de cinco días, o sea, el próximo lunes.
PACIENTE	Gracias, doctora, nos vemos en cinco días.
DOCTORA	Nos vemos el lunes. ¡Cuídese mucho, Rafael!

Ejercicio 91

Now it's your turn! Throughout the chapters in this book, many typical medical situations have been covered. Of course, we realize that countless others exist that are not included here, but the point is that you now have all of the basic and necessary structures with which to work. It is merely a question of filling in the appropriate vocabulary related to your specific field. Go ahead and try! *Remember* to use the simplest forms with the key power verbs as your base. Try writing a dialogue that would be typically and routinely used in your everyday practice and in your specific area of expertise. ¡No tenga miedo de usar el diccionario!

Now it's time to move on to the dentist's office, followed by a routine eye visit, then on to the dermatologist, and ending at the pharmacy. In each instance, we present vocabulary and frequently used sentences that are typical of that field.

9.5 A trip to the dentist's office
Una visita al dentista

First, we'll begin with some vocabulary representative of the dental field, followed by expressions commonly used during a dental examination.

VOCABULARIO

orthodontics	**la ortodoncia**	endodontics	**la endodoncia**
braces	**los frenos,**	root canal	**la endodoncia**
	los frenillos	rubber dam	**el hule protector**

---

[26]**¿Me explico?** means, literally, "Am I explaining myself?", which places the responsibility for clear communication on the health care professional. This is more polite than "¿Entendió?", which means "Did you understand?" and could be perceived by the patient as accusatory.

oral surgeon	**el cirujano de boca**	periodontal	**periodontal**
a bridge	**un puente fijo**	to fill	**empastar, tapar,**
a partial	**un puente**		**rellenar**
	removible	gums	**las encías**
a denture	**una dentadura**	receding	**retrocediendo**
	completa	to bite	**morder**
a cap	**un frente estético**	tight	**apretado(-a)**
to extract	**extraer, sacar**	palate	**el paladar**
root canal	**extraer (sacar) el**	to reconstruct	**reconstruir**
	nervio	tartar	**el sarro**
root canal	**tratamiento de**	wisdom tooth	**la muela del juicio**
	conductos	almost done	**ya casi, ya mero**
crown	**la corona**		(*slang, Mex.*)
to bleed	**sangrar**	back molar	**la muela de atrás**
veneers	**los frentes estéticos**	toothbrush	**el cepillo de dientes**
blood	**la sangre**	dental floss	**el hilo dental**
ring, clamp	**el anillo**	noise	**el ruido**
the bleeding	**el sangrado**	to rinse	**rociar, enjuagar**
cavities	**las caries,**	loose	**flojo(-a)**
	las picaduras	drill	**el taladro**
molars	**las muelas**	to stop	**parar**
abscess	**el absceso**	bonding	**"bonding"**
gingivitis	**la gingivitis**	saliva	**la saliva**
filling	**la amalgama, el**		
	relleno, el empaste		

The following typical sentences can be used during dental exams and procedures.

Good morning, come in, and take a seat, please.	**Buenos días, pásele, por favor. Siéntese, por favor.**
How can I help you?	**¿En qué puedo ayudarle?**
Are you nervous? Don't worry!	**¿Está nervioso/nerviosa? ¡No se preocupe!**
Which tooth hurts?	**¿Qué diente le duele? (¿Cuál de los dientes le duele?)**
Where is the problem, above or below?	**¿Dónde está el problema? ¿Arriba o abajo?**
Is it bleeding?	**¿Está sangrando?**
Open your mouth, please.	**Abra la boca, por favor (Favor de abrir la boca).**
Stick out your tongue, please.	**Saque la lengua, por favor (Favor de sacar la lengua).**
I need to take an X ray of your tooth.	**Necesito sacar una radiografía de su diente (muela).**

I need to anesthetize your tooth.	Necesito anestesiar (adormecer, entumecer) su diente.
Is your lip/tooth/tongue asleep or numb?	¿Está dormido su labio? ¿Está dormido su diente? ¿Está dormida su lengua?
I can't save your tooth. I need to pull (remove) it/take it out.	No puedo salvar su diente. Necesito sacarlo.
I need to take out your tooth because it is loose.	Necesito extraer (sacar) su diente porque está flojo.
You are going to feel a lot of pressure, but not pain.	Va a sentir mucha presión, pero sin dolor.
I can save your tooth, but I need to extract the nerve (do a root canal).	Puedo salvar su diente, pero necesito extraer (sacar) el nervio.
I need to fill it.	Necesito taparlo (empastarlo).
Does the filling feel okay, or does it feel a little high?	¿Siente bien el relleno o está un poco alto?
Your gums are (gum line is) receding.	Se suben (bajan, retroceden) las encías.
I need to rinse your tooth with water.	Necesito rociar (enjuagar) su diente con agua.
I have a special toothbrush that makes a lot of noise.	Tengo un cepillo de dientes especial que hace mucho ruido.
If it hurts, raise your hand, and I'll stop.	Si le duele, levante la mano y yo paro.
Please bite down on the gauze for a half hour.	Por favor, muerda (Favor de morder) la gasa por media hora.
Please close your mouth gently.	Por favor, cierre (Favor de cerrar) la boca suavemente.
Don't cry; it won't hurt at all.	No llores; no le va a doler nada.
This ring is tight.	Este anillo está apretado.
Very good. Look at me.	Muy bien. Mírame.
Just about done/almost there.	Ya mero.
I'm almost finished.	Ya casi termino.
I'm going to prescribe medicine for the pain (the infection).	Voy a recetar medicina para el dolor (la infección).
Do you understand? (*literally,* Am I explaining myself?)	¿Me explico?
Please speak more slowly.	Hable más despacio, por favor (Favor de hablar más despacio).
You need another appointment in one month.	Necesita otra cita en un mes.

9.6 An appointment with the ophthalmologist
Una cita con el oftalmólogo

Now, we'll look at some vocabulary representative of the ophthalmologist's field.

VOCABULARIO

ophthalmology	**la oftalmología**
sight	**la vista**
color-blind/color-blindness	**daltónico/el daltonismo**
(I am) nearsighted	**(Soy) miope**
(I am) farsighted	**(Soy) hiperópico(-a)**
eye chart	**la carta, el gráfico, la gráfica**
glasses	**los lentes, las gafas, los anteojos, los espejuelos**
bifocals	**los bifocales, los lentes bifocales**
contact lenses	**los lentes de contacto, los pupilentes**
hard/soft/extended wear	**los lentes duros/suaves/de uso extendido**
Do your eyes itch?	**¿Tiene comezón/picazón en los ojos?**
Which eye or both?	**¿Qué ojo o los dos?/¿Cuál de los ojos, o los dos?**
both	**los dos/ambos**
Look at my left ear.	**Mire mi oído izquierdo.**
Read the next line, please.	**Lea la próxima línea, por favor.**
to appear, to seem	**parecer**
only/it's just that . . .	**nada más...**
to cover up	**tapar, cubrir**
still	**todavía**
you don't . . . yet	**todavía no...**
Which is better: the first lens or the second?	**¿Cuál es mejor—la primera lente[27] o la segunda?**
Which is better: a or b?	**¿Cuál es mejor: a o b?**
Is it the same?	**¿Es igual?**
infection	**una infección**
sty	**un orzuelo, una perrilla**
eyelash	**la pestaña**
eyelid	**el párpado**
to blink	**parpadear**
Blink! (*command*)	**¡Parpadée!/¡Favor de parpadear!**

---

[27]**El primer lente** is also acceptable.

astigmatism	**el astigmatismo**
scratch	**un rasguño**
dry eyes	**los ojos secos**
watery eyes	**los ojos llorosos**
tear duct	**el conducto lacrimal/lagrimal, el conducto lacrimógeno**
pinkeye (conjunctivitis)	**la conjuntivitis**
cataracts	**las cataratas**
blind	**ciego(-a)**
cross-eyed	**bizco(-a)**
to lubricate	**lubricar, mojar**
entropion	**la entropión**
ectropion	**la ectropión**
presbyopia	**la presbiopía, la presbicia**
ptosis	**ptosis, la caída de párpado**
glaucoma	**el glaucoma**
corneal ulcers	**las úlceras en la córnea**
redness	**el enrojecimiento**
episcleritis	**la episcleritis**
iritis	**la iritis, la inflamación del iris**
scleritis	**la escleritis**
iridectomy	**la iridectomía**
macular degeneration	**la degeneración de la mácula**
diabetic retinopathy	**la retinopatía diabética**
retinal artery (vein) occlusion	**la oclusión de la arteria (vena) retinal**
orbital cellulitis	**la celulitis orbital**
choroiditis	**la coroiditis**
exophthalmos	**exoftalmos**
ophthalmologist	**el oftalmólogo, la oftalmóloga**

9.7 Dermatology
La dermatología

This section is for those in the dermatological field.

VOCABULARIO

dermatologist	**el dermatólogo, la dermatóloga**	skin complexion	**la cutis, la tez**
		physical build	**la complexión**
dermatitis	**la dermatitis**	acne	**el acné**

pimples	**los granos,**	to burst open	**reventar**
	los granitos,	(don't burst)	**(no reviente)**
	los barros	to squeeze	**apretar**
blackheads	**las espinillas**	(don't squeeze)	**(no apriete)**
pores	**los poros**	to apply (apply)	**aplicar (aplique)**
sebaceous glands	**las glándulas**	an antibiotic	**una preparación**
	sebáceas	preparation	**antibiótica**
scar, scars	**la cicatriz,**	cream	**una crema**
	las cicatrices	lotion	**una loción**
skin	**la piel**	solution	**una solución**
oily skin	**la piel grasosa**	ointment	**un ungüento**
dry skin	**la piel reseca**	gel	**un gel**
follicles	**los folículos**	reddening	**el enrojecimiento**
cells	**las células**	swelling	**la hinchazón**
to foment	**fomentar la**	inflammation	**la inflamación**
bacterial	**proliferación**	minimize	**minimizar**
proliferation	**de bacteria**	increase	**aumentar**
nodule	**el nódulo**	dose, dosage	**la dosis**
a mole	**un lunar**	quantity	**la cantidad**
a birthmark	**una marca de**	wrinkles	**las arrugas**
	nacimiento	hormones	**las hormonas**
a lump	**una bolita**	a shot, injection	**la inyección**
a cyst	**un quiste**	collagen	**el colágeno**
a tumor	**un tumor**	laser treatment	**el tratamiento**
a biopsy	**una biopsia**		**con láser** (*m.*)
to pinch	**pellizcar**	veins	**las venas**
(don't pinch)	**(no pellizque)**	blood vessels	**los vasos**
to scratch	**rascar**		**sanguíneos**
(don't scratch)	**(no rasque)**		

9.8 The pharmacy
La farmacia

And finally, a section for pharmacists. (See also Chapter 7.2.)

VOCABULARIO

to indicate	**indicar**
to signal	**señalar**
should, must, ought	**deber**
until it is all gone	**hasta terminar todo**

until they are all finished	**hasta terminar con todo**
three days ago	**hace tres días**
between	**entre**
to speak	**hablar**
to read	**leer**
today	**hoy**
How does your doctor say . . . ?	**¿Cómo dice su doctor...?**
about, concerning	**de, acerca de, sobre**
Did you consult your doctor about . . . ?	**¿Consultó con su doctor de (acerca de, sobre)...?**
adverse	**adverso(s)**
side, secondary	**secundario(s)**
effects	**efectos** (as in, **efectos secundarios**)
to include; they include	**incluir; incluyen**
to taste	**saber a**
It tastes like . . .	**Sabe a...**
It has the taste of . . .	**Tiene sabor a...**
a different taste	**un sabor diferente**
to find	**encontrar (ue)**
a list	**una lista**
inside	**adentro, dentro de**
the package	**el paquete, el envase**
I/you/he/she would like	**quisiera**
to buy	**comprar**
our	**nuestro(-a)**
It is ready.	**Está listo(-a).**
It will be ready.	**Estará (Va a estar) listo(-a).**
to wait (to hope, to expect)	**esperar**
For what?	**¿Para qué?**
is it for, it is for	**sirve** (as in **¿Para qué (De qué) sirve?** ["What is it for?"])
In order to be sure . . .	**Para estar seguro(-a)...**
to pick up (pick up)	**recoger (recoja,** command form)
to pay (pay)	**pagar (pague,** command form)
at the cash register	**en la caja**
to remember	**recordar (ue)**
to explain	**explicar**
to repeat (please repeat)	**repetir (repita, por favor)**
to say, to tell	**decir**
to tell me	**decirme**
It's normal to feel . . .	**Es normal sentir(se)...**
Don't worry.	**No se preocupe.**
It's a pleasure.	**Es un placer.**

10

What you will learn in this lesson:

- how to utilize interpreter services in a medical setting
- cultural courtesies and formalities in Spanish related to greetings, foods, time, space, privacy issues, family, and circular v. linear thought processes
- the nonexistent concept of preventive medicine v. a doctor/dental visit only when feeling extremely ill or when toothache or throbbing is intolerable
- the concept of walk-in clinic v. doctor appointments
- prescriptions v. OTC meds v. consulting at the **farmacia** in Latin America (and subsequently purchasing medication without a prescription or without a previous doctor visit)
- to distinguish some "culture-bound syndromes"
- vocabulary related to medications
- vocabulary related to illnesses and symptoms
- medically related "layman" and slang terms

The first goal of this lesson is to be introduced to and understand some Latino cultural values and belief systems, as well as to be aware of the differences between "Anglo" and Latino behavioral patterns and subsequently to be able to apply this knowledge successfully during a Latino patient interview and exam.

The second goal is to use and recognize medically related terminology in order to express yourself, understand, and make yourself understood by all your Latino Spanish-speaking patients, no matter what their background may be.

This lesson is divided into two principal parts. The first is "Cross-cultural communication" and discusses interpreter techniques, as well as many cultural factors and culture-bound syndromes to provide insight into your Latino patients' varied belief systems and needs. It is hoped that this, in turn, will aid in creating a better rapport between the healthcare professional and patients.

The second part consists of vocabulary related to herbal remedies and medicines, which are listed in alphabetical order. Following this is a list of illnesses and symptoms, grouped by body systems and ordered alphabetically.

10.1 Cross-cultural communication

THE INTERPRETER

There are three basic forms of interpreting: simultaneous, consecutive, and paraphrasing. Let's examine the strengths and weaknesses of each method.

Simultaneous interpretation. This method consists of speaking concurrently in one language while listening in the other. The interpreter tracks approximately one or two words behind the speaker and renders the most precise translation possible.

Simultaneous translation is helpful when conserving time is a predominant factor. It does not necessarily provide for establishing close physician–patient contact or personal communication, however. The best use of this technique is for interpreting conferences, where a large number of persons can listen to the translation using headsets. In a medical setting, some find this method too distracting because it is difficult to listen to two people speaking simultaneously in different languages.

Consecutive interpretation. This technique consists of interpreting several phrases as precisely as possible, *after* the speaker has paused. This method, depending upon the interpreter's ability to retain and recall information, may foster a better physician–patient rapport because the doctor and patient can establish eye contact more easily while "speaking" to one another. They can "listen" to each other, first comprehending what they can, and then resort to the interpreter's "rendition" for confirmation. The drawback is that consecutive interpretation is more time-consuming.

Paraphrasing. This method allows the doctor and patient to express several sentences or paragraphs, which the interpreter then summarizes. It is quicker than the consecutive method, but slower than the simultaneous method. Paraphrasing is not always as accurate as the other two techniques, but it does allow for the interpreter to "soften" the language or to take into account cultural differences in expressions, courtesy, etc. The use of this method, however, can lead to a great deal of inaccuracy because salient factors may be lost by the interpreter's potential inability to recognize the important points and thus fail to convey crucial information.

Often a combination of all the techniques is used. Skilled interpreters usually defer to the doctor and patient regarding their preferences first, whenever possible.

Using an interpreter. When employing the services of an interpreter, the medical professional should first brief the interpreter on the upcoming procedure and examination and then request that the interpreter meet with the patient beforehand in order to explain what to expect during the procedure or exam, as well as what to expect in terms of the doctor, nurse, or technician. In this way, the interpreter can explain that a U.S.-trained doctor may seem more curt, brusque, dryer, and colder than a Hispanic doctor and that the patient should please not be offended. It also seems to be more effective, more comfortable, and less embarrassing for the patient when the interpreter is of the same sex.

In a hospital setting, the medical interpreter delicately balances the following four roles:

Direct translator	Must find a term with the exact equivalent.
Cultural broker	Must grasp two, often opposing backgrounds and take them into account within a split second while interpreting the concepts and content.
Biomedical interpreter	Must be a facilitator by linking healthcare knowledge, procedures, and analogies that properly convey the idea.
Patient advocate	Must help patients deal with red tape, and make their needs known in general. Often the interpreter must assist in finding locations, filling out forms, and guiding the patient.

Interpreters must be aware of various Spanish dialects, regionalisms, educational backgrounds, and untranslatable terms. Therefore, it is not necessarily true that being bilingual is equivalent to being a capable, competent interpreter. Interpreting is a highly developed academic skill and a discipline. It should be noted, as well, that a good medical interpreter is an integral part of the professional medical team when treating a non–English-speaking patient. He or she should not, however, offer personal opinions and impressions or give advice if the patient asks what the interpreter thinks. Nor should an interpreter release any information concerning the patient's condition unless it is given by the doctor or nurse to be translated. The interpreter is the conduit from one culture and language to another.

The Medical Interpreters' and Translators' Code of Ethics states: "A medical interpreter/translator is a specially trained professional who has proficient knowledge and skills in a primary language or languages and employs that training in a medical or health-related setting in order to make possible communication among parties using different languages."

The skills of a medical interpreter/translator include cultural sensitivity and awareness with respect to all parties involved, as well as mastery of medical and colloquial terminology, which make possible conditions of mutual trust and accurate communication leading to effective provision of medical-health services.

GENERAL INFORMATION CONCERNING INTERPRETERS

The interpreter speaks in the first person ("I" form), as though he or she were the patient or healthcare provider. "He says," "She says," etc. are professionally improper.

The interpreter should maintain strictly confidential all information learned during an interpretation. If the content to be interpreted may be perceived as unwittingly or unintentionally offensive or insensitive to the dignity or well-being of the patient, the interpreter should tactfully inform the health professional. He or she should also make every effort to understand and communicate the social and cultural context in which the patient is operating because it may affect the patient's medical needs. It is the interpreter's responsibility to be aware of the cultural and social realities of the patient and to educate or inform those who might misunderstand.

The interpreter should not accept any assignment for which he or she is not adequately qualified due to lack of language skill or knowledge of the subject matter, unless these limitations are understood by both the patient and the healthcare provider.

Confidentiality and comfort zones: Socioeconomic class differences openly exist in many Spanish-speaking countries, and attitudes formed by this system often continue to be manifested in the new country. An interpreter from a higher class may not show the same dignity or respect for a patient from a lower class background. The patient may feel embarrassed or uncomfortable. On the other hand, a patient from a higher class background may feel uneasy confiding to the healthcare professional through an interpreter who could have been her maid or laundry woman in her own country.

No matter what the socioeconomic situation, confidentiality is a real problem in a small town or community where the patient can encounter the interpreter in the supermarket or at a neighborhood gathering. There is no assurance that the interpreter hasn't announced the patient's problems to the entire **barrio**. (If the interpreter is professional and/or ethical, the aforementioned should not occur, but the patient won't necessarily know or believe it.)

THE LATINO PATIENT

In this section, we will look at general aspects to take into account concerning the Latino or Hispanic patient. Naturally, the authors are well aware that each individual is different and wish to avoid over-generalization. However, cultural differences simply do exist and are a fact of life, and it is incumbent upon healthcare professionals to be aware of them in order to avoid unwittingly offending a patient.

Within the Hispanic culture the extended family plays an extremely important role. The Hispanic family tends to be very close-knit. A patient may often be accompanied by other family members for moral support, due to *cariño* (affection), or merely out of habit. The "Anglo" healthcare professional may feel somewhat overwhelmed by this, perhaps even somewhat defensive or frustrated, but there is no need to feel so. It is fairly customary.

Hispanics also tend to be more expressive with their feelings, hand gestures, and body movements, in general, often touching each other in an affectionate or soothing manner, mentioning one another's names frequently within a conversation (a lovely personal touch), and/or often standing together at a much closer proximity than, for example, Anglo speakers would without feeling awkward or uncomfortable.

The Spanish language, which is reflective of Hispanic culture and vice versa, also observes more formal courtesies than does the mainstream culture in the United States. When meeting, greeting, interviewing, and leave-taking within the Hispanic culture, it is *extremely important,* customary, and courteous to shake hands. Formalities and courtesies are stressed, while political correctness is not a recognized concept.

Latino children are generally taught not to question others, especially people in authority, because this is considered impolite and disrespectful. This attitude may carry over into adulthood. In the medical setting, it is not typical to ask questions or clarify points, as it is for mainstream U.S. patients. Thus, a healthcare professional may want to explain or emphasize some points a bit more or make sure all the patient's questions are answered. Remember, great respect is shown for priests, healthcare professionals, and the elderly. Out of respect for the healthcare providers, the patient may tend to agree with everything they say, so as not to "challenge" their authority and/or to avoid wasting the doctors' or nurses' valuable time.

Another cultural point to be aware of is that some Hispanics adhere to the "homeostasis concept" that ill health may be interpreted as a lack of balance in the body. For example, it may be believed that a loss of blood affects sexual performance. Thus, the statement "The doctor needs to take blood" may result in a negative reaction unless the speaker also explains that there will be no ill effects from taking the sample. The concept of balance may affect other health issues; for example, parents may feel that they need to restore fluids that their baby has lost because of diarrhea.

Clearly, sensitivity to and awareness of cultural dynamics can greatly improve the relationship between the healthcare provider and the patient.

Attitudes toward food and family

Partaking, offering, and sharing food in an extended family environment is an integral part of Hispanic life. Food is not merely nutrition; it can signify security, warmth, survival, love, and acceptance. Thus, if dietary instructions are given in the following sense: "You should eat A, B, and C, but must stay away from D, E, and F" (which is concise and to the point in English), it would be construed as being harsh and unfeeling in Spanish. A more "apologetic" attitude, while also alluding to the family who loves and needs the patient, would be appropriate: "I am very sorry that you will need to be more careful of what you eat. Unfortunately, for your own health as well as your family's well-being, . . ."

Since the sharing and eating of food is such an important aspect of Latino life, it is understandable that bringing food to a hospital patient during a visit is considered a warm and caring gesture. By the same token, it is common for family members and friends to visit a patient in the hospital even when the "crisis" is over. It would be considered cruel, cold, and uncaring not to visit or to visit without arms laden with food. Generally speaking, even the patient expects this support, and would feel saddened and grieve (thus taking longer to recover) without it. Although these visits en masse may be extremely annoying to the medical staff (who may well be understaffed, overoccupied with completing interminable documents, and busy dealing with multiple services), as well as to the other patients who share the room, at least it may help to understand why this "behavior" takes place.

Doctor-patient relationship

In order to establish a stronger, trusting doctor-patient relationship, the Hispanic patient would experience less stress if the doctor would do the following:

- Shake hands and introduce him- or herself.
- Try to pronounce the patient's name (**nombre**) and surnames (**apellidos**) correctly.
- Attempt to speak some Spanish, even if only a few initial courtesy phrases.
- Sit down for a moment with the patient to inquire about the family, the children, and how the patient has been feeling in general lately, etc. Even though the doctor may be pressed for time, this initial conversation smooths the way for more open dialogue and a more relaxed patient, allowing the remainder of the interview to be conducted more easily.

The Spanish language and Latino culture often result in circular or branching thought processes; conversely, the English language and U.S. culture often result in linear thought processes. Whereas in the United States, it is considered efficient to be brief, concise, and to the point, in Latin American countries, such "efficiency" would be considered the result of poor upbringing and the height of rudeness and offensiveness. Any meeting of Hispanics is preceded by standard courtesies and polite small talk, and only after these preliminaries can the reason for meeting be addressed. In a U.S. medical setting, the healthcare professional may find the preliminaries to be exceedingly frustrating. However, knowledge of the reasons behind them and acquaintance with the language and cultures should help explain why the patient may not be answering questions succinctly or may appear to go off on tangents without necessarily returning to the point. (In such cases, a gentle reminder may be all that is needed.)

In Latin America, patients will often talk to a doctor in the same manner as they would to a priest or a therapist. It is not as common nor as accepted to attend counseling sessions or see psychiatrists as it is in the Anglo population. As a result, the role of the doctor expands to include general counseling duties.

In Latin America it is still sometimes routine for doctors to make house calls. It is also not uncommon for the doctor or nurse to phone the patient the following day in order to check on his or her progress.

In other words, Hispanics are accustomed to a more personal touch in health care. Once again, if an interpreter has not had time to speak with the patient and brief him or her on procedures or on what to expect during the interview, it would be very helpful for someone who speaks Spanish to do so. If this is not possible, hopefully the doctor will take the time to explain what he or she is going to be doing and why, in order to reassure the patient as much as possible.

Typical cultural differences

The following attitudes, beliefs, practices, and behaviors are generalizations. However, they are based on the authors' experiences and observations while interpreting doctor–patient interviews and talking with Hispanic patients.

1. It is still somewhat more common for Hispanics to believe that the fatter a baby is, the healthier she or he is. This is changing somewhat, however.

2. More sugar, salt, oil, and spicy seasonings are utilized in the "typical" Mexican diet than in the "typical" Anglo diet. (The food of most other Latin American countries is not as highly seasoned as that of Mexico.)

3. The concept of regular checkups and preventive medicine does not exist in Spanish-speaking countries. For adults, a yearly physical or a six-month dental checkup and teeth cleaning is almost inconceivable. The general attitude is, "If I feel really sick or am in great pain, I may go to see the doctor." First, however, the ailing adult usually tries home remedies, leftover medications, medicine suggested by the pharmacist, or treatments by other healers such as **curanderos**, **yerberos**, or **santeros**. When the decision is finally made to go to the doctor, appointments are usually on a first-come, first-served basis. As a result, Latin Americans in the United States are often dismayed and alarmed when they finally call the doctor's office and are given an appointment in three to four weeks. Their reaction is, "I'll either be dead or better by then!" (In the United States, economics may also play a part in the delay in seeking medical help early on.)

Children, however, are an exception to the rule. They are considered God's treasure and are often taken to see the doctor for the slightest change in bodily functions, a fever, the sniffles, or unusual behavior. Preventive medicine is still not usual, even for children. (Recall from Chapter 4 that well-baby visits are rare to nonexistent in Latin America.)

4. The Latin American patient is more likely to drink liquids at room temperature than with ice in order to avoid "catching a cold." If a medication (particularly in liquid form) requires refrigeration, you

may suggest removing it from the refrigerator some 10–15 minutes beforehand. This will allow it to return to room temperature (**a tiempo**), thus satisfying the patient and improving the possibility of compliance.

5. Latin Americans will often go in for an antibiotic shot (frequently at the **farmacia** or other business location where **inyecciones** are administered) in order to clear up a cold. In Mexico, as well as in many parts of Latin America, the pharmacy clerks are, at times, consulted for small ailments and will then recommend medication. Most medications (except amphetamines and some tranquilizers) can be purchased without a doctor's prescription. The pharmacists are not required to have any specialized training or university studies; however, a great many of them do. Those who do not have generally learned the trade through daily contact and experience and usually have a Mexican *PDR* at hand.

6. The Latin American patient also often feels that if the doctor has not prescribed any medication, he or she has not really "treated" the patient's illness.

7. The following is a saying in Mexico referring to mealtimes: **Hay que desayunar como rey, almorzar como príncipe y cenar como mendigo,** which means "One should have breakfast like a king, lunch like a prince, and dinner like a pauper/beggar." It is believed healthier not to eat late at night. The large meal is eaten between 2:00 P.M. and 4:00 P.M. The wisdom of this practice has only been recognized here in the United States somewhat recently.

8. For some reason Anglos seem to complain of suffering more from headaches and backaches, whereas Latin American patients seem to mention bladder and liver problems with more frequency. According to Harvard medical anthropologist Arthur Kleinman, ". . . in the United States when we get stressed, we often get headaches. . . ." He goes on to quote Dr. Spann, who states, "In the Southern cone of Latin America—Argentina, Uruguay, and Paraguay—people frequently somatize to the liver. If they have a headache, they say the liver is bothering them."[1]

9. For some Latinos it is considered a punishment to be sick, which may be linked to religious as well as cultural beliefs.

10. It is often quite difficult to become acculturated to a new society, especially for Latino parents. Their children may assimilate more easily due to friends made at school or at play who are from other ethnic backgrounds. This can, in turn, cause great stress within the family, which can be manifested in a medical setting. Thus, since it is

---

[1]Robert P. Carlson, "Talking with your Hispanic immigrant patients," *Texas Medicine,* Oct. 1996, 91 (1996) 10:90.

difficult to determine the degree of assimilation or acculturation of a patient, the medical professional is faced with additional obstacles when assessing the situation. Please keep in mind that a patient's country of origin, socioeconomic background, and formal education may also come into play.

11. We have noted in our classes during recent years that several healthcare professionals have mentioned more frequently instances of young pregnant girls with no family or social support system. In some cases, her family may be back in her native country. This presents difficulties, and one (albeit perhaps glib) solution is to put the young girl in contact with **promotoras** who serve as mediators and liaisons between the community and the health clinic or health care system. The **promotoras** often live in the community or barrio and are accepted as friends, relatives, or trusted members of that area. Another potential solution is to put the girl in contact with a church group in her neighborhood.

CULTURE-BOUND SYNDROMES

Another significant area to be aware of is the existence of several "culture-bound syndromes" that are mentioned with a fair amount of frequency among Hispanic patients. The following are four of the most common: **caída de mollera** (fallen or depressed anterior fontanelle), **susto** (reactive depression or posttraumatic stress disorder), **empacho** (a blockage of the intestines), and **mal de ojo**.

Caída de mollera

The medical diagnosis is dehydration, which is believed to be caused by pulling the baby from the breast or bottle too quickly, holding the baby incorrectly, or allowing the baby to fall. Some of the symptoms are diarrhea, loss of appetite, fever, irritability, or vomiting, among others. **No debes de agitar mucho a los hijos porque se les cae la mollera**. Perceived cure: Push the thumb up in palate to try to raise and reshape the fallen area, which could cause more serious repercussions; turn the baby upside down and shake him or pat salt over his head.

Susto or mal de susto

The medical diagnosis may be reactive depression, an anxiety reaction, or posttraumatic stress syndrome and is believed to be caused by a startling or frightening event. Some of the symptoms are irritability, diarrhea, depression, insomnia at night, daytime drowsiness, and lack of appetite or weight loss. **El susto** is considered by some to be a departure of the soul from the body, which may be held captive by supernatural beings. This can bring on TB, diabetes, miscarriages, and other disorders. Perceived cure: In some cases ritual cleansings or herbal teas are suggested. A healer might give the following instructions: prepare an herbal potion, put the potion in a spray bottle or have someone take a mouthful of the liquid and spray it on the patient while someone else suddenly covers the patient with a towel so that he or she continues to breathe in the vapors. In this way, the **susto** is cured with another **susto**.

Empacho

The medical diagnosis may be gastroenteritis, appendicitis, intestinal parasites, or food poisoning. **Empacho** is thought to be caused by a bolus of food that sticks to the intestinal wall as a result of eating certain foods at incorrect times, swallowing gum, swallowing too much saliva during teething, or eating too many sweets, among other things. The symptoms are diarrhea, constipation, vomiting, indigestion, and feeling bloated and/or lethargic. The word *empacho* derives from the Indo-European word *ped* ("foot") and *impedire* ("to prevent"). The undigested food sticking to the wall of the digestive tract is perceived to differ from "regular" indigestion, perhaps as a result of social and psychological forces. For example, **empacho** in a child may occur if the child is forced to stop playing in order to eat dinner or is made to eat a dish or a food that he or she strongly dislikes. Perceived cure: Treatment may consist of having the back massaged, rubbing a raw egg over the area, and/or drinking herbal teas.

Mal de ojo

Admiring or covetous looks are to blame for **mal de ojo**, which historically has been translated as "evil eye." Perceived symptoms include irritability, crying, sleeplessness, and fever. Prevention and treatment differ widely among Latinos from different regions. In the southwestern United States and Mexico, for example, **mal de ojo** can be warded off or prevented by touching a baby after looking at him or her with admiration or affection. Another preventive measure used is an amulet called **ojo de venado**[2] (made from a nut from a tree, **azabache**,[3]

---

[2]**ojo de venado** literally, "deer's eye"
[3]**azabache** jet lignite

and amber tied together with red string), which is hung around the baby's neck or wrist, or a red string is tied around the baby's waist. In contrast, in the Caribbean region, it is "harmful" to touch a child after he or she has received admiring or covetous looks because this action will pass on the **mal de ojo**. In Cuba, a mother is supposed to say, **Bésale el culito** ("Kiss his little ass/anus") after someone admires her baby. Around the Caribbean, **azabache** is used as a prophylactic. In many regions or countries, treatment may consist of passing an unbroken egg (a pure unborn entity) over the child's body.

NEGATIVE FORCES

Mal de ojo is a good example of the underlying concept of positive versus negative forces that is manifested in many beliefs and/or religions throughout the world. The "negative forces" (called evil, bad, the devil, dark, bad energy, etc.) make you ill, and the "positive forces" (called good, light, angels, etc.) make you well. In order to become better, healthier, richer, happier, etc., one must drive the negative out and replace it with something positive. A common practice worldwide is the use of an egg to attract the negative force from the person by drawing it into the egg, which is then disposed of so that it can no longer cause harm. In the case of **mal de ojo**, it is believed that when someone comments about a child (a pure and vulnerable entity), that person may be feeling envy, jealousy, or other negative emotions. This negative feeling sends out bad energy or "vibes" that may enter the child and make him or her sick. There are many methods of driving out the negative forces. In addition to eggs, animals are often used to attract the negative forces. Other methods consist of introducing goodness such as perfumes, incense, prayers, fire, or penance that will overwhelm the "negative" force and compel it to leave.

According to Robert T. Trotter II, Ph.D., in his article "Folk medicine in the Southwest," the first three illnesses, **caída de mollera**, **susto**, and **empacho**, "can be linked to recognized biologic conditions and therefore cannot be analyzed solely on the basis of socio-cultural factors. Clearly, it would be a mistake to continue ignoring these syndromes in the Southwest on the assumption that they are 'all in the mind' of the Mexican-American patients."[4] It can be added that these three illnesses are not only known by the above names within the Southwest of the United States, but in all of Latin America as well. It is

---

[4]Robert T. Trotter II, "Folk medicine in the Southwest," Interstate Postgraduate Medical Assembly, 78 (December, 1985) 8:169–170.

very important for non-Latino doctors to recognize their existence and symptoms, among those of other illnesses, in order to have a better understanding of their Hispanic patients.

VARIABLES

Naturally, each Hispanic patient's background must be taken into consideration regarding social and economic class, country and region, etc. These are all variable factors in any culture. They are particularly relevant when dealing with Spanish-speaking populations, since there are 20 countries in the Americas with native Spanish speakers, and each of these countries has its own indigenous populations with different customs and languages. Please bear this in mind while reviewing the following, some of which are also considered to be "culture-bound syndromes" or characteristics.

Giving birth. Some Hispanic women in U.S. hospitals may choose to deliver their babies in a squatting or kneeling position on the floor rather than in a hospital bed. These women are not accustomed to having their newborn whisked away to another room, but laid in their arms immediately after birth. This preference is in line with the holistic approach that some U.S. hospitals are beginning to accept as an alternative.

Attitudes toward hospitals. Because illness is often perceived as a weakness of character or a punishment from God, it merits mention that the Latin American patient often believes, as stated by Antonio Zavaleta, ". . . that if you go into a hospital you will not come out alive, that you will die there. For many Hispanic immigrants, this fear is real!"[5]

Mal aire. Literally, this means "bad air." The medical diagnosis may be angina pectoris, pneumonia, or even a peptic ulcer. **Mal aire** is believed to be night air that can enter any body cavity and cause gas and distention. Perceived preventions are many and varied. For example, placing a raisin on the umbilical cord of a newborn, covering an infant's ears with a cap, and, for mothers, avoiding sexual activity for 40 days after giving birth are all perceived as measures to prevent contracting **mal aire**.

In addition to exposure to night air, **mal aire** also applies to extremes of temperature, especially going from the heat into the cold. Situations in which **mal aire** can be contracted include the following:

---

[5]Quoted in "Talking with your Hispanic immigrant patients" by Robert P. Carlson, page 38.

- Having a pain in the side, chest, or back and being exposed to the cold
- Becoming hot while cooking or making tortillas and either going out into the cold or cool air or touching or drinking cold water
- Going out into the cold air when an eye is red or having red eyes from watching television or a movie and being exposed to cold air[6]

People who believe they have **mal aire** often state, **Me dio un aire** ("I caught an air [bad air]").

Treatment often consists of using a lighted candle and a glass to create suction, called **ventosa** in Spanish and "cupping" in English. Cupping of one kind or another is practiced all over the world. You can tell if a patient has tried this treatment by the circular pattern of superficial "hickeylike" indentations. Recognizing the results of this treatment can avoid a misguided call to the authorities to report abuse!

Mal de orin. A urinary tract infection, called "urine sickness," is manifested by frequency of urination or pain upon urination. (In Nicaragua, the term **chistata**, which means "cystitis," is often used.)

Algodoncillo. This disease or infection, called "thrush" in English, is believed to be provoked by heat rising from the body to the mouth. Concerned parents will often describe it as little bits of cotton (**algodoncillos**) between the lip and the teeth. It is actually a fungal infection that occurs in newborns and suckling babies up to six months of age.[7] The perceived cure is to put cotton on a stick or to use a cotton swab to remove the infection.

Erisipela. "Erysipelas" is red spots on the hands and arms that have been overexposed to sun. **Erisipela**, which is also called **jiotes** or **ersipela**, is also believed to be caused by a lack of vitamins.[8]

---

[6]Patients have explained this syndrome to the authors as follows: *"Cuando tienes un dolor en el costado, pecho o espalda o cuando sales de repente de la casa y hace frío afuera y tienes calor o si estás guisando y tienes calor. O si estás haciendo tortillas, no debes de agarrar el agua fría porque tienes calor y te puede dar un aire, o si el ojo se pone muy rojo, y sales con el frío, o si estás viendo la tele o un cine y sales al frío, quizás es conjuntivitis pero se dice, me dio un aire."*

[7]This syndrome has been described as follows: *"Es una cosita blanca que les forma a los bebés recién nacidos hasta los 6 meses. Es como algodoncillos entre el labio y el diente. Pones algodón en un palito y lo quitas. Es como lama en la boca. Esto nada más ocurre con los bebés o niños lactantes—entre recién nacidos hasta los seis meses de edad."*

[8]This syndrome has been described as follows: *"O puede ser falta de vitaminas que también se llama 'jiotes' o ersipela."*

Fogaso. It is believed that heat rising from the center of the body causes tiny red dots on the mouth and tongue, stressed feet, and rashes.

Postemillas; fuegos. Toothaches or abscessed teeth are common ailments. **Fuegos** (literally, "fires") is used to describe chancre sores, fever blisters, or cold sores.[9]

Chípil. This disease that children have after weaning is believed to be caused by crawling on a cold floor and is connected with cold and rejection. As an adjective, **chipilo(-a)** is used to describe a younger child. It is believed that jealousy or envy of a younger sibling causes a child to become **chípil** and demonstrate behaviors of crying, whining, or throwing tantrums. A child can even become **chipilón** from jealousy during the mother's pregnancy with another child.[10]

Hot and Cold Syndrome. Many common problems and complaints are believed to come from either heat or cold. For example, cold is believed to lead to chest cramps, earaches, headaches, stiffness, paralysis, pain due to strains, teething pain, stomach cramps, and maladies resulting from cold air on certain parts of the body. Tuberculosis may be provoked by the "cold theory." The Hot and Cold Syndrome is more than likely based on the early Hippocratic theory of disease and the four body "humors." The theory may well have spread through Spain between the 700s and 1400s while the Moors (Arabic culture) invaded and settled Spain and then from Spain to the New World (Latin America).

The disrupted relationship between these humors is often considered to be the cause of disease. Thus when all four "humors" are balanced, the body is healthy.

Blood	hot and wet	**Yellow bile**	hot and dry
Phlegm	cold and wet	**Black bile**	cold and dry

For example, if an illness is classified as "hot," it must be treated with a cold substance. To maintain balance, "hot" foods should not be combined; they should be eaten with "cold" foods. It is also suggested, for example, that after delivering a baby, which is considered a "hot" experience, a woman should not eat pork, a "hot" food, but should eat something "cold" to restore her balance.

Some "cold" foods are avocados, bananas, white beans, lima beans, coconut, and sugar cane. Some "hot" foods are chocolate, cof-

---

[9]This syndrome has been described as follows: *"Son los 'fuegos' de la boca o úlceras o ulceritas."*

[10]This syndrome has been described as follows: *"Si estás embarazada con otro bebé, el niño se pone chípil o chillón y hace berrinches y llora."*

fee, alcohol, corn meal, garlic, kidney beans, onions, and peas. (There is no logic by which to determine the category of a food; the classifications are simply "known" and passed down.)

Some illnesses and conditions that are considered "cold" are arthritis, colds, menstruation, and joint pains; while some "hot" illnesses are constipation, diarrhea, rashes, and ulcers.

It is believed that penicillin is a "hot" medication and cannot be used to treat a "hot" disease. Unfortunately, for healthcare providers, the concepts of hot and cold can vary from country to country and even from region to region. Nevertheless, an awareness of patients' perceptions of hot and cold diseases, foods, and remedies can result in understanding why a patient may react strongly or fearfully to a doctor's recommendation, treatment program, or even diagnosis. Even in the mainstream U.S. culture, cold is associated with threatening aspects of existence, and heat is associated with secure and comforting aspects of existence.

SUMMARY

As can be seen, many concepts that underlie folk culture medicine have a basis, and the cures have been handed down through the years, some being very effective. The point here, however, is to be aware of common complaints, beliefs, and treatments and to recognize them within the context of the culture.

Dr. Zavaleta also has issued the following caution: "There's an ill-informed belief that culturally based health-care delivery systems like folk healers are declining, and that is absolutely not true." He continues by stating, "What we find is these delivery systems are very often not right out there for you to see. When you ask people, they are not going to tell you about them. It's the kind of thing you have to spend almost a lifetime studying in order to really see it and have people tell you the truth."[11]

After a great deal of study, much discussion with many Latino friends, acquaintances, and family, as well as firsthand knowledge, the authors wholeheartedly agree with Dr. Zavaleta. If anyone suggests that **curanderos** are very rare nowadays, he or she either has not won the patient's **confianza** ("trust") or is a Latino embarrassed to admit his or her belief for fear of ridicule.

---

[11]Quoted in "Talking with your Hispanic immigrant patients" by Robert P. Carlson, page 40.

As we conclude this section on cross-cultural communication and understanding, it bears repeating that the Latino patients' concerns and complaints should not be ridiculed or dismissed as inconsequential social and cultural phenomena. Latino patients, like all patients, should be accorded compassion, understanding, and respect by members of the medical profession.

10.2 Herbal remedies

The following is a list of some herbal remedies with their English names, Spanish name equivalents, and cures as perceived by the patient. Most are taken in the form of teas or applied as topical lotions. Many are also used as food seasonings.

English	Spanish	Perceived use
aloe, aloe vera	**sábila**	burns, cancer, asthma, scars, swelling of the extremities
chamomile (tea)	**manzanilla**	upset stomach, cramps, diarrhea, colic
camphor (tea, lotion)	**alcanfor**	laxative
coriander (tea)	**cilantro**	laxative, purgative, cramps
corn silk (tea)	**pelos, cabellos de elote**	urinary infection, kidney stones
garlic (garlic water)	**ajo**	blood pressure, asthma, TB, worms
gordolobo	**gordolobo, mullein, mullen**	cough, bronchitis, hemorrhoids, varicose veins
linden	**tila**	nervousness, sleeplessness
mint (tea)	**yerba, hierba buena**	stomachaches, colic, nerves
olive oil (oil)	**aceite de olivo**	burns, fever, constipation
onion (food)	**cebolla**	burns, coughs, tumors, warts
orange blossom (tea)	**flor de azahar**	nerves, tranquilizer, insomnia
rue (tea)	**ruda**	nerves, hysteria, headache, menstrual cramps, abortion during the first to second month

| sage (tea) | **salvia** | high cholesterol, dysentery, headache, stomachache, phlegm |
| worm seed (tea, lotion) | **epazote** | fungus, as a diuretic, stomachache |

10.3 Medicines
Medicinas

adrenaline	**la adrenalina**	liniment	**el linimento**
analgesics	**los analgésicos**	lozenges	**los trocitos,**
antacids	**los antiácidos**		**las pastillas**
antibiotics	**los antibióticos**		**para chupar**
antidote	**el antídoto**	ointment	**el ungüento**
antihistamines	**los antihistamí-**	paregoric	**el paregórico**
	nicos	penicillin	**la penicilina**
aspirin	**la aspirina**	pills	**las píldoras,**
atropine	**la atropina**		**las pastillas**
barbiturates	**los barbitúricos**	plasters/patches	**los parches**
belladonna	**la belladona**	pomade	**la pomada**
bicarbonate	**el bicarbonato**	purgative	**el purgante**
bromide	**el bromuro**	sedative	**el sedante**
capsules	**las cápsulas**	sulfa	**la sulfa**
codeine	**la codeína**	suppository	**el supositorio**
cortisone	**la cortisona**	syrup	**el jarabe**
estrogen	**el estrógeno**	tablets	**las tabletas**
hormones	**las hormonas**	tonic	**el tónico**
insulin	**la insulina**	tranquilizers	**los tranquilizantes,**
laxative	**el laxante**		**los calmantes**

10.4 Illnesses and symptoms (by area)

Note: The Spanish definitions that are enclosed in quotation marks are slang or less refined terms, which you should not use unless your patient does not understand the standard layman's terms. Your patient, however, may express him- or herself in this fashion depending on educational level or socioeconomic or regional background. Therefore, it is helpful to be aware of these definitions.

The head	La cabeza
acne, dermatitis	acné (*m.*), dermatitis (*f.*)
adenoids	adenoides (*m.*)
bad breath	mal aliento (*m.*)
bald, hairless	calvo, sin pelo, "el pelón"
baldness	calvicie (*f.*)
bleeding of the gums	sangrar de las encías
blurred vision	vista (*f.*) borrosa/nublada/empañada
buzzing in the ears	zumbido (*m.*) de/en los oídos
canker sore, chancre	pequeña úlcera (*f.*) en la boca, fuego (*m.*), chancro (*m.*)
cavities	caries (*f.*), dientes (*m. pl.*) podridos
cleft palate	paladar (*m.*) hendido, grietas (*f. pl.*) en el paladar
cross-eyed	bizco (*m.*)
dandruff	caspa (*f.*)
deaf-mute	sordomudo (*m.*), sordomuda (*f.*)
deafness; deaf	sordera (*f.*); sordo(-a)
depressed, or fallen fontanelle	fontanela (*f.*) caída o deprimida, "mollera (*f.*) caída"
coated "dirty" tongue	"lengua (*f.*) sucia"
diphtheria	difteria (*f.*), "diteria" (*f.*)
earache	dolor (*m.*) de oído
ear wax	cera (*f.*), cerumen (*m.*), "cerilla" (*f.*)
facial discoloration, chloasma	paño (*m.*), cloasma (*m.*)
facial paralysis	parálisis (*f.*) facial
goiter	bocio (*m.*), "buche" (*m.*)
harelip, cleft lip	labihendido (*m.*), el labio leporino, "comido (*m.*) de la luna"
halitosis	halitosis (*f.*)
headache	dolor (*m.*) de cabeza, jaqueca (*f.*)
hoarseness; hoarse	ronquera (*f.*); ronco(-a)
inflammation of the thyroid gland	inflamación (*f.*) de la glándula tiroides
inflamed eyelids	párpados (*m. pl.*) inflamados
laryngitis	laringitis (*f.*)
lisping	ceceo (*m.*)
mental illness	enfermedades (*f.*) mentales
migraine	migraña (*f.*)
mumps	paperas (*f. pl.*), "bolas" (*f. pl.*), "chanza" (*f.*)
pain or irritation in the eyes	dolor (*m.*) o irritación (*f.*) de los ojos

paleness, pale	**palidez** (*f.*), **pálido(-a)**
perforated eardrum	**tambor** (*m.*) **roto, tímpano** (*m.*) **roto**
persistent headaches	**cefalgia** (*f.*), **cefalea** (*f.*), **dolores** (*m. pl.*) **de cabeza persistentes**
pimples, blackheads	**barros** (*m. pl.*), **granitos** (*m. pl.*), **espinillas** (*f. pl.*), **"espinas"** (*f. pl.*)
salivation	**sialorrea** (*f.*), **mucha saliva** (*f.*)
sinusitis	**sinusitis** (*f.*)
sore gums	**encías** (*f. pl.*) **dolorosas**
stiff neck	**tortícolis** (*f.*), **"cuello tieso"** (*m.*)
stuffed-up nose	**nariz** (*f.*) **tapada, "mormado(-a)"**
to stutter, to stammer	**tartamudear**
sty	**orzuelo** (*m.*), **"perrilla"** (*f.*)
swollen tonsils	**amígdalas** (*f. pl.*) **o anginas** (*f. pl.*) **inflamadas/ hinchadas**
tired eyes, eye strain	**ojos** (*m. pl.*) **cansados/fatigados**
tonsillitis	**amigdalitis** (*f.*)
toothache	**dolor** (*m.*) **de diente, dolor** (*m.*) **de muela**
unconsciousness	**pérdida** (*f.*) **del conocimiento**

The thorax   El tórax o pecho

allergy	**alergia** (*f.*)
asthma	**asma** (*f.*)[12]
asthmatic respiration	**respiración** (*f.*) **asmática**
back pain	**dolor** (*f.*) **de espalda**
blood in the sputum	**sangre** (*f.*) **en el esputo o en la saliva**
both lungs affected	**ambos pulmones** (*m. pl.*) **afectados**
heavy, painful breasts	**senos** (*m. pl.*) **o pechos** (*m. pl.*) **adoloridos/ pesados**
broken, fractured rib	**costilla** (*f.*) **rota/fracturada**
bronchitis	**bronquitis** (*f.*)
chest cold	**catarro** (*m.*) **o resfriado** (*m.*) **en el pecho**
chest pain	**dolor** (*m.*) **en el pecho**
to choke	**ahogarse, "atragantarse," "dar al galillo"**
congenital heart defect	**defecto** (*m.*) **congénito del corazón**
congestion	**congestión** (*f.*)
cough; dry cough	**tos** (*f.*); **tos seca**
cough with phlegm	**tos** (*f.*) **con flema** (*f.*), **"desgarrando"**
difficulty breathing	**respiración** (*f.*) **dificultosa, dificultad** (*f.*) **en respirar**

---

[12]Although **asma** is feminine, it takes a masculine article; for example, you would say **el asma crónica** ("chronic asthma").

double pneumonia	**pulmonía** (*f.*) **doble**
emphysema	**enfisema** (*m.*)
hay fever	**fiebre** (*f.*) **de heno, "romadizo"** (*m.*)
heart attack, infarct	**ataque** (*m.*) **al corazón, ataque cardíaco, infarto** (*m.*)
heart diseases	**enfermedades** (*f. pl.*) **del corazón**
heart murmur	**soplo** (*m.*) **del corazón**
indigestion	**indigestión** (*f.*), **indigesto** (*m.*)
inflamed spleen	**bazo** (*m.*) **inflamado**
palpitations	**palpitaciones** (*f. pl.*)
pleurisy	**pleuresía** (*f.*)
pneumonia	**pulmonía**
pulmonary edema	**edema** (*f.*) **pulmonar**
rheumatic fever	**fiebre** (*f.*) **reumática**
rheumatic heart	**reumatismo** (*m.*) **del corazón**
shortness of breath	**falta** (*f.*) **de respiración, dificultad** (*f.*) **en/al respirar**
shoulder pain, bursitis	**dolor** (*m.*) **en el hombro, bursitis** (*f.*)
side pain	**dolor** (*m.*) **del costado/del lado**
thrombosis	**trombosis** (*f.*)
tightness in the chest	**presión** (*f.*) **o dolor** (*m.*) **en el pecho**
tuberculosis, TB	**tuberculosis** (*f.*), **"tisis"** (*f.*), **"tis"** (*f.*)
whooping cough	**tos** (*f.*) **ferina, "coqueluche"** (*f.*)

The abdomen — El abdomen

abdominal cramps	**retorcijones** (*m. pl.*), **retortijones** (*m. pl.*)
appendix	**apéndice** (*m.*), **"tripita"** (*f.*)
black or dark stool	**excremento** (*m.*) **negro u obscuro/oscuro**
bloated	**inflamado(-a), aventado(-a)**
to burp	**eructar**
colic	**cólico** (*m.*)
constipated	**estreñido(-a), "constipado(-a)"**
cramps	**calambres** (*m. pl.*) (*muscle*), **cólicos** (*m. pl.*) (*period*)
diarrhea, loose bowels	**diarrea** (*f.*), **"estómago** (*m.*) **suelto," "chorro** (*m.*)**/chorrillo** (*m.*)**"**
dysentery	**disentería** (*f.*), **"cursio"** (*m.*)
enlargement of the kidney/liver	**agrandamiento** (*m.*) **del riñón/hígado**
expel gas (to)	**tener gas, "echar un pedo," "tirar un pedo"**
gall, bile	**hiel** (*f.*), **bilis** (*f.*), **"yel"** (*m.*)
gall bladder	**vesícula** (*f.*) **biliar**
gallstones	**cálculos** (*m. pl.*) **biliares, piedras** (*f. pl.*) **biliares**

gastritis	gastritis (*f.*), inflamación (*f.*) del estómago
heartbeat (hunger pang)	latido (*m.*)
heartburn, acidity	agruras (*f. pl.*), acidez (*f.*)
"heat in the bladder"	"calor (*m.*) en la vejiga"
hepatitis	hepatitis (*f.*)
hernia	hernia (*f.*)
jaundice	ictericia (*f.*), piel (*f.*) amarillenta
kidney infection	infección (*f.*) de los riñones
nausea, vomiting	náuseas (*f.*), vómitos (*m.*)
pancreas	páncreas (*m.*)
peritonitis	peritonitis (*f.*)
stomach gas	gases (*m. pl.*) en el estómago
stomach pain	dolor (*m.*) de estómago
"spilling of bile"	derrame (*m.*) de bilis
swollen glands (in groin)	incordio (*m.*), encordio (*m.*)
swollen spleen	bazo (*m.*) inflamado/hinchado
upset stomach, nausea	estómago (*m.*) revuelto
upset stomach, indigestion, impaction, obstruction	empacho (*m.*)
ulcers	úlceras (*f. pl.*)
to vomit	vomitar

Anus, rectum, and genital organs	**Ano, recto, y órganos genitales**
amenorrhea	amenorrea (*f.*), ausencia (*f.*) de menstruación
atrophy of the testicles	atrofia (*f.*) de los testículos/de los "bolas"/ de los "huevos"/de las "talagas"
bleeding	desangramiento (*m.*), pérdida (*f.*) de sangre
blennorrhagia, gonorrhea	blenorragia (*f.*), gonorrea (*f.*), purgación (*f.*)
bowel movement (to have a)	obrar, defecar
blood in the urine	sangre (*f.*) en la orina
burning sensation when urinating	ardor (*m.*) al orinar, "quemazón" (*f.*)
circumcision	circuncisión (*f.*)
"cold in the womb"	"frío (*m.*) en la matriz"
cyst in the ovaries	quiste (*m.*) en los ovarios
cyst on the penis	quiste (*m.*) en el pene
discharge from the penis/vagina	secreción (*f.*)/desecho (*m.*) del pene/ de la vagina

dysmenorrhea	dismenorrea (*f.*)
excessive pain during period	dolor (*f.*) excesivo durante la regla
fibroids, tumors	fibroma (*f.*), fibroides (*m. pl.*), tumores (*m. pl.*)
fistula in the anus	fístula (*f.*) en el ano
fissure in the anus	fisura (*f.*) en el ano
flow, menstrual flow	sangrado (*m.*), flujo (*m.*), flujo menstrual
frigidity	frigidez (*f.*)
gonorrhea	gonorrea (*f.*), purgación (*f.*), blenorragia (*f.*)
heavy feeling in the abdomen	pesadez (*f.*) en el abdomen
hydrocele	hidrocele (*f.*)
hypertrophy of the prostate	hipertrofia (*f.*) de la próstata
hysterectomy	histerectomía (*f.*)
inflammation of the epidermis	epidermitis (*f.*)
loss of sexual desire	pérdida (*f.*) de deseo sexual
menopause, change of life	menopausia (*f.*), cambio (*m.*) de vida
menstrual period	regla (*f.*), menstruación (*f.*), período (*m.*), "mes" (*m.*)
pain during sexual intercourse	dolor (*m.*) durante las relaciones sexuales
pain or soreness in the ovaries	dolor (*m.*) en los ovarios
pain or soreness in the womb	dolor (*m.*) en la matriz
piles, hemorrhoids	almorranas (*f. pl.*), hemorroides (*m. pl.*)
polyps in the uterus	pólipos (*m. pl.*), fibromas (*f. pl.*) en la matriz
prolapse of the uterus	"caída (*f.*) de la matriz"
sterility	esterilidad (*f.*)
syphilis	sífilis (*f.*), "sangre (*f.*) mala"
torsion, twisting of testicles	torsión (*f.*) de los testículos
tumors	tumores (*m. pl.*)
to urinate	orinar
varicocele	varicocele (*f.*)
venereal disease, STDs, STIs	enfermedades (*f. pl.*) venéreas
venereal lesion, chancre	úlceras (*f.*), chancro (*m.*), grano (*m.*)

Extremities	**Extremidades o miembros**
to amputate	**amputar**
any defect of foot, ankle, knee	**patizambo** (*m.*), **chueco** (*m.*)
athlete's foot	**pie** (*m.*) **atleta**
blisters on the foot	**ampollas** (*f. pl.*) **en pie**
bow-legged	**corvo(-a)**, **cascorvo(-a)**, **"zambo(-a)"**
bunion	**juanete** (*m.*)
bursitis	**bursitis** (*f.*)
cold moist hands	**manos** (*m. pl.*) **frías y** (*f. pl.*) **húmedas**
corns; soft corns	**callos** (*m. pl.*); **callos** (*m. pl.*) **blandos**
enlargement/pain of joints	**engrandecimiento** (*m.*) **de/ dolor** (*m.*) **en las coyunturas/articulaciones**
flat foot	**pie** (*m.*) **plano**
fracture, broken bones	**fractura** (*f.*)/**quebradura** (*f.*)/ **rotura** (*f.*) **de los huesos**
gout	**gota** (*f.*), **podagra** (*f.*)
ingrown nail	**uña** (*f.*) **enterrada**
sprain	**torcedura** (*f.*), **"falseado"** (*as in* **me falseé**, *from* **falsear**)
to sprain, to twist	**torcer, descoyuntar, dislocar, desconcertar**
swelling of the ankles	**hinchazón** (*f.*)/**inflamación** (*f.*) **de los tobillos**
torn ligament; "pulled muscle"	**ligamento** (*m.*) **roto; "un desgarre"**
varicose veins	**várices** (*f. pl.*), **venas** (*f. pl.*) **varicosas**
wart	**verruga** (*f.*), **mezquino** (*m.*)
bottom of the foot (sole)	**planta** (*f.*) **del pie**

The skin	**La piel**
abrasion	**raspadura** (*f.*)
abscess	**absceso** (*m.*), **postema** (*f.*)
birthmark	**lunar** (*m.*), **"mancha** (*f.*) **de nacimiento"**
blister	**ampolla** (*f.*)
boil, carbuncle	**grano** (*m.*) **enterrado, nacido** (*m.*), **"tacotillo"** (*m.*)
bruise	**moretón** (*m.*)
burn	**quemadura** (*f.*)
chapped skin; to chap	**grieta** (*f.*); **agrietarse, "rajarse"**
chilblain	**sabañones** (*m. pl.*), **"saballones"** (*f. pl.*)
cut (*noun*)	**cortada** (*f.*)
cyanosis	**cianosis** (*f.*), **"piel** (*f.*) **azulada"**
dermatitis	**dermatitis** (*f.*)

dry skin	**piel** (*f.*) **seca, piel reseca**
eczema	**eczema** (*m.*), **eccema** (*m.*)
eruption	**erupción** (*f.*)
erysipelas	**erisipela** (*f.*)
fester, a sore, bedsore	**llaga** (*f.*)
itch	**picazón** (*f.*), **"comezón"** (*f.*)
oily skin (face)	**piel** (*f.*) **grasosa (cara)**

APPENDIX A

Verb Tables

PRESENT TENSE: REGULAR VERBS

tomar		comer		vivir	
tomo	tomamos	como	comemos	vivo	vivimos
tomas		comes		vives	
toma	toman	come	comen	vive	viven

PRESENT TENSE: IRREGULAR VERBS

cerrar (e → ie)		dormir (o → ue)		hacer	
cierro	cerramos	duermo	dormimos	hago	hacemos
cierras		duermes		haces	
cierra	cierran	duerme	duermen	hace	hacen

Verbs with similar changes

cerrar	pensar, perder, sentarse
dormir	volver, poder, contar, encontrar
hacer	poner, salir, venir, decir, tener, oír, traer

FUTURE TENSE

ir a + infinitive			
voy a	tomar	vamos a	cerrar
vas a	comer		
va a	vivir	van a	dormir

PAST TENSE: REGULAR VERBS

tomar		comer		vivir	
tomé	tomamos	comí	comimos	viví	vivimos
tomaste		comiste		viviste	
tomó	tomaron	comió	comieron	vivió	vivieron

PAST TENSE: IRREGULAR VERBS

hacer	poner	venir	tener	estar
hice	puse	vine	tuve	estuve
hiciste	pusiste	viniste	tuviste	estuviste
hizo	puso	vino	tuvo	estuvo
hicimos	pusimos	vinimos	tuvimos	estuvimos
hicieron	pusieron	vinieron	tuvieron	estuvieron

decir	ser	ir	traer
dije	fui	fui	traje
dijiste	fuiste	fuiste	trajiste
dijo	fue	fue	trajo
dijimos	fuimos	fuimos	trajimos
dijeron	fueron	fueron	trajeron

IMPERATIVE OR COMMAND FORM: REGULAR VERBS

	tomar	comer	vivir
tú form affirmative	toma	come	vive
tú form negative	no tomes	no comas	no vivas
singular formal	tome	coma	viva
plural formal	tomen	coman	vivan

IMPERATIVE OR COMMAND FORM: IRREGULAR VERBS

	hacer	poner	salir	venir
tú affirmative	haz	pon	sal	ven
tú negative	no hagas	no pongas	no salgas	no vengas
singular formal	haga	ponga	salga	venga
plural formal	hagan	pongan	salgan	vengan

	tener	oír	decir	ir
tú affirmative	ten	oye	di	ve
tú negative	no tengas	no oigas	no digas	no vayas
singular formal	tenga	oiga	diga	vaya
plural formal	tengan	oigan	digan	vayan

	traer	cerrar	pensar	perder
tú affirmative	trae	cierra	piensa	pierde
tú negative	no traigas	no cierres	no pienses	no pierdas
singular formal	traiga	cierre	piense	pierda
plural formal	traigan	cierren	piensen	pierdan

	volver	acostarse	sentarse
tú affirmative	vuelve	acuéstate	siéntate
tú negative	no vuelvas	no te acuestes	no te sientes
singular formal	vuelva	acuéstese	siéntese
plural formal	vuelvan	acuéstense	siéntense

PRESENT PERFECT TENSE

haber + verb in the past participle			
he	tom**ado**	hemos	cerr**ado**
has	com**ido**		
ha	viv**ido**	han	dorm**ido**

PRESENT SUBJUNCTIVE

tomar	comer	vivir			
tome	tom**emos**	coma	com**amos**	viva	viv**amos**
tom**es**		com**as**		viv**as**	
tome	tom**en**	coma	com**an**	viva	viv**an**

The subjunctive is required after expressions of emotion, fear, desire, or doubt.

Estoy alegre de que usted se sienta mejor. I'm happy you feel better. (*emotion*)

Tengo miedo de que él no tome la medicina. I'm afraid he is not taking the medicine. (*fear*)

Espero que usted se mejore pronto. I hope you get better soon. (*desire*)

Dudo que ella tome toda la medicina. I doubt she is taking all the medicine. (*doubt*)

Dialogues and Monologues: English Translations

Note: The terms in brackets are either literal translations or words and expressions not stated in Spanish that are implicitly understood when translated into English. The terms in parentheses are the alternatives given in the dialogue or monologue.

DIÁLOGO 1.1 | Introductions—Greeting your patient

DOCTOR/NURSE	Good morning, Mrs. Gómez. I'm Dr. Pérez. (I'm Bob/ Sandra, your nurse.)
PATIENT	It's nice to meet you!
DOCTOR/NURSE	Do you prefer [to be called] Juana or Mrs. Gómez?
PATIENT	I prefer Juana, please.
DOCTOR/NURSE	Fine, Juana. Come right this way and please take a seat. [Come in and sit down.]
PATIENT	Thank you, doctor. (Thank you, sir/madam.)

DIÁLOGO 1.8 | Beginning a patient interview

DOCTOR/NURSE	Good morning, Mrs. Gómez. I'm Dr. Pérez. (I'm Bob/ Sandra, your nurse.)
PATIENT	It's nice to meet you!
DOCTOR/NURSE	Do you prefer [to be called] Juana or Mrs. Gómez?
PATIENT	I prefer Juana, please.
DOCTOR/NURSE	Fine, Juana. Come right this way and please have a seat. [Come in and sit down.]
PATIENT	Thank you, doctor. (Thank you, sir/madam.)
DOCTOR/NURSE	What seems to be the problem? [What brings you here today?] How do you feel? [How are you feeling?]
PATIENT	Oh, doctor (sir/madam), my head hurts and my eyes hurt me.

DOCTOR/NURSE   Where does your head hurt? What part?
PATIENT   Here, doctor (sir/madam).

DIÁLOGO 2.2 | Taking vital signs

NURSE   Good morning, Mrs. Gómez. I'm Bob/Sandra, your nurse.
PATIENT   Nice to meet you.
NURSE   Do you prefer Juana or Mrs. Gómez?
PATIENT   I prefer Juana, please.
NURSE   Fine [Very well], Juana. Come right in and sit down.
PATIENT   Thank you, sir (madam).
NURSE   Is this your first visit?
PATIENT   No, it's the [my] second.
NURSE   Ah, okay [good]. Please get on the scale. I need to weigh you. Fine. You weigh 50 kilos.
PATIENT   Oh, no! I weigh a lot!
NURSE   No, it's not much. I also need to take your blood pressure—your arm, please.
PATIENT   Okay, here it is.
NURSE   Fine. It's 160 over 100.
PATIENT   Is it okay [all right/good]?
NURSE   It's a little [a bit] high, and now for your pulse. . . . Good, it's 72. Please open your mouth. I need to take your temperature.
PATIENT   Okay, sir (madam).
NURSE   It's 98 point 6 degrees.
PATIENT   Is it normal?
NURSE   Yes, Juana, it's fine, too. Thank you. The doctor will be here in just a moment.

DIÁLOGO 2.6 | Chief complaints

DOCTOR   What seems to be the problem? [What brings you here today?] How are you feeling?
PATIENT   Oh, doctor, my head hurts and my eyes hurt me.
DOCTOR   Where does it hurt? What part of your head?
PATIENT   Here, doctor. What do I need?
DOCTOR   Well, let's see . . . your blood pressure is a bit high. Your temperature is normal and your pulse [is] too. It's neither fast nor slow. For the moment, Juana, you need to take two aspirins for your headache.
PATIENT   How often?

DOCTOR   You need to take two aspirins, four times a [per] day. Also, the lab tech needs to take a urine and blood sample.

PATIENT   Okay, doctor, and [by] when do you need the samples?

DOCTOR   First, Juana, you need to make an appointment with the receptionist for tomorrow.

PATIENT   Okay [Fine], thank you, doctor.

DIÁLOGO 3.6 | Basic interview

DOCTOR   Good morning, Mrs. Sánchez. I'm Dr. Brown.

SEÑORA   Good morning, doctor. It's nice to meet you.

DOCTOR   How are you?

SEÑORA   I'm sick. I don't feel well [I'm not well], doctor.

DOCTOR   What seems to be the problem? (What hurts?)

SEÑORA   My head, stomach, and nose hurt me, and my whole body in general.

DOCTOR   How long have you had these problems? [For how much time do you have these problems?]

SEÑORA   It's been two days. [For two days./It makes two days.]

DOCTOR   Are you taking [Do you take] any medicine or remedies now, ma'am?

SEÑORA   Yes, doctor, I'm drinking [I drink/take] tea and some pills.

DOCTOR   What are the pills and tea called?

SEÑORA   Well, doctor, it's chamomile tea, and they're little white pills.

DOCTOR   Okay, you need to call the receptionist with the names of the pills. Do the pills help you, ma'am?

SEÑORA   "Wull" [Well], I don't know. They relieve the discomforts a bit, but tea is always helpful [always helps].

DOCTOR   Okay, then, very well, and now you need a physical exam. Please take off your clothes and put on the gown. Excuse me. I'll be back in a moment. (I'll be right back.)

SEÑORA   Yes, doctor.

DIÁLOGO 3.6 | Basic interview (take II)

DOCTOR   What seems to be the problem? (What hurts?)

SEÑORA   My head, stomach, and nose hurt me, and [actually] my whole body in general.

DOCTOR   For how long have you had the [these] problems?

SEÑORA   Well, I don't know, doctor, it's been two or three days.

DOCTOR   Are you taking medicine or any remedies now, ma'am?

SEÑORA   Yes, doctor, I'm drinking tea and [taking] some pills.

DOCTOR   What are the pills and tea called?

SEÑORA   Well, doctor, it's chamomile tea and [some] little white pills. I don't know the name; they're from my friend [my child's godmother].

DOCTOR   Okay, ma'am, you need to call the receptionist with the names of the pills. Do the pills help?

SEÑORA   "Wull," I don't know. They relieve the discomforts a bit, but the tea always helps.

DOCTOR   Okay, ma'am. Do you have a fever, chills, or exhaustion?

SEÑORA   Yes, I have a fever and some chills, but I'm not very exhausted [I don't have exhaustion]. But I've been vomiting, also.

DOCTOR   Oh, but are you dizzy, have a runny nose, or feel weak?

SEÑORA   Well, you see, [It's just that] doctor, yes, I am dizzy and I feel weak. Doctor, it's just that generally I'm constipated, but now I have diarrhea. I feel like my body is aching all over. [I feel like that I have my body all cut up].

DOCTOR   Um . . . Do you have a cough or phlegm as well [also]?

SEÑORA   I have a slight [a bit of a] cough, but I don't have phlegm.

DOCTOR   Okay [Oh], and it's been two or three days that you've been having these problems. (Well, ma'am,) You [You'll] need a physical exam. Please take off your clothing and put on the [this] gown. Excuse me and I'll be back in a moment.

SEÑORA   Okay [Yes], doctor.

DIÁLOGO 3.7 | Qualifying and quantifying pain

DOCTOR   Sir, what kind of pain is it? Is it sharp like needles or [sharp] like a knife or not [any of these]?

SEÑOR   No, doctor, it just comes and goes.

DOCTOR   Is the pain slight, moderate, or strong?

SEÑOR   No, well, doctor, it's just that it's strong when it comes [does come].

DIÁLOGO 4.8 | A pediatric visit

DOCTOR   Good morning, Mrs. Sánchez. I'm Dr. Brown.

SEÑORA   Good morning, doctor. It's nice to meet you.

DOCTOR   How are you [doing]?

SEÑORA   I'm fine, doctor. It's [just] that my son, Joselito Manuel [Little Joey] is sick.

DOCTOR	Oh, poor thing. What seems to be the little one's problem? What (Such) a strong, manly boy!
SEÑORA	Thank you, doctor. His head, stomach, and throat hurt him, and his whole body in general.
DOCTOR	For how long has he had these problems?
SEÑORA	I don't know, doctor, for [about] two or three days.
DOCTOR	Is he taking medicine, tea or (any) home remedies now, Mrs. [Sánchez]?
SEÑORA	Yes, doctor, he's drinking tea, and [takes/is taking] some pills for children.
DOCTOR	What pills and tea? [What are the pills and tea called?]
SEÑORA	Well, doctor, it's chamomile tea, and they're little white pills. I don't know their name. They're from my friend.
DOCTOR	Okay, Mrs. Sánchez, you need to call the receptionist with the names of the pills. Do the pills help Joselito, ma'am?
SEÑORA	Well, I don't know. They relieve the discomfort a bit, but the tea always helps.
DOCTOR	Okay, Mrs. Sánchez. Does little Joselito have a fever or chills? Does he eat [Is he eating] well?
SEÑORA	Yes, he has a fever and chills, but he doesn't have (much) appetite.
DOCTOR	How high is the fever, Mrs. Sánchez?
SEÑORA	Well, doctor, it's just that, I don't know. I don't have a thermometer at home.
DOCTOR	Don't worry! We'll take his temperature now. Um, does he have a cough?
SEÑORA	Yes, doctor, he has a slight cough and he also has phlegm.
DOCTOR	What color is the phlegm?
SEÑORA	It doesn't have a [any] color, doctor, it's clear.
DOCTOR	Well [that's] good, now little José needs a physical exam. I need to take off [remove] your son's clothes and examine him.
SEÑORA	Oh, of course, doctor. [Okay, yes, doctor.]

DIÁLOGO 4.10 | Emergency room—difficulty breathing

DOCTOR	Good morning, Mrs. Valdez. How are you [doing]? And your husband and your other children?
SEÑORA	Very well [Just fine], doctor, we're all [doing] very well, except José Manuelito here. He has a cold and a cough.
DOCTOR	Oh, I see [understand], Mrs. Valdez. Well, then I need to examine José Manuelito [little José] now. I'm going to look at

his ears and throat, and also [am going to] listen to his lungs and heart.

SEÑORA   Is there a problem, doctor?

DOCTOR   When did the cough begin? (For how long has he had a cough?)

SEÑORA   Well, more or less three days ago.

DOCTOR   Is this the first time that he has had [suffered from] these symptoms? Does he have a lot of colds and coughing?

SEÑORA   Yes, doctor, every winter.

DOCTOR   Oh, I understand. Does he cough more in the morning or at night?

SEÑORA   Well, doctor, he coughs more at night when he goes to bed (I put him to bed). But sometimes he coughs in the morning too.

DOCTOR   What kind of cough is it? [What is the cough like?] What does it sound like? Is it a dry, hoarse cough or a cough with phlegm?

SEÑORA   It's a strong cough, like a seal's bark [dog's bark]. He also has a lot of difficulty breathing when he coughs.

DOCTOR   Is there anyone else [Are there other people] sick in your house (household) now?

SEÑORA   Well, we're all fine; except it's just that [it's only that] all the [my] kids [do] have the flu.

DOCTOR   Then, [your answer is] yes, they are all sick.

SEÑORA   Well, yes, doctor. But, what does my son need . . . does he need IV fluids, shots, amoxicillin . . . ?

DOCTOR   Don't worry, Mrs. Valdez. In just a while I'm going to prescribe medicine [for him].

MONÓLOGO 5.1 | The family

Let's meet the García family.

WOMAN   My name is Carmen Romero de García, and I am a woman. I am also a mother and a wife. I have a husband and his name is Carlos García.

MAN   My name is Carlos García Flores, and I am a man. I am also a father and a husband. I have a wife and her name is Carmen Romero de García.

NARRATOR   The mother and the father are the parents. The parents have two children.

GIRL   Hi! I am the Garcías' daughter. I am a child or a young girl. My name is Carmencita. I have a mother, a father, and a brother. My brother's name is Carlitos. He is eight years old. I am ten. I am older and he is younger.

BOY   Hi! I am the Garcías' son. I am a child or a young boy. My name is Carlitos. I have a mother, a father, and a sister. My sister's name is Carmencita. She is ten years old. I am eight.

NARRATOR   Carmencita and Carlitos are the García children. The Garcías—Mrs. and Mr.—are the parents. Carmencita and Carlitos are siblings [sister and brother].

MONÓLOGO 6.6 | A physical exam

(The doctor is conducting a physical exam.)

Good morning, Mrs. . . . I need to [I'm going to] examine you, okay? / First, I'm going to examine your eyes. Please, look at the [this] light. / Good, stick out your tongue, please. / Thank you, [now] please open your mouth and say "Ah." / Swallow, please. / Thank you. Now I want to listen to your lungs. / Take a deep breath through your mouth, please. [Breathe deeply through your mouth, please.] / Again . . . again. / Cough, please. / Lie down! / Bend your knees, please. / Relax, I need to palpate [examine] your stomach. / Thank you. Sit up again. / Relax your leg . . . thank you. / Fine, that's all. / You can [may] get dressed now and I'll return in a moment. (I'll be right back.)

MONÓLOGO 6.7 | A neurological exam

Good afternoon. . . . Come in, please. . . . Have a seat here. [Sit down, here.] / I'm going to give you a neurological exam. / Please look here. / Follow my finger with your eyes, but don't move your head. / Do you hear this? (Can you hear this?) / Lift [Raise] your eyebrows. Lower your eyebrows. / Close your eyes. Open your eyes. / [Give me] A big smile, please. / Do this. Inflate your cheeks. / Push against my hand with your head. Resist. / Now against my other hand. Resist. / Bite [down] very hard. Like this. Lift up [Shrug or raise] your shoulders. / Squeeze my fingers hard. / Push against my hands. Resist. Pull my hands. Resist. / Stand up. Close your eyes. Open your eyes. Walk straight ahead. / Turn around and walk on your heels. / Turn around and walk on your tiptoes. / Touch my finger with your finger. Touch your nose with your finger. Again. [Another time.] Again. / Raise your arms in front of you, palms up [upward]. Now, palms down, palms up, palms down, . . . Faster. Fine. Thank you. / Sit down and extend your legs (feet). Do you feel this? / Do you feel more here or here? / Thank you very much. Wait here, [for just] a moment.

MONÓLOGO 7.3 | Pap smear

Is it [this] your first pap smear? / I am going to examine you in general, and examine your breasts and genital area, as well. / I need to examine your thyroid gland. I am going to listen to your heart. / I am going to listen to your lungs. Please, take a deep breath [breathe deeply] through your mouth. / Lie down, please. / Place (Put) your feet here. / I am going to listen to your heart again—and now your stomach. / Now I need to examine your breasts. Do you examine your breasts at home? Do you notice anything that worries you? / Now I am going to apply [put] pressure on your stomach. Does it [this] hurt? / Move down, please. [Move more toward me, please.] / These are [That's just] my hands . . . These are [That's just] my fingers. / Now, I am going to insert the speculum. You are going to feel [You will feel] a bit of pressure now. / Here are the cultures and the exam sample. / And now I am going to insert my fingers [in order] to examine you. / Okay, that's all. You can move back and sit up now. / In [just] a moment the nurse will take the samples to the lab. Later [Then] I'll return with some of the results and we'll talk more. / You can get dressed now.

MONÓLOGO 7.7 | Blood test

Madam, [give me] your right arm, please. I want to get a blood sample. / Hold out your arm, and please keep it straight. / Don't bend it. / Hold still, please. I'm going to put on the tourniquet. / Please make a fist. / The needle hurts a little at first, but not for long. / Don't be afraid. It's fast. / Now, open your hand and put pressure on your arm to hold the cotton in place.

MONÓLOGO 7.8 | Urine test

Now I need a sample of your urine.

(For women) Take the disposable towels with you to the bathroom and wash your hands. Separate your labia with the disposable towels. Then, you need to clean each labium [side] from the front toward the back and between the labia. Begin to urinate (You can urinate) in the toilet, then in the jar, and finish urinating in the toilet. Put the lid [top] on the jar and leave it in the little window (on the shelf/cabinet). And wash your hands afterwards.

(For men) You need to clean yourself around your penis. Begin by urinating in the toilet, then in the jar, and you need to finish by urinating in the toilet. Put the lid [top] on and leave the jar on the shelf (on the cabinet, in the little window). And wash your hands afterwards.

MONÓLOGO 7.9 | Sputum test

Take this jar home with you. / Tomorrow morning, cough deeply two or three times. / Spit the phlegm in the jar. / Then [Later], please bring it to the lab.

MONÓLOGO 7.10 | Skin tests

Please hold out your arm and don't move [hold still]. The technician is going to do some skin tests [on you]. One is for TB and the other is for valley fever [coccidioidomycosis]. / The first is in your right arm. The second is in your left arm. / Please observe your skin for a swelling or reddening reaction. / Please do not scratch the area. / If you have any of these reactions after 24 hours, return to the clinic [doctor's office]. / I want to see you in my office the day after tomorrow.

MONÓLOGO 7.11 | Taking X rays

The technician needs to take X rays. / So, come tomorrow at 8:00 in the morning. / You can wash out [brush] your mouth or teeth, without swallowing water. / Then, you need to drink a liquid in order to [so that we can] see your internal organs.

DIÁLOGO 7.12 | Results and diagnosis

DOCTOR   Okay, sir, your blood, urine, and sputum are normal. But the skin test and X ray show a slight variation in your right lung. This indicates that you have the beginnings of an illness that's very common in this area and climate called valley fever.

SEÑOR   What should I do, doctor?

DOCTOR   Don't worry. With a diet high in proteins [a high-protein diet] and with a lot of rest, you will get better in [about] three months.

SEÑOR   At least I know what I have. I feel a little calmer [knowing]. But, I can't miss so much work.

DOCTOR   Well, sir, you [just] need to get better. I'm going to prescribe some vitamins for you, and continue with [stay on] this diet for two months.

DIÁLOGO 8.7 | **An emergency room visit for a failed treatment of an ear infection**

DOCTOR   Good morning, Mrs. Soto. How is it [are things] going for you? How is little Jaime coming along with his ear infection?

SEÑORA   Well, doctor, I'm fine, but my son is still sick. He hasn't gotten better. He still has a fever and a cold.

DOCTOR   Did you give little Jaime the antibiotics that I prescribed for him the last visit?

SEÑORA   Yes, doctor, but it seems to me that the medicine didn't work.

DOCTOR   Let's see, Mrs. [Soto]. How did you give him the medicine? How much and how many times a day did you give him the antibiotics?

SEÑORA   Well, I gave him a teaspoonful once a day, doctor.

DOCTOR   *(Thinking to himself)* That's why . . . no wonder . . . she didn't listen to me. She could have avoided this visit, but she didn't follow my instructions the first time.

DOCTOR   *(Speaking aloud)* Aha, well, Mrs. [Soto], a teaspoonful is fine, but he needs to take the medicine three times a day for ten days. It's very important to take the exact dosage [amount].

SEÑORA   Ay! How embarrassing, doctor. What should I do?

DOCTOR   Well, Mrs. Soto, I'm going to prescribe antibiotics for him again, but you need to be very careful with the instructions. This time *(because it's the second time)* you have to give little Jaime one teaspoonful, but two times per day for a period of one week. Am I being clear?

SEÑORA   Yes, doctor, now I understand . . . a teaspoonful two times each day and for a whole week. But, can I give him Tylenol or is it okay to give him Motrin as well, with the medicine you prescribed?

DOCTOR   Yes, the antibiotic works well with either Tylenol or Motrin for the pain and fever. It's okay, but only [give him] the antibiotic with Tylenol or the antibiotic with Motrin, he shouldn't take the three medicines together. Am I being clear? [Do you understand?]

SEÑORA   Yes, doctor.

DOCTOR   Do you have any other question or concern?

SEÑORA   No, doctor, I think that's all.

DOCTOR   Good, Mrs. Soto, call me if you have [any] questions or doubts, and take care of yourself and little Jaime. May it go well for you!

SEÑORA   The same to you, doctor, thank you.

DIÁLOGO 8.8 | An asthma attack in the emergency room

(The emergency room: an adult with an asthma attack)

DOCTOR Good evening, sir. I know you have difficulty breathing. Try not to speak, please, and breathe deeply into this nebulizer. Very good, Mr. López. Afterwards, I am going to speak with you about your medical history and examine you in general. But now I need to listen to your heart and lungs.

DOCTOR *(after 10 minutes)* Do you feel better now? I see that you are no longer wheezing.

SEÑOR Yes, doctor, I can breathe better now. I feel better, thank you. I've had asthma for twenty years, but this is the worst attack that I've [ever] had in my whole life.

DOCTOR Ah, well, what happened this time, Mr. López?

SEÑOR Well, this attack came on suddenly. I was at home, I was working and painting and I began to cough. Then I began to wheeze. I grabbed my inhaler and took [gave myself] two puffs, but it didn't help me. After a half hour of suffering, my wife finally took [brought] me to the hospital.

DOCTOR That's good [then]. Aside from [Besides] asthma, do you have any other illnesses?

SEÑOR Yes, doctor, I have high blood pressure and take Vasotec.

DOCTOR Do you have allergies to any medication [problems with or allergic reactions to any medicines]?

SEÑOR Well, when I took penicillin once, I got a rash.

DOCTOR Do you have any relatives [family members] who have or have had diabetes or heart problems?

SEÑOR Yes, diabetes, but, thank God, I don't yet.

DOCTOR Okay, Mr. López, the lab tech is going to take some X rays of your lungs, and then I am going to examine you completely [give you a complete exam].

SEÑOR That's fine, doctor. Thank you very much.

DOCTOR Good, I'll be right back.

DIÁLOGO 9.3 | Monthly breast self-examination

NURSE Do you examine your breasts at home each [every] month?

PATIENT Well, it's just that, uh . . . no. Do I need to examine myself? I don't know how to do it. Can you explain to me how to examine them?

NURSE Of course. There are three very easy steps. First, examine your breasts when you are bathing [taking a bath]. It's easier to feel lumps with wet skin. After bathing, look at yourself in the mirror and examine your breasts again. Then, lie down and put your right hand behind your head, like this. Use the opposite hand, in other words, your left hand to touch your right breast. Use your finger pads [the flat part of your fingers] to search for lumps. Move your finger pads around your breast. Then, use your right hand to examine your left breast . . . like this. Then squeeze your nipples, softly, to see if there is any secretion or discharge.

PATIENT   How often should I examine my breasts?

NURSE   You should examine yourself after your period, not before.

PATIENT   And if I no longer get my period because of my change of life [menopause] . . . ?

NURSE   If you have had a hysterectomy or are in menopause, you should do it at the beginning of each month.

PATIENT   And if I find something, what do I do?

NURSE   Call us to make an appointment. Your doctor is going to examine you in more detail.

PATIENT   Thank you, miss. I think I understand now. I'm going to begin to examine myself every month. Thank you very much, and see you soon.

NURSE   You're welcome, ma'am, take good care of yourself and may it go well for you.

DIÁLOGO 9.4 | A patient with abdominal pain

DOCTOR   Good morning, Mr. Gómez. Come in and have a seat, please. I'm Doctor Martínez.

PATIENT   Thank you, doctor. It's nice to meet you.

DOCTOR   Fine, do you prefer Rafael or Mr. Gómez?

PATIENT   I prefer Rafael, please.

DOCTOR   Well, then, Rafael, tell me, what seems to be the problem?

PATIENT   Well, doctor, my gut hurts.

DOCTOR   Since when (For how long) has it been hurting you, Rafael?

PATIENT   Okay, well, doctor, it's [just] that the pain began about two or three days ago.

DOCTOR   What kind of pain is it? Is it sharp, fixed [in one place], or does it come and go?

PATIENT   Well, doctor, it comes and goes, but when I have it, it's very strong [painful].

DOCTOR   Well, is it like cramps (abdominal pains)?

PATIENT   Yes, doctor. That's how it is . . . like a cramp.

DOCTOR   Okay. Do you have other symptoms like diarrhea, vomiting, or a fever?

PATIENT   About two or three days ago I had a fever and diarrhea. I've never had vomiting, but I don't have any of these symptoms now, and that's why this pain concerns me [has me worried], doctor.

DOCTOR   Don't worry, Rafael. Tell me, how did the pain begin: after eating, spontaneously [suddenly, without warning], or after some physical exertion?

PATIENT   Ay, doctor! The truth is that it happened a few days ago at my daughter's birthday party. I think I ate too much, and at night the pain came on very strong with diarrhea. Afterward, in the morning I had a fever, but it went away with some aspirins, and I haven't had any diarrhea since yesterday.

DOCTOR   Okay, Rafael, don't be distressed [don't get upset]. I need to examine your abdomen. Please lie down here. Rafael, show me with your finger where it hurts. Tell me if it hurts when I apply pressure.

PATIENT   It's there, doctor, right there when you put pressure [on it]. Ay, it hurts!

DOCTOR   It's over [I'm done] now, Rafael. Stand up, but first sit up and then you can stand to avoid dizziness. It appears that your pain will be relieved with this medication, but the technician also needs to do [to run] some tests.

PATIENT   Okay, doctor, and how do [should] I take the medicine?

DOCTOR   I'll explain it to you now. Take one tablet every eight hours for five days. Is that clear? (Did you understand?) Or in other words, three times a day, before breakfast, before lunch, and before dinner.

PATIENT   I understand, and when do I need to go for the analysis [tests]?

DOCTOR   Make the appointment for tomorrow and return here within five days, in other words, next Monday.

PATIENT   Thank you, doctor; see you [we'll see each other] in five days.

DOCTOR   I'll see you [We'll see each other] on Monday. Take good care of yourself, Rafael!

Answer Key

Chapter 1

1A 1. las casas 2. las plumas 3. las agujas 4. las bolsas 5. las recetas
6. las sillas 7. las básculas 8. las mesas 9. las cervezas 10. las cápsulas

1B 1. los carros 2. los palos 3. los pisos 4. los vasos 5. los libros
6. los termómetros 7. los helados 8. los goteros

1C 1. las bases 2. las calles 3. los nombres 4. los trámites

1D 1. las inyecciones 2. los pulmones 3. las infecciones 4. los tamales
5. los frijoles 6. las mujeres

1E 1. unas inyecciones 2. unos papeles 3. unas infecciones
4. unas clínicas 5. unos sueros 6. unos termómetros

1F *The question for each answer is* ¿Qué es esto? 1. Es una báscula.
2. Es una cerveza. 3. Es una silla. 4. Es una mesa. 5. Es un sombrero.
6. Es un libro. 7. Es un otoscopio. 8. Es una aguja. 9. Es un termómetro.

1G 1. Es una casa. 2. Es un depresor. 3. Es un termómetro. 4. Es una
aguja. 5. Es una silla. 6. Es un suero. 7. Es (el) vino. 8. Es dinero.
9. Es una puerta. 10. Es un carro.

1H 1. El sombrero grande está en la silla (chica). 2. El vaso chico está en
la mesa (grande). 3. El libro está en la silla (grande). 4. El termómetro grande
está en la mesa (grande). 5. La pluma está en el piso. 6. El baño está derecho.

1I 1. Necesito un vaso grande, por favor. 2. Necesito un sombrero grande,
por favor. 3. Necesito un depresor chico, por favor. 4. Necesito un termómetro
grande, por favor. 5. Necesito una aguja chica, por favor. 6. Necesita una
pastilla.

1J (el *or* la *could be replaced by* mi) 1. el brazo 2. el ojo 3. la cabeza
4. la oreja/el oído 5. la espalda 6. el pie 7. la pierna 8. el tobillo
9. la rodilla 10. el estómago

1K (los *or* las *could be replaced by* mis) 1. los ojos 2. las piernas
3. los brazos 4. las orejas/los oídos 5. las manos 6. los tobillos 7. los pies
8. los dedos 9. las rodillas 10. las caderas

Chapter 2

2A   1. quince   2. veinte y ocho *or* veintiocho   3. ciento diez y nueve *or* ciento diecinueve   4. doscientos cincuenta y seis   5. trescientos setenta y cuatro 6. cuatrocientos setenta y tres

2B   1. No, es la segunda visita de la señora Gómez.   2. La paciente prefiere Juana.   3. La señora Gómez pesa cincuenta (50) kilos.   4. La presión arterial de Juana Gómez es ciento sesenta sobre cien.   5. El pulso es normal y la temperatura es normal.

2C   (*possible answers*)   1. El paciente necesita una receta.   2. (Usted) necesita la inyección en el brazo.   3. Sí, (necesita una receta) porque necesita antibióticos.   4. Necesita una inyección ahora/cada día/dos veces por día, etc. 5. Necesita tomar la medicina cuatro veces por día.   6. Necesita tomar la medicina en pastillas.   7. Prefiero tomar tabletas/cápsulas.   8. Tomo las pastillas con agua.

2D   (*possible answers*)   1. ¿Qué es esto?   2. ¿Cuándo toma (usted) la medicina?   3. ¿Dónde está el baño/el hospital/usted?   4. ¿Cuánto vino toma al día?   5. ¿Cada cuándo necesito tomar el té?   6. ¿Cuántas pastillas toma usted al día?   7. ¿Cuál prefiere (usted) tomar—té de manzanilla o medicina? 8. ¿Por qué toma usted la medicina?

2E   1. Le duele la cabeza y le duelen los ojos.   2. La presión arterial de la paciente es un poco alta.   3. La paciente necesita tomar aspirinas y hacer una cita con la recepcionista.   4. Necesita tomar dos pastillas cuatro veces al día. 5. El técnico necesita tomar una muestra de orina y de la sangre.

2F   *Horizontales:*   1. puerta   2. silla   3. carro   *Verticales:*   4. aguja 5. libro   6. mesa   7. bolsa

Chapter 3

3A   hablar: (yo) hablo, (tú) hablas, (él) habla, (ella) habla, (Ud.) habla, (nosotros) hablamos, (ellos) hablan, (ellas) hablan, (Uds.) hablan; pesar: (yo) peso, (tú) pesas, (él) pesa, (ella) pesa, (Ud.) pesa, (nosotros) pesamos, (ellos) pesan, (ellas) pesan, (Uds.) pesan

3B   1. toma   2. toma   3. tomamos   4. tomas   5. toman   6. toma 7. toman/tomamos   8. toman   9. toma

3C   1. hablas   2. hablamos   3. hablamos   4. hablamos   5. hablan   6. habla 7. hablan   8. hablan

3D   1. tomo vino   2. toma leche   3. toman cerveza   4. tomamos té 5. toman café   6. toman sopa   7. tomamos helado   8. toman Tylenol

3E   (*possible answers*)   1. Sí, toman mucho vino en Francia. 2. Tomo mucho café y mucha cerveza.   3. Tomamos agua en el desierto. 4. Toman mucho tequila en México.   5.   No, no tomo mucha medicina. 6. Sí, los norteamericanos toman mucha aspirina.   7. Tomamos la temperatura en la clínica.   8. Tomo (el) café por la mañana.

3F   1. Los norteamericanos no toman mucha salsa picante.   2. Uds. no toman té.   3. María no toma leche en el carro.   4. Yo no tomo vino en la clase.

3G   1. No, nuestro presidente no habla español.   2. No, no hablo español en el hospital.   3. No, no hablan francés en Cuba.   4. No, no hablamos inglés y español en la clínica.

3H   (*possible answers*)   1. No, no bajo de peso rápido.   2. No, no escucho a los pacientes siempre.   3. Sí, examino a los pacientes.   4. El doctor visita a los pacientes en el hospital.   5. No, no peso mucho.   6. Trabajo en el hospital/en la clínica.   7. No, no llevo una maleta al hospital.   8. Toman aspirinas los pacientes/los doctores/los dos.   9. Los pacientes toman Tylenol.   10. Sí, toman hielo después de la diálisis.   11. No, no respiro bien cuando tengo gripe.   12. Sí, los pacientes vomitan mucho.   13. El polen y los animales/Los dos causan la alergia.   14. Sí, inmunizo a los pacientes.   15. No, no limpio mi carro en el hospital.   16. Tomo Tylenol.   17. Sí, el paciente con asma respira con dificultad.   18. No, no saco muchas radiografías.   19. Sí, vacuno a muchos niños.   20. No, no orino con dificultad. Orino poco por lo general.

3I   1. Necesita las inyecciones.   2. Necesita dos inyecciones por día.   3. Necesita las inyecciones en el glúteo.   4. Juan necesita las inyecciones.   5. Necesita las inyecciones para controlar los síntomas de su enfermedad. Necesita dos por día por un período de diez días en el glúteo.

3J   1. Necesito examinar su oreja/oído.   2. Necesito tomar su pulso.   3. Necesito inyectar su glúteo.   4. Necesito recetar las pastillas/píldoras.   5. (Usted) necesita tomar su medicina.   6. (Usted) necesita examinar los senos en casa.   7. (Usted) necesita tomar muchos líquidos.

3K   1. estamos enfermos   2. están enfermos   3. está enfermo   4. estoy enfermo(-a)   5. están enfermos   6. estás enfermo(-a)   7. están enfermos

3L   (*possible answers*)   1. Estoy en casa hoy.   2. Tucsón está en Arizona.   3. Están en el hospital.   4. Estamos en la clínica.   5. Estoy en una cantina.   6. Está en el vaso.

3M   1. No está contenta cuando está cruda.   2. No están contentos cuando están crudos.   3. No estamos contentos cuando estamos crudos.   4. No estás contento(-a) cuando estás crudo(-a).   5. No estamos contentos cuando estamos crudos.   6. No están contentos cuando están crudos.

3N   (*possible answers*)   1. Estoy bien, gracias.   2. No, no estoy triste cuando no trabajo.   3. Sí, Uds. están (*or* nosotros estamos) contentos cuando Uds. escuchan (*or* nosotros escuchamos) música.   4. Sí, está alegre si toma mucho vino.   5. Sí, estamos enfermos cuando fumamos puros todo el día.   6. Sí, están borrachos si toman demasiado licor.   7. Sí, están crudos después.   8. No, no está enfermo hoy.   9. No, no está borracho hoy.   10. Sí, están nerviosos la primera vez.

3O   1. Se llama la señora Sánchez.   2. Está mal; no está bien.   3. Le duele la cabeza, el estómago, la nariz y todo el cuerpo.   4. Le duele hace (*or* desde hace) dos días.   5. Toma té de manzanilla y unas pastillas.   6. Alivian las molestias un poco, pero el té siempre ayuda.   7. Toma pastillas blancas y chicas. 8. Se llama té de manzanilla.   9. Necesita un examen físico.

3P   1. sombrero   2. maleta   3. té   4. tomo   5. hablo   6. cerveza   7. gotero 8. leche

Chapter 4

4A   1. eres   2. son   3. son   4. somos   5. es   6. somos   7. es   8. son   9. es

4B   (*possible answers*)   1. No, no es de los Estados Unidos.   2. Soy de los Estados Unidos.   3. Son de México.   4. Es de Canadá.   5. Son de Italia.

4C   1. Son las dos.   2. Son las cuatro y quince.   3. Son las siete y media. 4. Son las cinco y diez.   5. Son las tres y cinco.   6. Son las dos y veinte. 7. Son las nueve y siete.

4D   1. Son las ocho y treinta y cinco. (Son veinte y cinco para las nueve/las nueve menos veinte y cinco.)   2. Son las once y cincuenta y cinco. (Son cinco para las doce/las doce menos cinco.)   3. Son las tres y cincuenta. (Son diez para las cuatro/las cuatro menos diez.)   4. Son las cuatro y cuarenta y cinco. (Son quince para las cinco/las cinco menos quince.)   5. Son las dos y cuarenta. (Son veinte para las tres/las tres menos veinte.)   6. Son las ocho y cincuenta y cinco. (Son cinco para las nueve/las nueve menos cinco.)

4E   1. ¿De qué color es el sombrero? El sombrero es negro.   2. ¿De qué color es la mesa? La mesa es blanca.   3. ¿De qué color es el dinero? El dinero es verde.   4. ¿De qué color es la máquina? La máquina es gris.   5. ¿De qué color es la aguja? La aguja es café (de color café).   6. ¿De qué color es la pluma? La pluma es azul.   7. ¿De qué color es la cobija? La cobija es café (de color café).   8. ¿De qué color es la almohada? La almohada es amarilla.   9. ¿De qué color es la casa? La casa es roja.

4F   1. ¿De qué color son los libros? Los libros son rojos.   2. ¿De qué color son los relojes? Los relojes son blancos.   3. ¿De qué color son las sillas? Las sillas son verdes.   4. ¿De qué color es el mostrador? El mostrador es negro. 5. ¿De qué color son las bolsas? Las bolsas son cafés (de color café).   6. ¿De qué color es el sombrero? El sombrero es azul.   7. ¿De qué color es el termómetro? El termómetro es rosa (rosado/de color rosa).   8. ¿De qué color son las cervezas? Las cervezas son naranjas (anaranjadas/de color naranja).   9. ¿De qué color son las mesas? Las mesas son rojas.

4G   1. Hay un sombrero.   2. Hay seis sombreros.   3. Hay cuatro sombreros.

4H   1. comes   2. comemos   3. come   4. comen   5. come   6. comen 7. comemos   8. comen (*or* comemos)   9. come

4I   (*possible answers*)   1. Sí, Uds. comen (*or* comemos) muchos tacos.
2. Como tacos y enchiladas.   3. No, no comemos enchiladas por la mañana.
4. Comemos enchiladas por la tarde.   5. Los mexicanos comen chiles.
6. No, no como chiles con salsa picante.   7. Comen tortillas en el restaurante.
8. No, no como mucha grasa.   9. Como a las ocho de la mañana, a las doce
de la tarde y a las siete de la noche.   10. Come cereal a las siete de la mañana.

4J   (*possible answers*)   1. Leo las revistas *Time* y *Newsweek*.   2. Sí, aprendo
muy rápido el español.   3. Bebo leche a las seis de la mañana.   4. Sí, Uds.
comprenden (*or* nosotros comprendemos) bien el inglés.   5. Sí, corro en el
parque cada día.   6. Sí, cree que está enfermo.   7. No, no respondo a todas las
preguntas.   8. No, no venden Uds. (*or* no vendemos) carros usados en el
hospital.   9. Uds. ven (*or* Nosotros vemos) a los pacientes en la sala de
emergencias.   10. No, no come chiles.   11. Sí, es difícil correr.   12. No, no debe
dinero al hospital.   13. Sí, es difícil leer la receta del doctor.   14. Sí, muchos
pacientes tienen dolor de cabeza por el estrés.

4K   1. viven   2. vive   3. viven   4. vivimos   5. vive   6. viven   7. vive

4L   (*possible answers*)   1. Macho Camacho vive en Puerto Rico. Es boxeador.
2. Vivo en Florida, en los Estados Unidos.   3. Viven en los Estados Unidos
o Canadá.   4. Vive en los Estados Unidos.   5. Fidel Castro vive en Cuba.
6. Los franceses viven en Francia.   7. Los italianos viven en Italia.   8. Octavio
Paz fue[1] de México.

4M   1. abres   2. abre   3. abrimos   4. abren   5. abre

4N   1. abro la maleta   2. abres la bolsa   3. abren las cervezas   4. abren
el vino   5. abrimos la puerta   6. abre

4O   (*possible answers*)   1. Abrimos los libros de español mucho.   2. Viven
en Chile.   3. No, no abro los libros de español durante "Monday Night
Football."   4. Una mujer en la clase vive en Chihuahua. Un hombre en la clase
tiene un chihuahua.   5. Yo abro la ventana en la clase.

4P   1. El hijo de la señora Sánchez está enfermo.   2. Le duelen (*or* Tiene
dolor de) la cabeza, el estómago, la garganta y todo el cuerpo en general.
3. Toma un té y unas pastillas para niños.   4. Sí, tiene un poco de tos y flemas.
5. Necesita hacer un examen físico.

4Q   1. vas a tomar   2. van a tomar   3. vamos a tomar   4. van a tomar
5. va a tomar   6. van/vamos a tomar   7. va a tomar   8. va a tomar   9. va a
tomar

4R   voy, vas, va, vamos, van

---

[1] **fue** was (he died in 1998)

4S (*possible answers*) 1. Pedro va a la clínica. 2. Vamos al cine a las ocho. 3. Voy a comer tacos a las ocho. 4. Marta va a ir al hospital mañana. 5. Cuarenta personas van a la clínica. 6. No, no voy a comer tacos en la noche. 7. Sí, vamos a aprender español en la clase. 8. Van a traer una cobija si un paciente tiene frío. 9. Sí, voy a hablar español con los pacientes mexicanos. 10. Sí, van a mirar la televisión.

4T (*possible answers*) 1. Voy a ir a la clínica después de la clase. 2. Voy a recetar antibióticos.

4U 1. José Manuelito no está bien; tiene un resfriado y tos. 2. Los hermanos de José tienen gripa. 3. Comenzó hace tres días. Tose más por la noche cuando se acuesta. 4. Es una tos muy fuerte. Suena como tos de perro.

4V 1. es 2. es 3. está 4. está 5. son 6. es 7. está 8. es 9. estoy 10. es

Chapter 5

5A (*sample response*) En mi familia somos cinco personas: mi esposo, mis dos hijos, mi hija y yo.

5B 1. abuela 2. sobrino 3. hermano/cuñado 4. sobrina 5. suegro 6. nieta 7. abuelo 8. tíos 9. cuñada 10. prometido(-a) *or* novio(-a)/ esposo(-a)

5C *Each healthcare professional will have his or her own answers.*

5D (*possible answers*) 1. Usamos una cuchara para tomar sopa. 2. Usamos un tenedor y un cuchillo. 3. No, comemos chícharos con una cuchara/ un tenedor. 4. Tomo café en una taza. 5. Dejo una propina a un mesero. 6. Tomamos el almuerzo a las doce y media. 7. El tenedor va al lado izquierdo del plato. 8. Me gusta cuándo mi hijo limpiar la boca con la servilleta.

5E *Each healthcare professional will have his or her own answers.*

5F (*possible answers*) 1. me gusta 2. me gusta 3. me gusta el flan con chiles 4. Sí, me gustan las almejas. 5. No, no me gustan las uvas. 6. Sí, me gustan las zanahorias. 7. Me gustan las naranjas y las manzanas. 8. Me gustan los tacos, los pasteles y el helado.

5G (*possible answers*) 1. Sí, me gusta comer los frijoles. 2. Me gusta comer en el restaurante. 3. No, no me gusta tomar sopa caliente y picante en el desierto. 4. Me gusta comer huevos en la mañana. 5. Sí, me gusta beber las cervezas mexicanas. 6. No, no me gusta comer chícharos con las manos.

5H 1. tienes 2. tiene 3. tiene 4. tiene 5. tenemos 6. tienen 7. tenemos 8. tiene

5I (*possible answers*) 1. No, no tengo una aguja grande. 2. La enfermera tiene la aguja grande. 3. Sí, tengo dos Tylenol. 4. Tengo el Valium en casa (*or* en el baño). 5. No, no tenemos anestesia para el dolor hoy. 6. Sí, los pacientes tienen náusea a veces. 7. Sí, el doctor tiene alta presión.

5J   1. tienes   2. tiene   3. tiene   4. tenemos   5. tienen   6. tienen   7. tienen

5K   1. vienen, ponen   2. viene, pone   3. venimos, ponemos   4. vienen, ponen   5. vengo, pongo   6. vienes, pones   7. vienen, ponen

5L   (*possible answers*)   1. No, no tengo frío.   2. Tengo comezón en el brazo (*or* en el pie).   3. El paciente tiene calambres.   4. Sí, tenemos miedo de las agujas.   5. Sí, me duele el brazo después de tantas inyecciones.   6. Sí, tengo náuseas después de comer tripas.   7. No, no tengo la medicina que está tomando.   8. Sí, tengo algo/medicina para la náusea.

5M   *Horizontales:*   1. dedo   2. pierna   3. estómago   4. brazo   5. pelo   6. mano   7. corazón   *Verticales:*   8. pie   9. nariz   10. dientes   11. cabeza   12. boca   13. oído   14. espalda   15. ojo

Chapter 6

6A   1. pongo, hago, salgo   2. pones, haces, sales   3. pone, hace, sale   4. ponen, hacen, salen   5. pone, hace, sale   6. pone, hace, sale

6B   1. traigo, caigo   2. trae, cae   3. traes, caes   4. traen, caen   5. trae, cae   6. trae, cae   7. traemos, caemos   8. traen, caen   9. traen, caen   10. traen, caen

6C   1. voy, doy   2. va, da   3. va, da   4. va, da   5. van, dan   6. van, dan   7. vamos, damos   8. van, dan   9. va, da   10. va, da

6D   1. quiere   2. quiere   3. quiero   4. quiere   5. quieren   6. quieren

6E   (*possible answers*)   1. Tú quieres comer las galletas y el pan dulce.   2. Ella quiere comer las tortas y los tacos.   3. Nosotros queremos comer las enchiladas.   4. Los pacientes quieren comer las uvas.   5. Ud. quiere comer el queso.

6F   1. puedo   2. puede   3. podemos   4. puedo   5. pueden

6G   (*possible answers*)   1. El paciente puede sentarse en la silla.   2. Puedo comprar tacos y enchiladas en el restaurante mexicano.   3. Podemos venir a la clínica a las siete y media de la tarde.   4. Yo puedo hablar español.   5. Podemos/Pueden ir al cine mañana.

6H   1. vuelvo, cierro, duermo   2. vuelve, cierra, duerme   3. vuelven, cierran, duermen   4. vuelve, cierra, duerme   5. vuelven, cierran, duermen   6. vuelve, cierra, duerme

6I   (*possible answers*)   1. Hoy es miércoles.   2. Mañana es jueves.   3. Pasado mañana es viernes.   4. Mañana es martes.   5. Pasado mañana es miércoles.   6. Mañana es viernes.   7. Pasado mañana es sábado.   8. Hay clases de español los viernes.   9. Hay trabajo los lunes, martes, miércoles, jueves y viernes.   10. Vamos a la iglesia el domingo.

6J   1. Domingo es después del sábado.   2. Viernes es antes del sábado.
3. Lunes es después del domingo.   4. Sábado es antes del domingo.   5. Noventa
y seis es después del número 95.   6. Cien es antes del número 101.   7. Las
cuatro de la tarde son después de las tres de la tarde.   8. La una es antes de las
dos de la tarde.

6K   1. Enero es antes de febrero.   2. Abril es antes de mayo.   3. Julio es
antes de agosto.   4. Octubre es antes de noviembre.   5. Marzo es antes de abril.
6. Junio es antes de julio.   7. Septiembre es antes de octubre.   8. Diciembre
es antes de enero.

6L   (*possible answers*)   1. Mi cumpleaños es el veinte y dos[2] de febrero.
2. El cumpleaños de mi madre es el cuatro de junio.   3. El cumpleaños de mi
padre es el doce de noviembre.   4. El Día de las Madres es en mayo.   5. El Día
de los Padres es en junio.   6. El Día de la Independencia norteamericana es en
julio.   7. El Día de la Independencia mexicana es en septiembre.   8. El Día de
dar Gracias es en noviembre.   9. El Día de los Novios es en febrero.   10. El Día
de la Raza es en octubre.   11. El Día de los Muertos es en noviembre.
12. Navidad es en diciembre.

6M   1. ¡Abra Ud.!   2. ¡Abran Uds.!   3. ¡Corra Ud.!   4. ¡No corra Ud.!   5.
¡No camine Ud.!   6. ¡Caminen Uds.!   7. ¡No tome Ud.!   8. ¡No tomen Uds.!
9. ¡Estudie Ud.!   10. ¡Estudien Uds.!   11. ¡Suba Ud.!   12. ¡No suban Uds.!
13. ¡Cante Ud.!   14. ¡No canten Uds.!   15. ¡Escriba Ud.!   16. ¡Escriban Uds.!
17. ¡No fume Ud.!   18. ¡No fumen Uds.!

6N   1. Primero va a examinar los ojos del paciente.   2. Dice al paciente
"Mire la luz."   3. (*possible answers*) Saque la lengua. Abra la boca. Diga "Ah."
Pase saliva. Respire profundo por la boca. Tosa. Acuéstese. Doble las rodillas.
Relájese. Siéntese otra vez. Afloje la pierna. Puede vestirse.

6O   pase (pasar), siéntese (sentarse), mire (mirar), siga (seguir), mueva
(mover), levante (levantar), baje (bajar), cierre (cerrar), abra (abrir), haga
(hacer), infle (inflar), empuje (empujar), resista (resistir), muerda (morder),
suba (subir), apriete (apretar), empuje (empujar), jale (jalar), resista (resistir),
levántese (levantarse), cierre (cerrar), abra (abrir), camine (caminar), dé (dar),
camine (caminar), dé (dar), camine (caminar), toque (tocar), toque (tocar),
levante (levantar), siéntese (sentarse), extienda (extender), espere (esperar)

Chapter 7

7A   (*possible answers*) Necesito examinarle. ¿Dónde quiere hacer el ejercicio?
¿Cuándo va a sacar me los rayos X? ¿Me permite sacarle sangre? ¿Por qué es
necesario decir "ah"? Favor de extender el brazo. ¿Por qué necesito traer mis
medicinas? Debe hacerle una prueba. Voy a pesarle. ¿Cuándo quisiera hacer
una cita?

---

[2] more commonly written **veintidós**

7B   1. Take two pills three times a day for ten days until you finish all the pills.   2. Insert the suppository into your rectum each night before you go to bed for a period of two weeks.   3. Apply the cream on the bedsores three times a day for a week.

7C   *Answers will vary.*

7D   1. Muévase más hacia mí.   2. Voy a introducir el espéculo. 3. Ahora Ud. puede vestirse.

7E   (*possible answers*)   1. Necesita salir de la puerta del hospital y dé vuelta a la izquierda. Camine derecho por una cuadra y dé vuelta a la derecha. Camine derecho por dos cuadras. Necesita cruzar la calle y allí está la clínica. 2. Necesita salir de la puerta del hospital y dé vuelta a la derecha. Camine derecho por tres cuadras y dé vuelta a la izquierda. Camine derecho por cuatro cuadras. Necesita cruzar la calle y allí está el consultorio de dentistas. 3. Necesita salir de la puerta del hospital y dé vuelta a la derecha. Camine derecho por dos cuadras y dé vuelta a la izquierda. Camine derecho por dos cuadras. Necesita cruzar la calle y allí está la Cruz Roja.   4. Necesita salir/Salga de la puerta del hospital y dé vuelta a la derecha. Camine derecho por una cuadra y dé vuelta a la izquierda. Camine derecho por cuatro cuadras. Necesita cruzar la glorieta. Allí está el baile.   5. Necesita salir de la puerta del hospital y dé vuelta a la derecha. Camine derecho por dos cuadras y dé vuelta a la izquierda. Camine derecho por tres cuadras. Necesita cruzar la calle y allí está el banco.

7F   1. estás tomando   2. está tomando   3. están tomando   4. estamos tomando   5. está tomando

7G   1. estás comiendo   2. está comiendo   3. están comiendo   4. estamos comiendo   5. está comiendo

7H   1. La técnica quiere obtener una muestra de sangre del brazo derecho de la paciente.   2. Tiene que extender el brazo y mantenerlo derecho. 3. La técnica va a poner el torniquete.   4. La paciente necesita cerrar la mano. 5. La aguja duele un poco.   6. La señora tiene que poner presión en el brazo.

7I   1. El enfermero necesita una prueba de orina.   2. Necesita llevar las toallas desechables al baño.   3. Tiene que lavarse las (*or* lavar sus) manos. 4. Tiene que orinar en el frasco y en el excusado.   5. Necesita dejar el frasco en la ventanilla.

7J   1. Una es la prueba tuberculina y la otra es para la fiebre del valle. 2. Sacan las pruebas en los brazos.   3. Necesita observar la reacción de la piel por hinchazón o enrojecimiento.   4. La paciente tiene que regresar al consultorio si observa algunas de estas reacciones.   5. La doctora quiere ver a la paciente pasado mañana.

7K   1. La sangre, la orina y el esputo del señor están normales.
2. Las pruebas y la radiografía muestran una pequeña variante en el pulmón derecho.   3. Estos resultados indican que el paciente tiene los principios de la fiebre del valle.   4. La doctora sugiere una dieta alta en proteínas y mucho descanso.   5. La doctora le da unas vitaminas. *or* La doctora da al señor una receta para vitaminas.

Chapter 8

8A   1. mis, mi, mi, mis   2. tu, tus, tu, tu   3. mis, mis, mi, mis   4. tu, tu, tus, tu

8B   1. nuestra, nuestra, nuestra, nuestras   2. nuestros, nuestros, nuestra, nuestro   3. nuestra, nuestra, nuestras, nuestra   4. nuestras, nuestros, nuestro, nuestros

8C   1. su pato   2. su bata   3. sus jeringas   4. su martillo   5. sus píldoras
6. sus goteros   7. su estetoscopio   8. sus otoscopios   9. su aguja   10. su receta
11. sus vendas   12. sus libros

8D   1. Aquí se fuman pipas.   2. Aquí se fuma tabaco.   3. Aquí se prepara la comida mexicana.   4. Aquí se preparan platos franceses.   5. Aquí se dan las inyecciones.   6. Aquí se da la vacuna.   7. Aquí se enyesa el brazo.   8. Aquí se enyesan los dedos.   9. Aquí se vende aspirina.   10. Aquí se vende gasa.

8E   1. Aquí se habla español.   2. Aquí se venden medicinas.   3. Se lee en la sala de espera.   4. Se compra medicina en la farmacia.   5. Se venden vendas aquí.   6. Se venden drogas en la calle.   7. Se abre la clínica a las ocho.   8. Allí se llevan guayaberas también.

8F   1. Esa   2. Estas   3. Esas   4. Esta   5. Esa

8G   1. Estos   2. Esos   3. Ese   4. Este   5. Ese

8H   1. tomaste   2. tomamos   3. tomó   4. tomaron   5. tomó   6. tomamos
7. tomaron   8. tomaron

8I   (*possible answers*)   1. Tomamos el vaso de vino el otro día.   2. Sí, Juan tomó el agua en México.   3. Ellos tomaron cerveza en la fiesta anoche.
4. Tomamos cinco tazas de café la mañana después de la fiesta.   5. Marta tomó la limonada en la cantina antier.   6. Sí, los turistas tomaron mucha agua en el desierto.

8J   1. comió   2. comiste   3. comimos   4. comió   5. comieron   6. comió
7. comimos   8. comieron

8K   1. comieron   2. comió   3. comiste   4. comimos   5. comieron   6. comí
7. comieron

8L   1. abrieron   2. abrió   3. abriste   4. abrió   5. abrió   6. abrí

8M   1. Tú recibiste una visita ayer.   2. Ella compró unos termómetros ayer.
3. Uds. vendieron unos otoscopios ayer.   4. Nosotros necesitamos unas vendas
ayer.   5. Juan y María corrieron un kilómetro ayer.   6. Yo caminé una cuadra
ayer.   7. Ud. aprendió unos verbos ayer.   8. Tú escribiste unas instrucciones
ayer.   9. Mis hermanos limpiaron unos cuartos ayer.   10. Uds. visitaron al
hospital ayer.

8N   1. El técnico perdió la jeringa y no sacó muestras de la sangre.
2. Uds. oyeron la música y durmieron profundamente.   3. Yo mostré y expliqué
los resultados a los pacientes.   4. Los niños salieron de la clínica pero no
cerraron la puerta.   5. Yo no alcancé la repisa alto y pedí ayuda.
6. Los farmacéuticos leyeron la receta pero no entendieron las instrucciones.
7. La doctora Ríos cayó en la nieve y mordió la lengua.   8. Indiqué dónde me
dolió, pero la enfermera no comprendió.   9. Yo oí las noticias y desperté a mis
hijos.   10. Yo toqué la guitarra y mis hermanos huyeron del cuarto.

8O   1. hizo   2. hizo   3. hiciste   4. hicimos   5. hicimos   6. hicieron   7. hice

8P   1. Hiciste   2. Hizo   3. Hizo   4. Hicimos   5. Hicieron   6. Hicieron
7. Hiciste   8. Hice

8Q   *Answers will vary.*

8R   1. fuiste   2. fue   3. fuimos   4. fueron   5. fue   6. fuimos

8S   1. tuvo   2. tuviste   3. tuvo   4. tuvieron   5. tuvimos   6. tuvieron
7. tuvieron   8. tuve

8T   1. tuvo, fue   2. tuvimos, fuimos   3. tuviste, fuiste   4. tuvieron, fueron
5. tuvo, fue   6. tuvieron, fueron   7. tuvieron, fueron   8. tuve, fui

8U   1. estuvo   2. estuvieron   3. estuvieron   4. estuve   5. estuviste
6. estuvimos

8V   (*possible answers*)   1. Sí, estuvieron (*or* estuvimos) bien ayer en
la clínica.   2. No, no estuvieron (*or* estuvimos) enfermos durante el examen.
3. Sí, estuvieron (*or* estuvimos) contentos en la fiesta.   4. Sí, el baile folklórico
estuvo bonito.   5. Sí, estuve cansado al esperar en el hospital.

8W   1. Jaimito sigue mal, con calentura y gripa.   2. No, no sirvió la medicina
que recetó el doctor.   3. Ella dio una cucharadita de los antibióticos a Jaimito
una vez por día.   4. El doctor dijo, "Es muy importante tomar la dosis exacta."
La dosis exacta debe ser una cucharadita tres veces al día.   5. Ella preguntó al
doctor, "¿Puedo darle Tylenol o está bien darle Motrin también con la medicina
que me recetó?"   6. El doctor contestó a la señora, "Sí, el antibiótico sirve con
o Tylenol o Motrin."

8X   1. Primero, la doctora da explicaciones al paciente.   2. Ella preguntó al paciente primero, "¿Se siente mejor ahora?"   3. Sufre del asma y sufre de alta presión. Toma Vasotec.   4. Sí, fue el peor ataque que ha tenido en toda su vida. 5. El paciente estuvo en su casa, estuvo trabajando y pintando y comenzó a toser. Luego, empezó a respirar con un silbido. Agarró su inhalador y se dio dos bombazos.   6. Sí, tiene familiares que han sufrido de diabetes.   7. El técnico va a sacar unas radiografías de sus pulmones.   8. La doctora va a examinarle completamente después.

Chapter 9

9A   1. lavo   2. me lavo   3. lavas   4. lavas   5. se lava   6. lava
7. nos lavamos   8. lavamos   9. lavan   10. se lavan

9B   1. pongo   2. me pongo   3. pone   4. te pones   5. ponen   6. se ponen
7. ponen, se pone   8. pones   9. nos ponemos   10. pone

9C   1. irnos   2. ingresarme   3. vestirse   4. sentarnos   5. levantarme
6. bajarse   7. llamarme   8. moverte   9. bañarme   10. limpiarme

9D   *Answers will vary.*

9E   1. el   2. a la   3. el   4. al   5. la   6. a la   7. el   8. al (*or* a la)

9F   1. La compra.   2. La hacemos.   3. Lo busco.   4. La toman.
5. Lo vemos en la mañana.   6. La venden en el mercado.   7. Lo escribe.
8. El doctor lo receta.   9. La miro.   10. Lo veo en la calle.

9G   1. Los llevo.   2. Las mira.   3. Los tocan.   4. Las comen.   5. Los toman por la tarde.   6. Las compramos en la tienda.   7. Las ves en el baño.
8. Los llamo.   9. Los empacan en la maleta.   10. Las miras en la playa.

9H   1. ¿Ud. se examina? (Do you examine?), examinarme (to check myself), explicarme (to explain to me), examínese (check yourself), al bañarse (while bathing yourself), después de bañarse (after bathing yourself), mírese (look at yourself), examínese los senos (check your breasts), acuéstese (lie down), tocarse el seno (to touch your breast), examinarse el seno izquierdo (to check your left breast), apriétese los pezones (squeeze your nipples), examinarme los pechos (to check my breasts), examinarse (to examine yourself), examinarme (to examine myself), cuídese (take care of yourself)

2. examínese los senos (examine your breasts), mírese (look at yourself), examínese los senos (examine your breasts), acuéstese (lie down), ponga (place), use (use), use (use), mueva (move), use (use), apriétese (squeeze), llámenos (call us), cuídese (take care of yourself).

3. *Answers will vary for each healthcare professional.*

English-Spanish Glossary

a little/a little bit: poco

a lot: mucho(a)(s)

abdomen: abdomen (*m.*)

abdominal cramps: retorcijones, retortijones (*m.*)

abortion: aborto (*m.*)

abrasion: raspadura (*f.*)

abscess: absceso (*m.*), postema (*f.*)

abscessed tooth: postemilla (*f.*)

abused: maltratado(a)

according to: según

aching all over, flu-like symptoms: el cuerpo cortado (*Mex., Sp.*)

acidity: acidez (*f.*)

acne: acné (*m.*)

activities: actividades (*f.*)

adenoids: adenoides (*m.*)

admired: admirado(a)

admit to hospital (to): ingresar, internar

adrenaline: adrenalina (*f.*)

after: después de

afterwards: después

aha: ajá

AIDS: SIDA (*m.*)

alcoholic beverages: bebidas (*f.*) alcohólicas

all (*pl.*): todo(a)(s)

allergy: alergia (*f.*), coriza (*f.*) (*Cuba*)

alleviate (to): aliviar, ayudar

almost done: ya casi, ya mero (*Mex.*)

aloe, aloe vera: sábila (*f.*)

also, too: también

always: siempre

amenorrhea: amenorrea (*f.*), (ausencia de menstruación)

amoebas: amebas (*f.*) o amoebas (*f.*)

amputate (to): amputar

analgesic: analgésico (*m.*)

analysis: análisis (*m.*)

and: y

and so, and then, therefore: entonces

anemia or problems related to the blood: anemia (*f.*)

anguish: angustia (*f.*)

anguished: angustiado(a)

ankle: tobillo (*m.*)

another: otro(a)

answer (to): contestar, responder

antacid: antiácido (*m.*)

antibiotic: antibiótico (*m.*)

antibiotic preparation: preparación (*f.*) antibiótica

antidote: antídoto (*m.*)

antihistamine: antihistamínico (*m.*)

anus: ano (*m.*)

anxiety: ansiedad (*f.*)

anxious: ansioso(a)

any: algún, alguna

appear (to), seem (to): parecer (z)

appendix: apéndice (*m.*), "tripita" (*f.*)

apple: manzana (*f.*)

applicator: aplicador (*m.*)

apply (to): aplicar

appointment: cita (*f.*)

April: abril
are you . . . ? (*sing.*),(*pl.*): ¿Está . . . ?,
    Están . . . ?
are, they are: son
arm: brazo (*m.*)
arm pit: axila (*f.*)
around: alrededor (de)
artery: arteria (*f.*)
arthritis: artritis (*f.*)
ascend (to): subir
ashamed: avergonzado(a)
ask (to): preguntar
ask for, request (to): pedir
aspirin: aspirina (*f.*)
asthma: asma (*m.*)
asthmatic respiration: respiración (*f.*)
    asmática
astigmatism: astigmatismo (*m.*)
astonished/in shock: atónito(a)
at: a, en
at least: por lo menos
at what age?: ¿A qué edad?
athlete's foot: pie (*m.*) de atleta
atrophy: atrofia (*f.*)
atropine: atropina (*f.*)
attend (to), (a meeting, a course):
    asistir a
audiology: audiología (*f.*)
August: agosto
aunt: tía (*f.*)
aunt and uncle (as a unit): tíos (*m.*)
authorization: autorización (*f.*)
avoid (to): evitar, evadir

back: espalda (*f.*)
back molar: muela (*f.*) de atrás
back pain: dolor (*m.*) de espalda (*f.*)
bacon: tocino (*m.*)
bacteriologist: bacteriólogo(a)
bacteriology: bacteriología (*f.*)
bad: mal (*m.*)
bad breath: mal aliento (*m.*)

bald: calvo (*m.*), sin pelo, "el pelón"
baldness: calvicie (*f.*)
banana: plátano (*m.*) (*Mex.*), banana
    (*f.*), banano (*m.*), guineo (*m.*) (*C.A.*
    and Carib.*)
bandage: venda (*f.*), vendaje (*m.*)
barbiturates: barbitúricos (*m.*)
bathe oneself (to): bañarse
be (to): estar, ser
be able (to): poder
be in bed (to): guardar (estar en) cama
    (*f.*)
beans: frijoles (*m.*), habas (*f.*),
    habichuelas (*f.*) (*P.R.*)
beans, green: ejotes (*m.*) (*Mex.*),
    habichuelas verdes (*f.*) (*Cuba*),
    judías verdes (*f.*) (*Sp.*)
beat up (to): golpear
because: porque
become infected (to): contagiar
become pregnant (to): embarazarse
bed sore: llaga (*f.*)
beer: cerveza (*f.*)
before: antes (de)
began: comenzó, empezó
    (Ud./he/she/it)
begin (to): comenzar, empezar
beginnings: principios (*m.*)
believe (to): creer
belladonna: belladona (*f.*)
belly button: ombligo (*m.*)
bend (to): doblar
be sick (to): estar enfermo(a), estar mal
better (to), better (to get): mejorar
beverages: bebidas (*f.*)
bicarbonate: bicarbonato (*m.*)
bifocals: bifocales (*m.*)
big: grande
bile: hiel (*f.*), bilis (*f.*), "yel" (*m.*)
bill: cuenta (*f.*)
biological: biológico(a)
biologist: biólogo(a)

biology: biología (*f.*)

biopsy: biopsia (*f.*)

birth control pill: píldora (*f.*), pastilla (*f.*) anticonceptiva

birth mark: marca (*f.*) de nacimiento

bite (to): morder

bitter: amargo(a)

black: negro(a)

blackheads: espinillas (*f.*)

bladder: vejiga (*f.*)

bleed (to): sangrar

bleeding: sangrado, desangramiento, pérdida de sangre

blennorrhagia: blenorragia (*f.*), purgación (*f.*)

blind: ciego(a)

blink (to): parpadear

blister: ampolla (*f.*)

bloated: inflado(a), aventado(a)

block (street): cuadra (*f.*)

blond: rubio(a), güero(a) (*Mex.*), chele (*El Salv.*)

blond, light hair or skin: güero(a) (*Mex.*)

blood: sangre (*f.*)

blood in the sputum: sangre (*f.*) en el esputo (*m.*) o la saliva (*f.*)

blood pressure, arterial pressure: presión (*f.*) arterial, presión sanguínea

blood transfusion: transfusión (*f.*) de sangre (*f.*)

blood vessel: vaso (*m.*) sanguíneo

blue: azul

blurred vision: vista (*f.*) borrosa, nublada, empañada

body hair: vello (*m.*)

boil, carbuncle: fornúculo (*m.*), abceso (de la piel), nacido (*Carib.*), "tacotillo" (*m.*), carbunco (*m.*)

bolt down food (to): tragar

bonding (dental): bonding

bone: hueso (*m.*)

book: libro (*m.*)

borage (tea): borraja

both: los dos, las dos, ambos(as)

both lungs affected: ambos pulmones (*m.*) afectados

bothers, dicomforts, problems: molestias (*f.*)

bowel movement (to have a): obrar, defecar

bow-legged: corvo (*m.*), cascorvo (*m.*), "zambo" (*m.*), las piernas arqueadas (*f.*)

boy (girl): niño(a)

boyfriend (girlfriend): novio(a)

braces: frenos (*m.*), frenillos (*m.*)

brain: cerebro (*m.*)

bread: pan (*m.*)

breaded veal: milanesa (*f.*)

breast: senos (*m.*), mamas (*f.*), pechos (*m.*)

breast feed (to): dar pecho (*m.*)

breathe (to): respirar

bride/groom: novia(o)

bridge (dental): puente (*m.*) fijo

broken: fracturado(a)(s), quebrado(a)(s), roto(a)(s)

bromide: bromuro (*m.*)

bronchitis: bronquitis (*f.*)

bronchium: bronquio (*m.*)

brother: hermano (*m.*)

brother-in-law: cuñado (*m.*)

brown: café (*m.*), marrón (*P.R.*), pardo(a)

bruise: moretón (*m.*)

bruised: moreteado(a)

building: edificio (*m.*)

bunion: juanete (*m.*)

burn: quemadura (*f.*)

burn (to): quemar

burning/stinging/burn (to)/sting (to): ardor (*m.*)/arder

burning sensation when urinating:
ardor al orinar, "quemazón" al
orinar

burnt: quemado(a)

burp (to): eructar

bursitis: bursitis (*f.*)

burst open (to): reventar

but: pero

butt cheeks: nalgas (*f.*), pompis (*f.*)

butter: mantequilla (*f.*)

buy (to): comprar

buzzing in the ears: tintineo (*m.*),
zumbido (*m.*) de/en los oídos (*m.*)

by: por

cabinet: gabinete (*m.*)

cake: pastel (*Mex.*)(*m.*), bizcocho (*m.*),
torta (*f.*), queque (*m.*) (*Carib., N.
Mex.*)

calcium: calcio (*m.*)

calf: pantorrilla (*f.*)

call oneself (to): llamarse

camphor (tea, lotion): alcanfor

cancer: cáncer (*m.*)

cancerous: canceroso(a)

canker sore, chancre: pequeña úlcera
(*f.*) en la boca (*f.*), fuego (*m.*),
chancro (*m.*)

capsule: cápsula (*f.*)

car: coche (*m.*), carro (*m.*), automóvil
(*m.*)

carbohydrates: carbohidratos (*m.*)

cardiologist: cardiólogo(a)

cardiology: cardiología (*f.*)

care for (to)/take care of (to): cuidar

carrot: zanahoria (*f.*)

carry (to): llevar, cargar

casualty: casualidad (*f.*)

cataracts: cataratas (*f.*)

catheter: sonda (*f.*), catéter (*m.*)

cauliflower: coliflor (*f.*)

cause (to): causar

cautious: cauteloso(a)

cavities: caries (*m.*), picaduras (*f.*)

cells: células (*f.*)

cerebral infarct: infarto (*m.*), derrame
(*m.*) cerebral

certain: cierto(a)(s)

cesarean: cesárea (*f.*)

chair: silla (*f.*)

chamomile tea: té (*m.*) de manzanilla

chancre: postemillas o fuego (*m.*)

chancre: chancro (*m.*), grano (*m.*)

**chancre sores, fever blisters or cold
sores:** fuegos (*m.*)

change: cambio (*m.*)

change (to): cambiar

change of life: cambio (*m.*) de vida (*f.*)

chap (to): agrietarse, "rajarse"

chapped skin: grieta (*f.*)

chat (to): charlar, platicar (Mex)

cheekbone: pómulos (*m.*)

cheese: queso (*m.*)

chemotherapy: quimioterapia (*f.*)

chest: pecho (*m.*)

chest cold: catarro (*m.*) o resfriado (*m.*)
en el pecho (*m.*)

chest pain: dolor (*m.*) en el pecho (*m.*)

chew (to): masticar, mascar

chicken: pollo (*m.*), gallina (*f.*)

chicken pox: viruela (*f.*) loca, varicela
(*f.*)

chilblain: sabañones (*f.*), "saballones"
(*f.*)

children: niños (*m.*)

chile: chile (*m.*), ají (*m.*) (*Carib.*)

chills: escalofríos (*m.*)

chin: barbilla (*f.*), mentón (*m.*)

chlamydia: clamidia (*f.*) o chlamydia

chloasma: cloasma (*f.*)

choke (to): ahogarse, "atragantarse,"
"dar al galillo"

cholesterol: colesterol (*m.*)

chop, i.e. pork chop: chuleta (*f.*)

choroiditis: coroiditis (*f.*)

chronic: crónico(a)

circumcision: circuncisión (f.)

clamp: pinza(s)

clams: almejas (f.)

clavicle: clavícula (f.)

clean (to): limpiar

cleft palate: paladar (m.) hendido, grietas (f.) en el paladar

clitoris: clítoris (m.)

close (to): cerrar

coated "dirty" tongue: lengua (f.) sucia

coated pill: gragea (f.)

coccidioidomycosis, valley fever: fiebre (f.) del valle, coccidioidomicosis

coccyx: cóccix (m.)

codeine: codeína (f.)

coffee: café (m.)

cold: frío (m.)

cold in the womb: frío en la matriz (f.)

cold moist hands: manos (f.) frías, húmedas

cold or flu: gripe (f.)

colic: cólicos (m.)

colitis: colitis (f.)

collagen: colágeno (m.)

color blind: daltónico(a)/daltonismo (m.)

come (to): venir (g)

complication: complicación (f.)

condoms, rubbers: condones (m.), preservativos (m.), hules (m.)

confused: confundido(a)

congenital heart defect: defecto (m.) congénito del corazón

congestion: congestión (f.)

conjunctivitis, pink eye: conjuntivitis (f.)

constant: constante, fijo (Carib.)

constipated: estreñido(a), estítico(a) (C.A.)

consult (to): consultar

contact lenses: lentes (m.) de contacto, pupilentes (m.)

contagious: contagioso(a)

container: frasco (m.)

contaminate (to): contaminar

content: contento(a)

continue (to): continuar, seguir

contraception: contracepción (f.)

control (to): controlar

contusion: contusión (f.), golpe (m.)

convalescence: convalecencia (f.)

converse (to): conversar

convulsions: convulsiones (f.), ataques (m.)

cookies: galletas (f.)

coriander (tea): cilantro (m.)

corn: maíz (m.)

corn silk (tea): pelos (m.) o cabellos (m.) de elote (m.)

cornea: córnea (f.)

corneal ulcers: úlceras (f.) en la córnea (f.)

corns, soft corns: callos (m.), callos (m.) blandos

cortisone: cortisona (f.)

cough: tos (f.)

cough (to): toser

cough with phlegm, wet cough: tos con flema (f.), "desgarrando"

cough, dry: tos (f.) seca

count (to): contar

counter: mostrador (m.)

cousin: primo(a)

cover (to): cubrir, tapar (Mex.)

cover, cap: tapadera (f.)

cover up (to): tapar, cubrir

cramps (abdomen): retortijones (m.), (re)torcijones (m.)

cramps (menstrual): cólicos (m.)

cramps (muscle): calambres (m.)

cranium: cráneo (m.)

crash (to): chocar

crawl (to): gatear

cream: crema (f.)

cross-eyed: bizco(a)

crown: corona (f.)

cup: taza (*f.*)
cure (to): curar
custard: flan (*m.*)
cut (noun): cortada (*f.*)
cut (to): cortar
cyanosis: cianosis, "piel azulada"
cycle (to)/circulate (to): circular
cyst: quiste (*m.*)
cytologist: citólogo(a)
cytology: citología (*f.*)

dance: baile (*m.*)
dandruff: caspa (*f.*)
dark: oscuro(a)
dark skin color: moreno(a)
dates (calendar): fechas (*f.*)
daughter: hija (*f.*)
daughter-in-law: nuera (*f.*)
day after tomorrow: pasado mañana
day before yesterday: anteayer (antier)
deaf: sordo(a)
deaf-mute: sordomudo(a)
deafness: sordera (*f.*)
December: diciembre
deer's eye (*lit.*): ojo (*m.*) de venado (*m.*)
defecate (to): defecar
defect of foot, ankle, knee: defecto (*m.*)
   del pie, del tobillo, de la rodilla,
   patizambo(a), chueco(a)
delicious: delicioso(a), sabroso(a),
   rico(a)
delivery: parto (*m.*)
denture: dentadura (*f.*) completa
Depo Provera®: inyecciones (Depo) (*f.*)
depressed: deprimido(a)
depression: depresión (*f.*), estar triste
dermatitis: dermatitis (*f.*)
dermatologist: dermatólogo(a)
dermatology: dermatología (*f.*)
descend (to), get out of (to), get off of
   (to): bajar
desire (to): desear

dessert spoon: cucharita (*f.*)
destination: destino (*m.*)
destiny: destino (*m.*)
diabetes: diabetes (*f.*)
diabetic retinopathy: retinopatía (*f.*)
   diabética
diaphragm: diafragma (*m.*)
diarrhea: diarrea (*f.*), "estómago (*m.*)
   suelto," "chorro/chorrillo "
die (to): morir (ue)
diet: dieta (*f.*)
difficulty breathing: respiración (*f.*)
   dificultosa, dificultad al respirar
diphtheria: difteria (*f.*), "diteria" (*f.*)
directory: directorio (*m.*)
discharge: desecho (*m.*), secreción (*f.*)
discomforts: molestias (*f.*)
disconnect (to): desconectar
dish: plato (*m.*)
disinfect (to): desinfectar
dislocation: dislocación (*f.*)
disposable: desechable
dizziness: mareos (*m.*)
dizzy: mareado(a)
do (to): hacer (g)
do it (to): hacerlo
Do this!: ¡Haga esto!
Do you feel . . . ?: ¿Se siente . . . ?
Do you pant (wheeze) when you
   walk?: ¿Jadea cuando camina?
Do you understand?: ¿Me explico?
   (literally, Am I explaining myself?),
   ¿entiende?, ¿comprende?
Do you/Does s/he have an appetite?:
   ¿Tiene apetito (*m.*)?
doctor: doctor(a)
Does it hurt when I apply pressure?:
   ¿Le duele cuándo pongo(aplico)
   presión?
Does it hurt when I remove the
   pressure?: ¿Le duele cuándo suelto
   (quito) la presión?

doll: muñeca (f.)
Don't worry!: ¡No se preocupe!
door: puerta (f.)
dosis: dosis (f.)
double pneumonia: pulmonía
doble (f.)
douches: duchas (f.), lavados (m.)
Down syndrome: síndrome (m.) de
Down
Dr.'s office: consultorio (m.)
dress oneself (to): vestirse
drill: taladro (m.)
drink (to): beber
drive (to): conducir, manejar
dropper: gotero (m.)
dry: seco(a)
dry (noun): reseca(o)
dry (to): secar
dry eyes: ojos (m.) secos
dry skin: piel (f.) reseca, piel seca
duck: pato (m.)
due date: fecha apróximada (f.) de parto
(m.)
due to that: por eso
dull: sordo(a)
during: durante
dysentery: disentería (f.), "cursio" (m.)
dysmenorrheal: dismenorrea (f.)

ear of corn: elote (Mex.) (m.), mazorca
(f.)
ear wax: cera (f.), cerumen (m.),
"cerilla" (f.)
earache: dolor de oído (m.)
eardrum: tímpano (m.)
early: temprano
eat (to): comer
ectropion: ectropión (f.)
eczema: eczema (f.)
edifice: edificio (m.)
eggs: huevos (m.), blanquillos (m.)
(N. Mex.)

elbow: codo (m.)
elective abortion: aborto (m.) inducido,
legrado (m.)
embarrassed: apenado(a),
avergonzado(a)
embolism: embolia (f.)
embryologist: embriólogo(a)
emergency: emergencia (f.)
emphysema: enfisema (f.)
encephalitis: encefalitis (f.)
enchilada: enchilada (f.)
end (to): acabar, terminar
endodontics: endodoncia (f.)
enemas: enemas (f.), lavativas (f.)
enlargement of the . . . : agrandamiento
del . . .
enter (to): entrar
entropion: entropión (m.)
epidemic: epidemia (f.), epidémico(a)
(adj)
epididymis: epidídimo
epilepsy: epilepsia (f.)
episcleritis: episcleritis (f.)
erisipela, erysipelas: erisipela (f.)
eruption: erupción (f.)
esophagus: esófago (m.)
estrogen: estrógeno (m.)
examine (to): examinar
exception: excepción (f.)
excuse me (when leaving room): con
permiso (m.)
exhausted: agotado(a)
exhaustion: agotamiento (m.)
exist (to): existir
expel gas (to)/fart (to): tener gas
(m.)/"echar un pedo" (m.), "tirar
un pedo"
expensive: caro(a)
extend (to): extender (ie)
extended wear: de uso extendido
extract (to): extraer, sacar
extremities: extremidades (f.)

eye: ojo (*m.*)
eye chart: carta (*f.*), gráfico(a) (*m., f.*)
eyebrow: ceja (*f.*)
eyelash: pestaña (*f.*)
eyelid: párpado (*m.*)

face: cara (*f.*)
facial discoloration: paño (*m.*)
facial paralysis: parálisis (*f.*) facial
faint (to): desmayar
fainting spells: desmayos (*m.*)
fall (to): caer(se), caer (g)
fallen fontanel: fontanela (*f.*) caída o deprimida, "mollera (*f.*) caída"
fallopian tube: trompa (*f.*), tubo (*m.*) de Falopio
family: familia (*f.*)
family members: familiares (*m.*)
far sighted (hyperopic): hiperópico (*m.*)
fast: rápido(a)
fasting, without eating in the morning: en ayunas
fat: gordo(a)
father: padre (*m.*)
father-in-law: suegro (*m.*)
fathers (in general): padres (*m.*) de familia
fatigue: fatigado(a)
fats: grasas (*f.*)
fear: miedo (*m.*), temor (*m.*)
feather: pluma (*f.*)
February: febrero
feed (to): alimentar, dar de comer
feel (oneself) (to): sentirse
female: hembra (*f.*)
fetal alcohol syndrome: síndrome (*m.*) fetal de alcohol (*m.*)
fetoscope: fetoscopio (*m.*)
fever: fiebre (*f.*), calentura (*f.*)
fiancé(e): prometido(a)
fiber: fibra (*f.*)

fibroids, tumors: fibroma (*f.*), fibroides (*m.*), tumores (*m.*)
fill (to) (dental): empastar, tapar, rellenar
filling (dental): amalgama (*f.*), relleno (*m.*)
find (to): encontrar, hallar
finger: dedo (*m.*)
finger pads: yemas (*f.*)
first: primer(o)(a)
first time: primera vez (*f.*)
fish: pescado(s)(*m.*)
fistula: fístula (*f.*)
flat foot: pie (*m.*) plano
flow: flujo (*m.*)
fluids: líquidos (*m.*)
foam: espuma (*f.*)
folk healer: curandero(a), santero(a) (*Carib.*)
follicle: folículo (*m.*)
follows (as): a continuación
foment (to) bacterial proliferation: fomentar la proliferación de bacteria (*f.*)
food: alimento (*m.*)
foot: pie (*m.*)
for: para, por
for two days: por dos días
for the first time: por primera vez (*f.*)
for tomorrow: para mañana
for, in order to: para
forearm: antebrazo (*m.*)
forehead: frente (*f.*)
foreskin: prepucio (*m.*)
fork: tenedor (*m.*)
fowl: aves (*f.*)
freeze (to): congelar
frequency: frecuencia (*f.*)
fresh: fresco(a)
friend: amigo(a)
fright/scare: susto (*m.*)
frightened: asustado(a), espantado(a)

frigidity: frigidez (*f.*)
from: de, desde
from the front: de frente
full term: nacido a tiempo (*m.*)

gain weight (to): subir de peso (*m.*)
gall: hiel (*f.*), bilis (*f.*), "yel" (*m.*)
gall bladder: vesícula (*f.*) biliar
gallstones: cálculos (*m.*) o piedras
    biliares (*f.*) or en la vesícula
garlic: ajo (*m.*)
gastritis: gastritis (*f.*), inflamación (*f.*)
    del estómago (*m.*)
gel: gel (*m.*)
gelatin: gelatina (*f.*)
generally: generalmente, por lo general
generous: generoso(a)
genital warts: verrugas (*f.*) genitales
genitalia: genitalia (*f.*), partes (*f.*)
    genitales
get down from, get off of (to): bajarse
Get dressed (command): Vístase.
get on, get in, ascend (to): subir
get sick (to): enfermarse
get up (to): levantar, levantar(se),
    subir
gingivitis: gingivitis (*f.*)
give (to): dar
gland: glándula (*f.*)
glass: vaso (*m.*)
glasses: lentes (*m.*), gafas, anteojos
    (*m.*), espejuelos (*m.*) (*Carib.*)
glaucoma: glaucoma (*f.*)
glue (to): pegar
gluteus: glúteo (*m.*)
go (to): ir
go up (to): subir
godfather, godmother: padrino(a)
godmother/father's relationship to
    godchild's mother/father: comadre
    (*f.*)/compadre (*m.*)
goiter: bocio (*m.*), "buche" (*m.*)

gonorrhea: gonorrea (*f.*), purgación (*f.*),
    blenorragia (*f.*)
good: bueno(a), bien
gourd: calabaza (*f.*)
gout: gota (*f.*), podagra (*f.*)
grab (to): agarrar
gram: gramo (*m.*)
grandfather (grandmother): abuelo(a)
grandson (granddaughter): nieto(a)
grapefruit: toronja (*f.*), pomelo (*m.*)
    (*Arg. and Sp.*)
grapes: uvas (*f.*)
green: verde
groin: ingle (*f.*)
groom: novio
guard (to): vigilar
gums: encías (*f.*)
gynecologist: ginecólogo(a)
gynecology: ginecología (*f.*)

hair: pelo (*m.*), cabello (*m.*)
hairless: calvo (*m.*), sin pelo, "el pelón"
halitosis: halitosis (*f.*)
hallucination: alucinación (*f.*)
ham: jamón (*m.*)
hamburger: hamburguesa (*f.*)
hammer: martillo (*m.*)
hand: mano (*f.*)
handicapped: deshabilitado(a),
    incapacitado(a), discapacitado(a),
    minusválido(a)
happen (to): pasar
happy: alegre
"harelip": labihendido(a), el labio (*m.*)
    leporino, "comido de la luna"
harm (to): dañar
hat: sombrero (*m.*)
have (to): tener (g)
Have you ever had . . . ?: ¿Alguna vez
    ha tenido (ha sufrido de) . . . ?
hay fever: fiebre de heno (*f.*),
    "romadizo" (*m.*)

head: cabeza (*f.*)

headaches: dolores (*m.*) de cabeza (*f.*), o jaquecas (*f.*)

heart: corazón (*m.*)

heart attack: ataque (*m.*) al corazón (*m.*), ataque cardíaco, infarto

heartbeat: latido (*m.*) del corazón

heartburn: agruras (*f.*), acidez (*f.*)

heart diseases: enfermedades (*f.*) del corazón (*m.*)

heart murmur: soplo del corazón (*m.*)

heat in the bladder: calor en la vejiga (*f.*)

heavy/painful breast: senos (*m.*) o pechos (*m.*) adoloridos/pesados

help (to): ayudar, aliviar

hematologist: hematólogo(a)

hematology: hematología (*f.*)

hemorrhoid: hemorroides (*f.*), almorranas (*f.*)

hepatitis A, B, C: hepatitis (*f.*) A, B, C

here: aquí, acá

hernia: hernia (*f.*)

herpes: herpes (*m.*)

hers: suyo(a)

high: alto(a)

hips: caderas (*f.*)

his: suyo(a)

histologist: histólogo(a)

hit (to): pegar

HIV: VIH (*m.*)

hives: urticaria (*f.*)

hoarse: ronco(a)

hoarseness: ronquera (*f.*)

home: casa (*f.*), hogar (*m.*)

home remedies: remedios (*m.*) caseros

homework: tarea (*f.*)

hormonal: hormonal

hormone treatment: tratamiento (*m.*) hormonal

hormones: hormonas (*f.*)

hospitalizations: hospitalizaciones (*f.*)

hospitalize (to): ingresar, internar

hot: calor (*m.*)

hot flashes: bochornos (*m.*), sofocos (*m.*)

hot sauce: salsa (*f.*) picante

hot water bottle: bolsa (*f.*) de agua caliente

hot water compresses: fomentos (*m.*) de agua caliente

house: casa (*f.*)

How?: ¿Cómo?

How do you feel?: ¿Cómo se siente?

How embarrassing!: ¡Qué pena!

How many?: ¿Cuántos(as)?

How much?: ¿Cuánto(a)?

How often?: ¿Cada cuándo?/¿Con que frecuencia?

hunger: hambre (*m.*)

hurt: lastimado(a)

hurt (to) (as in "It hurts me"): doler (ue)

husband: esposo (*m.*)

hydrocele: hidrocele (*f.*)

hymen: himen (*m.*)

hyper: acelerado(a)

hyperglycemia: hiperglucemia (*f.*)

hypertension: hipertensión (*f.*)

hypochondria: hipocondría (*f.*)

hypoglycemia: hipoglucemia (*f.*)

hysterectomy: histerectomía (*f.*)

hysteria: histeria (*f.*)

I.V.: suero (*m.*)

I'm very sorry.: Lo siento mucho.

ice: hielo (*m.*)

ice cream: helado (*m.*), mantecado (*m.*) (*Carib.*), nieve (*f.*) (*N. Mex.*)

ice pack: bolsa (*f.*) de hielo (*m.*)

identity: identidad (*f.*)

if: si

illicit drugs: drogas (*f.*)

illness: enfermedad (*f.*)

immunization: inmunización (*f.*), vacuna (*f.*)

immunize (to): inmunizar, vacunar

immunology: inmunología (f.)

impaction, obstruction (intestinal): empacho (m.)

importance: importancia (f.)

impotence: impotencia (f.)

in: en

in a little while: al rato

in front: frente (f.)

in order to: para

increase (to): aumentar

indicate (to): indicar

indication: indicación (f.)

indigestion: indigestión (f.), indigesto (m.)

induced abortion: aborto (m.) inducido, legrado (m.)

infarct: infarto (m.)

infect (to): infectar

infectious: infeccioso(a)

inflamed: inflamado(a)

inflamed eyelids: párpados (m.) inflamados

inflamed throat: garganta (f.) inflamada

inflammation: inflamación (f.)

inflammation of the thyroid gland: inflamación (f.) de la glándula tiroides

inflate (to): inflar

ingrown nail: uña (f.) enterrada

inject (to), give a shot (to): inyectar

injection: inyección (f.)

injured: lesionado(a)

inner ear, ear: oído (m.) (*Mex.*)

insert: introducir

insist (to): insistir

insistence: insistencia (f.)

insufficiency: insuficiencia (f.)

insulin: insulina (f.)

insurance: seguro (m.), aseguranza (slang) (f.)

intermittent: intermitente, va y viene

intestinal worms: lombrices (f.)

intravenous feeding: suero (m.), alimentación (f.) intravenosa

introduce (to): presentar

iridectomy: iridectomía (f.)

iris: iris (f.)

iritis: iritis (f.), inflamación de la iris

irregular: irregular

irregularities: irregularidades (f.)

irrigate (to): irrigar

irritation: irritación (f.)

Is there anything that alleviates the pain?: ¿Hay algo que alivia el dolor?

Is there anything that makes it feel better?: ¿Hay algo que le hace sentir mejor?, ¿Con qué se siente mejor?

Is there anything that makes it feel worse?: ¿Hay algo que le hace sentir peor?, ¿Con qué se siente peor?

Is there?/Are there?/There is/There are: ¿Hay?/Hay

is, it is: es

isolate (to): aislar

It comes and goes.: va y viene.

it just/it only: nada más, no más, sólamente, únicamente

it seems to me: me parece, se me hace

it's just that: nada más que, no más que

it's that: es que

itch: picazón (f.), comezón (f.)

IUD: dispositivo (m.), aparato (m.), DUI (*Cuba*)

January: enero

jar: frasco (m.)

jaundice: ictericia (f.), piel (f.) amarillenta

jet-lignite: azabache (m.)

joint: articulación (f.), coyuntura (f.)

juice: jugo (m.), zumo (m.)

July: julio

jumpy: acelerado(a)

June: junio

keep (to): guardar, mantener
kidney: riñón (*m.*)
kidney stones: cálculos (*m.*), piedras
    (*f.*) en los riñones (*m.*)
knee: rodilla (*f.*)
knife: cuchillo (*m.*)
knock (to): tocar
know (to): saber (facts), conocer
    (people or places)

lab tech: técnico(a)
labia: labios (*m.*) vaginales
laboratory: laboratorio (*m.*)
laceration: laceración (*f.*)
large: grande
large intestine: intestino (*m.*) grueso
laryngitis: laringitis (*f.*)
larynx: laringe (*f.*)
laser treatment: tratamiento del láser
    (*m.*)
last (to): durar
last night: anoche
last time: última (*f.*) vez
last week: semana (*f.*) pasada
late: tarde
later: luego, más tarde, después
laxative: laxante (*m.*)
learn (to): aprender
leave behind (to): dejar
leg: pierna (*f.*)
leg cramps: calambres (*m.*) en las
    piernas (*f.*)
lemon: limón (*m.*)
let's see: a ver
lettuce: lechuga (*f.*)
lie back, lie down (to): acostarse
    (*L. Am.*), tumbarse (*Sp.*)
ligaments: ligamentos (*m.*)
light: claro(a), luz
light (to): encender
light hair or skin: rubio(a), güero(a)
    (*Mex.*), chele (*m.*) (*El. Salv.*)
like, as if: como, como que
lime: lima (*f.*), limón (*Mex.*) (*m.*)

linden: tila (*f.*)
liniment: linimento (*m.*)
lips: labios (*m.*)
liquid: líquido (*m.*)
lisping: ceceo (*m.*)
listen (to): escuchar
little: pequeño(a), chico(a)
little one: pequeñito(a)
little window: ventanilla (*f.*)
live (to): vivir
liver: hígado (*m.*)
lobster: langosta (*f.*)
loin, i.e. pork loin: lomo (*m.*)
long (length): largo(a)
look for (to): buscar
look at (to): mirar
loose: flojo(a), suelto(a)
loose bowels: diarrea (*f.*), "estómago
    (*m.*) suelto," "chorro (*m.*)/chorrillo
    (*m.*)"
lose (to): perder
lose weight (to): bajar de peso (*m.*),
    perder peso
loss: pérdida (*f.*)
lotion: loción (*f.*)
love (to): querer (ie), amar
low: bajo(a)
lower (to): bajar
lozenges: trocitos (*m.*), pastillas (*f.*)
    para chupar
lubricate (to): lubricar, mojar
lump: bolita (*f.*), bulto (*m.*)
lung: pulmón (*m.*)
lung disease: enfermedad (*f.*) pulmonar

machine: máquina (*f.*)
macular degeneration: degeneración
    (*f.*) de la mácula (*f.*)
make (to): hacer (g)
malaria: malaria (*f.*), paludismo (*m.*)
males: machos (*m.*), varones (*m.*),
    hombres (*m.*)
man: hombre (*m.*)
manage (to): manejar

March: marzo
massage (to)/rub (to): masajear, dar un masaje (*m.*), sobar, frotar
maternity: maternidad (*f.*)
May: mayo
measles: sarampión (*m.*) o rubéola (*f.*)
measure (to): medir (i)
medical: médico(a)
medical doctor: médico (*m.*) (*f.*), doctor(a)
medical prescription: receta (*f.*) médica, prescripción (*f.*)
medication: medicamento (*m.*)
medicine: medicina (*f.*)
medicine man (woman): curandero(a), santero(a) (*Carib.*)
melted cheese in a tortilla: quesadilla (*f.*)
menopause: menopausia (*f.*), cambio (*m.*) de vida
menstrual cramps: cólicos (*m.*)
menstrual flow: flujo (*m.*) menstrual
menstrual period: regla (*f.*), período (*m.*), menstruación (*f.*), "mes" (*m.*)
mental illness: enfermedad (*f.*) mental
microscope: microscopio (*m.*)
migraine: migraña (*f.*)
mild rash: salpullido (*m.*), erupción (*f.*) en la piel (*f.*)
milk: leche (*f.*)
milliliter: mililitro (*m.*)
minimize (to): minimizar
mint (tea): yerba (*f.*) o hierba buena
mirror: espejo (*m.*)
miscarriages: malpartos (*m.*), abortos (*m.*) naturales o espontáneos
miss (to): faltar, perder (as in not attend or arrive)/extrañar (as in "I miss you")
moderate: así así, más o menos, moderado
moderately: así así, más o menos, regular
molar: molar (*m.*), muela (*f.*)
mole: lunar (*m.*)
moment: momento (*m.*)
money: dinero (*m.*)
mood, humor: humor (*m.*), estado de ánimo
more or less, sort of: más o menos
mortality: mortalidad (*f.*)
mortified, upset: mortificado(a)
mother: madre (*f.*)
mother-in-law: suegra (*f.*)
mothers (in general): madres (*f.*)
mouth: boca (*f.*)
move (to): mover
movie: película (*f.*), cine (*m.*)
movie theater: cine (*m.*)
mullein: gordolobo
mumps: paperas (*f.*), "bolas" (*f.*), "chanza" (*f.*)
museum: museo (*m.*)
must: deber
must, ought, owe (to): deber
myopic: miopía (*f.*)

nail: uña (*f.*)
name: nombre (*m.*)
nape: nuca (*f.*)
napkin: servilleta (*f.*)
narcotic: narcótico (*m.*)
nasal cavity: fosa (*f.*) nasal
nasal septum: tabique (*m.*)
natural fruit drinks made with water: aguas (*f.*) frescas
nausea: náusea (*f.*), asco (*m.*), basca (*f.*)
near sighted (myopic): miope (*m.*)
nebulizor: nebulizador (*m.*), tubito (*m.*)
neck: cuello (*m.*)
need (to): necesitar
needle: aguja (*f.*)
nephew: sobrino (*m.*)
nerve: nervio (*m.*)

nervous: estar nervioso(a), tener
    nervios
neurologist: neurólogo(a)
neurology: neurología (*f.*)
neurotic: neurótico(a)
never: nunca
niece: sobrina (*f.*)
night before last: antenoche
nipple: pezón (female) (*m.*), tetilla
    (male) (*f.*)
no longer: ya no
no wonder: con razón
nodule: nódulo (*m.*)
noise: ruido (*m.*)
normal: normal
Norplant®: implantes (*m.*), Norplan
nose: nariz (*f.*)
nostrils: ventanas (*f.*) de la nariz (*f.*),
    narices (*f.*)
not yet: todavía no
November: noviembre
now: ahora , ahorita, ya
numb: entumido(a), entumecido(a),
    adormedico(a)
nurse: enfermera(o)
nutritionist: nutricionista (*f.*) (*m.*),
    nutriólogo (a)

observe (to): observar
obstetrical: obstétrico(a)
October: octubre
octopus: pulpo (*m.*)
of, from: de
oily: grasoso(a)
oily skin (face): piel (*f.*) grasosa (cara)
ointment: ungüento (*m.*), pomada (*f.*)
older: mayor
olive oil: aceite (*m.*) de oliva
on: en
on one's back: boca arriba
on one's side: de lado
on one's stomach: boca abajo

**one that uses herbs for healing,
    herbalist:** yerbero(a), hierbero(a)
onion: cebolla (*f.*)
only/it's just that: solamente/nada
    más
open: abierto
open (to): abrir
operate (to): operar
operation: operación (*f.*), cirugía (*f.*)
ophthalmologist: oftalmólogo(a)
ophthalmology: oftalmología (*f.*)
or: o, ó
or, in other words: o sea
oral surgeon: cirujano(a) de la boca (*f.*)
orange: naranja (*f.*)
orange blossoms: flor de azahar (*f.*)
orbital cellulites: celulitis (*f.*) orbital
orthodontics: ortodoncia (*f.*)
others: otros(as)
otoscope: otoscopio (*m.*)
out loud: en voz alta
outer ear: oreja (*f.*)
ovary: ovario (*m.*)
over: sobre
overwhelmed: agobiado(a),
    acongojado(a), abrumado
owe (to), must, should: deber
oysters: ostras (*f.*), ostiones (*m.*)

pacifier: chupón (*m.*), bobo (*m.*) (*P.R.*)
pain (noun): dolor (*m.*)
pain or irritation in the eyes: dolor (*m.*)
    o irritación (*f.*) de los ojos (*m.*)
pain or pressure in the chest: dolor
    (*m.*) o presión (*f.*) en el pecho (*m.*)
painful/heavy breasts: senos (*m.*) o
    pechos (*m.*) adoloridos
painting: pintando(a)
palate: paladar (*m.*)
paleness, pale: palidez (*f.*), pálido(a)
palm: palma (*f.*)
palms down: palmas hacia abajo

palms up: palmas hacia arriba
palpate (to): palpar
palpitations: palpitaciones (*f.*)
pancreas: páncreas (*m.*)
paragraph: párrafo (*m.*)
parasites: parásitos (*m.*)
paregoric: paregórico
parents: padres (*m.*)
partial bridge (dental): puente (*m.*) removible
partner (business): socio(a)
partner (as in boy/girlfriend, husband/wife): pareja (*f.*)
pass (to): pasar
patch: parche (*m.*)
pathologist: patólogo(a)
pathology: patología (*f.*)
pay (to): pagar
peach: durazno (*m.*) (*Mex.*), melocotón (*m.*)
peanuts: cacahuates (*m.*) (*Mex.*), maní (*m.*) (*Carib.*), cacahuetes (*m.*) (*Sp.*)
pear: pera (*f.*)
peas: chícharos (*m.*) (*Mex.*), petit pois (*m.*) (*Carib. and C.A.*), guisantes (*m.*) (*Sp.*), arvejas (*f.*) (*S.Am.*)
pelvis: pelvis (*m.*)
pen: pluma (*f.*), bolígrafo (*m.*)
penicillin: penicilina (*f.*)
penis: pene (*m.*)
pepper: pimienta (*f.*)
per day: por día, al día
perforated eardrum: tambor (*m.*) o tímpano (*m.*) perforado/"roto"
period: regla (*f.*), período (*m.*), menstruación (*f.*)
periodontal: periodontal
peritonitis: peritonitis (*f.*)
persistent headaches: cefalgia (*f.*), cefalea (*f.*), dolores (*m.*) de cabeza persistentes

pharmacy: farmacia (*f.*)
pharyngitis: faringitis (*f.*)
phlegm: flema (*f.*)
phosphorous: fósforo (*m.*)
physical: físico(a)
physical build: complexión (*f.*)
physiological: fisiológico(a)
pie: pay (*Mex.*) (*m.*), tarta (*f.*)
piles: almorranas (*f.*), hemorroides (*f.*)
pill: píldora (*f.*), pastilla (*f.*)
pimples: granos (*m.*), granitos (*m.*), barros (*m.*)
pin (to): prender
pinch (to): pellizcar
pineapple: piña (*f.*), ananás (*f.*) (*Arg.*)
pink: rosa (*f.*), rosado (a)
pink-eye (conjunctivitus): conjuntivitis (*f.*)
pins: alfileres (*m.*)
plantain: plátano (*m.*) macho (*Mex.*), plátano (*m.*) (*Carib. and C.A.*)
plaster: yeso (*m.*), parche (*m.*)
play (an instrument) (to): tocar
play (to) (a game): jugar
please: por favor, favor de
pleurisy: pleuresía (*f.*)
pneumonia: neumonía (*f.*), pulmonía (*f.*)
point: punto (*m.*)
poisonous: ponzoñoso(a)
polio: poliomielitis (*f.*)
political: político(a)
polyps in the uterus: pólipos (*m.*), fibromas (*f.*) en la matriz (*f.*)
pomade: pomada (*f.*)
poor little one: pobrecito(a)
pore: poro (*m.*)
pork: puerco (*m.*)
potassium: potasio (*m.*)
potatoes: papas (*f.*) patatas (*f.*) (Sp)
pregnancy: embarazo (*m.*)
premature: prematuro(a)

preoccupied: preocupado(a)
prepare (to): preparar
presbyopia: prebiopia (*f.*)
prescribe (to): recetar
prescription: receta (*f.*)
pressure: presión (*f.*)
pressure in the chest: dolor (*m.*) o
  presión (*f.*) en el pecho (*m.*)
pressure or tightness in the chest:
  dolor (*m.*) o presión (*m.*) en el
  pecho (*m.*)
problems: problemas (*m.*), molestias
  (*f.*)
produce (to): producir (z)
prolapse of the uterus: caída de la
  matriz (*f.*)
prostrate: próstata (*f.*)
protect (to): proteger
proteins: protéinas (*f.*)
psychologist: psicólogo(a), sicólogo(a)
psychotic: sicótico(a), psicótico(a)
ptosis: ptosis/caída de párpado (*m.*)
pubic hair: vello (*m.*)
pubic lice: piojos (*m.*) púbicos (*m.*)
pull (to): jalar, halar
pulled muscle or torn ligament:
  desgarre (*m.*)
pulmonary edema: edema (*f.*)
  pulmonar
pulsating: pulsativo(a)
pulse: pulso (*m.*)
pumpkin: calabaza (*f.*)
pupil: pupila (*f.*), niña (*f.*) del ojo (*m.*)
purgative: purgante (*m.*)
purple: morado(a), púrpura
put (to): poner (g)
put a cast on (to): enyesar
put on a splint (to): entablillar

quantity: cantidad (*f.*)

radiation treatment: radiaciones (*f.*)
radiology: radiología (*f.*)

raise (to), lift (to): levantar
rapid: rápido(a)
rash: ronchas (*f.*), erupciones (*f.*)
rash (mild), heat rash: salpullido (*m.*) /
  sarpullido (*m.*)
raw (a little): crudo(a)
**raw fish in a tomato base, "cooked" in
  limes in the sun:** ceviche (*m.*)
reaction: reacción (*f.*)
read (to): leer
receding: retrocediendo
receptionist: recepcionista (*f.*) (*m.*)
reconstruct (to): reconstruir
rectum: recto (*m.*)
recuperation: recuperación (*f.*)
red (color): rojo(a)
red snapper: huachinango (*m.*), pargo
  (*m.*)
reddening: enrojecimiento (*m.*)
redness: enrojecimiento (*m.*)
regular: regular, normal
relax (to): relajar, relajarse, aflojar,
  aflojarse
relaxation: relajación (*f.*)
relieve (to): aliviar
remain (to): quedar, quedarse
remember (to): recordar, acordarse
remove (to): quitar, quitarse
resist (to): resistir
respond (to): responder
rest: descanso (*m.*)
rest (to): descansar
result: resultado (*m.*)
result (to): resultar
retinal artery (vein) occlusion:
  oclusión de la arteria (*f.*)/vena (*f.*)
  retinal
return (to): regresar, volver
rheumatic fever: fiebre (*f.*) reumática
rheumatic heart: reumatismo (*m.*) del
  corazón (*m.*)
rhythm method: método (*m.*) del
  ritmo (*m.*)

rib: costilla (f.)
rice: arroz (m.)
rice and milk dessert/rice pudding: arroz (m.) con leche (m.)
rich, delicious: rico(a)
ring: anillo (m.)
ringing in th ears: tintineo (m.), zumbido (m.)
rinse (to): rociar, enjuagar
ripe: maduro(a)
root canal: endodoncia (f.), extraer (sacar) el nervio, tratamiento (m.) de conductos
rose (tea): rosa de Castillo (f.)
rub (to): frotar, sobar, masajear
rubber dam (dental): hule (m.) protector
rubella: sarampión (m.), rubéola (f.)
rue (tea): ruda (f.)
run (to): correr
runny nose: nariz (f.) suelta

sacrum bones: huesos (m.) del sacro (m.)
sad: triste
sage: salvia (f.)
saliva: saliva (f.)
salivation: sialorrea (f.), mucha saliva (f.)
salt: sal (f.)
sample: muestra (f.)
sauce for chicken (made of chocolate, peanuts, and chiles): mole (m.)
save (a life) (to): salvar
scabies: sarna (f.)
scale: báscula (f.), balanza (f.)
scalp: cuero (m.) cabelludo
scar: cicatriz (f.)
scarlet fever: fiebre (f.) de escarlatina
schizophrenic: esquizofrénico(a)
scleritis: escleritis (f.)
scratch: rasguña (f.)
scratch (to): rascar

scrawny: raquítico(a)
scrotum: escroto (m.)
scurvy: escorbuto(a)
seal's bark: tos de perro (dog's cough (lit))
seat (to): sentar, sentarse
sebaceous glands: glándulas (f.) sebáceas
second: segundo(a)
secretion: secreción (f.)
sedative: sedante (m.)
see (to): ver
seizures: ataques (m.), convulsiones (f.)
sell (to): vender
senility: senilidad (f.)
separate (to): separar
September: se(p)tiembre
serious: serio(a)
service: servicio (m.)
sexuality: sexualidad (f.)
shark: tiburón (m.)
sharp: agudo(a), punzante
shave oneself (to): afeitarse, rasurarse
shelf: repisa (f.)
shellfish: mariscos (m.)
short (height): bajo(a)
short (length): corto(a)
shortness of breath: falta de respiración (f.), dificultad (f.) al respirar
shot: inyección (f.)
should, must, ought, owe (to): deber (m.)
shoulder: hombro (m.)
show (to): mostrar, enseñar, señalar
shrimp: camarón (m.)
siblings: hermano(a)(s)
sick: enfermo(a)
sign (to): firmar
signature: firma (f.)
sinus: seno (m.)
sinusitis: sinusitis (f.)

sister: hermana (*f.*)
sister-in-law: cuñada (*f.*)
sit (oneself) (to): sentarse
sit down (to): sentarse
sit up (to): sentarse
sitz bath: baño (*m.*) de asiento (*m.*)
skeleton: esqueleto (*m.*)
skin: piel (*f.*)
skin complexion: cutis (*m.*), tez (*f.*)
skinny: flaco(a),
slap (to): bofetear (*Carib.*), cachetear
(*Mex.*)
sleep (to): dormir(ue)
sleepy: tener sueño
slightly: poco(a)
slim: delgado(a)
slow: lento(a)
small: pequeño(a), chico(a)
small intestine: intestino (*m.*) delgado
small pox: viruela (*f.*)
smile: sonrisa (*f.*)
smoke (noun): humo (*m.*)
smoke (to): fumar
smoothie: licuado (*m.*) (*Mex.*), batida
(*f.*) (*Carib.*), batido (*m.*) (*C.A.*)
so much: tanto
social worker: trabajador(a) social
sodium: sodio (*m.*)
soft drink: soda (*f.*) refresco (*m.*), fresco
(*m.*) (*C.A.*)
sole fish: lenguado (*m.*)
solution: solución (*f.*)
some: algunos(as), unos(as)
somewhat depressed: un poco
deprimido(a), triste, agüitado(a)
(*Mex.*), achicopalado(a) (*Carib.*)
son (daughter): hijo(a)
son-in-law: yerno (*m.*)
sore: llaga (*f.*)
sore throat: garganta inflamada (*f.*)
soup: sopa (*f.*), caldo (*m.*)
sour: agrio(a)
Spanish: español (*m.*)

spasm: espasmo (*m.*)
spasmodic: espasmódico(a)
spasms: espasmos (*m.*)
speak (to): hablar
special: especial
speculum: espéculo (*m.*), pato (*m.*)
speedometer: velocímetro (*m.*)
spend (to): gastar (as in money), pasar
(as in time)
sphincter: esfínter (*m.*)
spilling of bile: derrame (*m.*) de bilis
spinach: espinacas (*f.*)
spinal column: columna (*f.*) vertebral
spirit: espíritu (*m.*)
spit (to): escupir
spleen: bazo (*m.*)
sponge: esponja (*f.*)
spouse: esposo(a)
sprain: torcedura (*f.*), "falseado" (as in
"me falseé")
squash: calabaza (*f.*)
squeeze (to): apretar (ie)
**stabbing like a blade or knife (shooting
pains):** punzante como una navaja
(*f.*) o cuchillo (*m.*)
stale: seco(a), viejo(a)
stammer (to): tartamudear
stand (to): parar(se)
STDs (STIs): enfermedades (*f.*)
venéreas
steak, minute steak: bistec (*m.*)
sterility: esterilidad (*f.*)
sterilization: esterilización (*f.*)
sterilize (to): esterilizar
stethoscope: estetoscopio (*m.*)
stew: guisado (*m.*)
stick (to): pegar
stiff neck: tortícolis (*f.*), "cuello tieso"
(*m.*)
still: todavía
still born: nacido muerto
stitches: puntos (*m.*) o puntadas (*f.*)
stomach: estómago (*m.*)

stomach gas: gases (*m.*) en el estómago
stool: excremento (*m.*)
stop (to): parar, dejar de
stop smoking: dejar de fumar
straight ahead: derecho
strawberry: fresa (*f.*)
straws: popotes (*m.*) (*Mex.*), pajillas (*f.*)
street: calle (*f.*)
stretch marks: estrías (*f.*)
strike (to): golpear, pegar
string beans: ejotes (*m.*) (*Mex.*), judías verdes (*f.*) (*Sp.*), habichuelas verdes (*f.*) (*Cuba*)
stroke: embolia (*f.*)
strong: fuerte
structure: estructura (*f.*)
study (to): estudiar
stuffed-up nasally: nariz (*f.*) tapada, mormado(a), nariz tupida (*Carib.*)
stutter (to): tartamudear
sty: orzuelo (*m.*), "perrilla" (*f.*) (*Mex.*)
suck (to): chupar
sudden mood swings or changes: cambio de humor (estado de ánimo) de repente
suddenly: de repente, repentinamente
suffer (to): sufrir
suffer from (to): padecer (z), sufrir de
sugar: azúcar (*f.*)(*m.*)
suggest (to): sugerir
suitcase: maleta (*f.*), velis (*m.*) (*Mex.*), petaca (*f.*) (*Mex.*)
sulfa: sulfa (*f.*)
suppository: supositorio (*m.*)
surgery: cirugía (*f.*)
surprised: sorprendido(a), admirado(a)
svelte: esbelto(a)
swallow (to): tragar o pasar saliva (*f.*)
sweats: sudores (*m.*)
sweet: dulce (*m.*)
sweet rolls (Danish): pan (*m.*) (de) dulce

swelling: hinchazón (*f.*)
swim (to): nadar
swollen: hinchado(a)
swollen glands: glándulas (*f.*) inflamadas
swollen glands (in groin): incordio (*m.*), encordio (*m.*)
swollen spleen: bazo (*m.*) inflamado/hinchado
syphilis: sífilis (*f.*), "sangre mala" (*f.*)
syringe: jeringa (*f.*)
syrup: jarabe (*m.*), sirope (*m.*)

table: mesa (*f.*)
table cloth: mantel (*m.*)
tablespoon: cucharada (*f.*)
tablet: tableta (*f.*)
tableware/utensils: cubiertos (*m.*)
taco: taco (*m.*)
take (to): tomar
take care of (to): cuidar
take off (to): quitar, quitarse
Take off or remove your clothing. (command): Quítese la ropa. (*f.*)
take out (to): sacar (also for taking photos or X-rays)
take someone (or something) somewhere (to): llevar
talk (to): hablar
tall: alto(a)
tapeworm: lombriz (*f.*) solitaria
tartar: sarro (*m.*)
tea: té (*m.*)
tear duct: conducto (*m.*) lacrimógeno, lacrimal, lagrimal
technician: técnico(a)
teeth: dientes (*m.*), muelas (*f.*) (*slang*)
telephone: teléfono (*m.*)
temperature: temperatura (*f.*)
tenderness in the breasts: senos/pechos (*m.*) adoloridos
terminate (to), end (to): terminar
test (to): probar

testicles: testículos (*m.*), "bolas" (*f.*),
    "huevos" (*m.*), "talagas" (*f.*) (*last
    three slang*)
tests: pruebas (*f.*)
texture: textura (*f.*)
That's good!: ¡Qué bueno!
That's why: Por eso
the bill, the account: cuenta (*f.*)
the last time: la última vez
the other day: el otro día
then (in a series), later: luego
then/and so: entonces
therapeutic abortion: aborto (*m.*)
    inducido, legrado (*m.*)
therapy: terapia (*f.*)
there: allí, allá
there is, there are: hay
thermometer: termómetro (*m.*)
these problems: estos problemas (*m.*)
thigh: muslo (*m.*)
thin: delgado(a)
think (to): pensar
thinking to oneself: pensando a solas
third: tercer(o)(a)
thirst: sed (*f.*)
thorax: tórax (*m.*), pecho (*m.*)
throat: garganta (*f.*)
throbbing: pulsativo(a)
thrombosis: trombosis (*f.*)
through: por
thrush: algodoncillo (*m.*)
thus, thusly, like this: así
thyroid gland: glándula (*f.*) tiroides
tight: apretado(a)
tightness in the chest: dolor (*m.*) o
    presión (*f.*) en el pecho (*m.*)
time: hora (*f.*), tiempo (*m.*)
time (sequence): vez
times (series): veces
tingling: hormigueo (*m.*)
tip: propina (*f.*)
tiptoes: puntas (*f.*) del pie
tired: cansado(a)

tired eyes, eye strain: ojos (*m.*)
    cansados/ fatigados
tissues: tejidos (*m.*)
to: a
to the left: a la izquierda
to the right: a la derecha
to tie the tubes/tubal ligation: amarrar
    los tubos/ligar las trompas
today: hoy
toilet: excusado (*m.*) (*Mex.*), inodoro
    (*m.*)
tomato: tomate (*m.*), jitomate (*m.*)
    (*Mex. City and S. Mex*)
tomorrow morning: mañana por la
    mañana (*f.*)
tongue: lengua (*f.*)
tongue depressor: depresor (*m.*),
    depressor de lengua
tonic: tónico (*m.*)
tonsillitis: amigdalitis (*f.*), tonsilitis (*f.*)
tonsils: amígdalas (*f.*) o anginas (*f.*)
too much: demasiado(a)
too, also: también
toothache: dolor de diente (*m.*), muela
    (*f.*)
toothbrush: cepillo (*m.*) de dientes
    (*m.*)
torn ligament "pulled muscle":
    desgarre (*m.*), ligamento (*m.*) roto
torsion, twisting of testicles: torsión (*f.*)
    de los testículos (*m.*)
tortilla (flour or corn): tortilla (*f.*)
touch (to): tocar
toward the back: hacia atrás
towards: hacia
towel: toalla (*f.*)
tranquilizers: tranquilizantes (*m.*),
    calmantes (*m.*)
traquea: tráquea (*f.*)
treat (to): tratar
try on (to): probar
tubal ligation: ligadura (*f.*) de trompas
    (*f.*)

tuberculosis, T.B.: tuberculosis (*f.*),
"tisis," "tis"
tumor: tumor (*m.*)
turkey: pavo (*m.*), guajolote (*m.*)
(*Mex.*), guanajo (*m.*) (*Cuba*)
turn (command form): dé vuelta
turn (to) (as in walking or driving):
dar vuelta, doblar
turn around (to), turn over (to) (when
lying down): voltear , voltearse
turn on (lights) (to): encender, prender
tush: pompis (*f.*)
twist (to): torcer, descoyuntar, dislocar,
desconcertar
twist or sprain (noun): torcedura (*f.*)
two days ago (lit., it makes two days):
hace dos días
typhoid: tifoidea (*f.*)

uh, um: em
ulcers: úlceras (*f.*)
umbilical cord: cordón (*m.*) umbilical
umbilicus: ombligo (*m.*)
uncle: tío (*m.*)
uncomfortable: incómodo (a)
unconscious (to be): perder el
conocimiento
understand (to): entender (ie),
comprender
Undress (command): Desvístase,
Quítese la ropa.
uneasy, restless: inquieto(a)
university: universidad (*f.*)
upon finishing: al terminar
upon getting up: al levantarse
upset: mortificado(a), molesto(a)
upset stomach: estómago (*m.*) revuelto
(*m.*)
urether: uréter (*m.*)
urethra: uretra (*f.*)
urinary tract infection: infección de la
vía orinaria, mal de orin (*m.*),
chistata (*Nica.*)

urinate (to): orinar
urine: orina (*f.*)
urologist: urólogo(a)
urology: urología (*f.*)
use (to): usar, utilizar
uterus: útero (*m.*), matriz (*f.*)

vaccinate (to): vacunar
vagina: vagina (*f.*)
valley fever, coccidioidomycosis:
fiebre (*f.*) del valle,
coccidioidomicosis
variation: variante (*f.*)
varicocele: varicocele (*f.*)
varicose veins: venas (*f.*) varicosas,
várices (*f.*)
vas deferens: vaso (*m.*) deferente
vasectomy: vasectomía (*f.*)
vegetables: vegetales (*m.*), verduras
(*f.*), legumbres (*f.*)
vein: vena (*f.*)
veneers (dental): frentes (*m.*) estéticos
venereal disease, STDs, STIs:
enfermedades (*f.*) venéreas
very good: muy bien
vessel: vaso (*m.*)
visit (to): visitar
vitamins: vitaminas (*f.*)
vomit: vómito (*m.*)
vomit (to): vomitar
vomiting: estar vomitando, tener
vómitos (*m.*)

waist: cintura (*f.*)
waiter, waitress, or server: mesero(a)
walk (to): caminar, andar
walker: andadera (*f.*)
want (to): querer (ie)
wash (to): lavar
wash oneself (to): lavarse
waste (to): gastar
watch over (to): vigilar
water: agua (*f., use "el" in the singular*)

watermelon: sandía (*f.*)
watery eyes: ojos (*m.*) llorosos
weak: débil
wean (to): destetar
wear (to): llevar, llevar puesto, usar
weigh (to): pesar
weight, a coin: peso (*m.*)
well: bueno, pues, entonces
wet (to): mojar
what?: ¿qué?
wheeze (to): respirar con
    silbidos/chiflidos (*m.*)
wheezing: respirando con silbidos
    (*m.*)/chiflidos (*m.*)
when: cuando
when or upon going to bed: al acostarse
when?: ¿cuándo?
where?: ¿dónde?
which one(s)?: ¿cuál(es)?
which?: ¿cuál?
white: blanco(a)
who?: ¿quién?
whooping cough: tosferina (*f.*), tos
    ferina (*f.*), "coqueluche"
why?: ¿por qué?
wife: esposa (*f.*)
window: ventana (*f.*)
wisdom tooth: muela (*f.*) del juicio

with: con
withdrawal (coitus interrupts): "Mi
    esposo me cuida." (*slang*)
without: sin
witness: testigo(a)
woman: mujer (*f.*)
work (to): trabajar
Worm Seed: epazote
wounded: herido(a)
wrinkles: arrugas (*f.*)
wrist: muñeca (*f.*)
write (to): escribir

X-rays: rayos X (*m.*), radiografías (*f.*),
    placas (*f.*)

yeast infection: infección (*f.*) por
    hongos (*m.*)
yellow: amarillo(a)
yes: sí
yesterday: ayer
You can get dressed now: Puede
    vestirse ahora, Se puede vestir
    ahora.
young: joven (m,f)
younger: menor
yours: suyo(a)(s)
youth: joven (*m., f.*)

Spanish-English Glossary

a: to, at

a continuación: the following

a la derecha: to the right

a la izquierda: to the left

¿A qué edad?: At what age?

a ver: let's see

abdomen (*m.*): abdomen

abierto: open (as in, "The door is open.")

aborto (*m.*): abortion

aborto (*m.*) **inducido, legrado** (*m.*): elective, induced or therapeutic abortion

abril: April

abrir: open (to)

absceso (*m.*)**, postema** (*f.*): abscess

abuelo(a): grandfather (grandmother)

aceite (*m.*) **de olivo/oliva:** olive oil

acelerado(a): hyper, jumpy

acidez (*f.*): acidity, heartburn

acné (*m.*): acne

acongojado(a): overwhelmed

acostarse: lie back, down (to)

actividad (*f.*): activity

adenoides (*m.*): adenoids

admirado(a): admired, surprised

adormecido(a): numb, sleepy

adrenalina (*f.*): adrenaline

afeitarse: shave oneself (to)

agarrar: grab (to)

agosto: August

agotado(a): exhausted

agotamiento (*m.*): exhaustion

agrandamiento del riñón (*m.*)**/hígado** (*m.*): enlargement of the kidney/liver

agrietarse, "rajarse": chap (to)

agrio(a): sour

agruras (*f.*)**, acidez** (*f.*): heart burn, acidity

agua (*f.*, use "el" in the singular): water

aguas (*f.*) **frescas:** natural fruit drinks made with water

agudo(a): sharp

agüitado(a) (*Mex.*)**, achicopalado(a)** (*Carib.*): somewhat depressed, down, feeling blah

aguja (*f.*): needle

ahogarse, "atragantarse," "dar al galillo": choke (to)

ahora, ahorita, ya: now

aislar: isolate (to)

ajá: aha

ajo (*m.*): garlic

al acostarse: upon going to bed, when going to bed

al levantarse: upon getting up

al rato: in a little while

al terminar: upon finishing

alcanfor: camphor (tea, lotion)

alegre: happy

alergia (*f.*)**, coriza** (*f.*) (*Cuba*): allergy

alfileres (*m.*): pins

algodoncillo: thrush

algun(a): any
**¿Alguna vez ha sufrido de (ha tenido) .
. . ?:** Have you ever had . . . ?
algunos(as): some
alimentar: feed (to)
alimento (*m.*)**:** food
aliviar, ayudar: alleviate (to), help (to)
allí o allá: there
almejas (*f.*)**:** clams
almorranas (*f.*)**:** piles, hemorrhoid
alrededor (de): around
alto(a): high, tall
alucinación (*f.*)**:** hallucination
amalgama (*f.*)**, relleno** (*m.*)**:** filling
amargo(a): bitter
amarillo(a): yellow
amarrar los tubos: to tie the tubes
ambos pulmones (*m.*) **afectados:** both
    lungs affected
amenorrea (*f.*)**, (ausencia de
    menstruación):** amenorrhea
amibas (*f.*) **o amoebas** (*f.*)**:** amoebas
amígdalas (*f.*) **o anginas** (*f.*)**:** tonsils
amigdalitis (*f.*)**:** tonsillitis
amigo(a): friend
ampolla (*f.*)**:** blister
amputar: amputate (to)
analgésico (*m.*)**:** analgesic
análisis (*m.*)**:** analysis
andadera (*f.*)**:** walker
anemia (*f.*)**:** anemia or problems related
    to the blood
angustia (*f.*)**:** anguish
angustiado(a): anguished
anillo (*m.*)**:** clamp (dental), ring
ano (*m.*)**:** anus
año (*m.*)**:** year
anoche: last night
ansiedad (*f.*)**:** anxiety
ansioso(a): anxious
anteayer (antier): day before yesterday
antebrazo (*m.*)**:** forearm

antenoche: night before last
antes (de): before
antiácido (*m.*)**:** antacid
antibiótico (*m.*)**:** antibiotic
antídoto (*m.*)**:** antidote
antihistamínico (*m.*)**:** antihistamine
apenado(a): embarrassed
apéndice (*m.*)**, "tripita"** (*f.*)**:** appendix
aplicador (*m.*)**:** applicator
aplicar: apply (to)
aprender: learn (to)
apretado(a): tight
apretar: squeeze (to)
aquí, acá: here
ardor (*m.*)**:** burning/stinging
ardor al orinar, "quemazón": burning
    sensation when (upon) urinating
arroz (*m.*)**:** rice
arroz (*m.*) **con leche** (*m.*)**:** rice
    pudding
arrugas (*f.*)**:** wrinkles
arteria (*f.*)**:** artery
articulación (*f.*)**, coyuntura** (*f.*)**:** joint
artritis (*f.*)**:** arthritis
arvejas (*f.*)**:** peas
así: thus, thusly, like this
asistir a: attend (to), (a meeting, a
    course)
asma (*m.*)**:** asthma
aspirina (*f.*)**:** aspirin
astigmatismo (*m.*)**:** astigmatism
asustado(a): frightened
ataque (*m.*) **al corazón** (*m.*)**, ataque
    cardíaco, infarto** (*m.*)**:** heart
    attack
ataque cardíaco, ataque (*m.*) **al
    corazón** (*m.*)**, infarto** (*m.*)**:** heart
    attack
ataques (*m.*)**, convulsiones** (*f.*)**:**
    seizures
atónito(a): astonished/in shock
atrofia (*f.*)**:** atrophy

atropina (*f.*): atropine
audiología (*f.*): audiology
aumentar: increase (to)
autorización (*f.*): authorization
avergonzado(a): ashamed
aves (*f.*): fowl
axila (*f.*): arm pit
ayer: yesterday
ayudar, aliviar: help (to), relieve (to)
azabache (*m.*): jet-lignite
azúcar(*m., f.*): sugar
azul: blue

bacteriología (*f.*): bacteriology
bacteriólogo(a): bacteriologist
baile (*m.*): dance
bajar: descend (to), get out or off (to), to lower
bajar de peso (*m.*): lose weight (to)
bajo(a): low, short
bañarse: bathe oneself (to)
baño (*m.*) **de asiento** (*m.*): sitz bath
barbilla (*f.*), **mentón** (*m.*): chin
barbitúricos (*m.*): barbiturates
báscula (*f.*): scale
bazo (*m.*): spleen
bazo (*m.*) **inflamado/hinchado:** swollen/inflamed spleen
beber: drink (to)
bebidas (*f.*): beverages
bebidas (*f.*) **alcohólicas:** alcoholic beverages
belladona (*f.*): belladonna
bicarbonato (*m.*): bicarbonate
bifocales (*m.*): bifocals
biología (*f.*): biology
biológico(a): biological
biólogo(a): biologist
biopsia (*f.*): biopsy
bistec (*m.*): steak, minute steak
bizco(a): cross-eyed

blanco(a): white
blenorragia (*f.*), **purgación** (*f.*): blennorrhagia
boca (*f.*): mouth
boca abajo: on one's stomach
boca arriba: on one's back
bochornos (*m.*), **sofocos** (*m.*): hot flashes
bocio (*m.*), "**buche**" (*m.*): goiter
bofetear (*Carib.*), **cachetear** (*Mex.*): slap (to)
bolita (*f.*), **bulto** (*m.*): lump
bolsa (*f.*) **de agua caliente:** hot water bottle
bolsa (*f.*) **de hielo** (*m.*): ice pack
bonding (dental): bonding
borraja: borage (tea)
brazo (*m.*): arm
bromuro (*m.*): bromide
bronquio (*m.*): bronchium
bronquitis (*f.*): bronchitis
bueno(a), bien: good
bursitis (*f.*): bursitis
buscar: look for (to)

cabeza (*f.*): head
cacahuates (*m.*), **maní** (*m.*) (*Carib.*), **cacahuetes** (*m.*) (*Sp.*): peanuts
¿Cada cuándo?, ¿Con qué frecuencia?: How often?
cadera (*f.*): hip
caerse (g): fall (to)
café (*m.*): brown, coffee
caída de la matriz (*f.*): prolapse of the uterus
calabaza (*f.*): squash, pumpkin, gourd
calambres (*m.*): cramps (muscle)
calambres (muscle) (*m.*), **cólicos (period)** (*m.*): cramps
calcio (*m.*): calcium
cálculos (*m.*) **piedras** (*f.*) **en los riñones** (*m.*): kidney stones

cálculos (*m.*) **o piedras** (*f.*) **en la vesícula biliar:** gallstones
calle (*f.*): street
callos (*m.*), **callos** (*m.*) **blandos:** corns, soft corns
calor (*m.*): heat
calvicie (*f.*): baldness
calvo (*m.*), **sin pelo, "el pelón":** bald, hairless
camarón (*m.*): shrimp
cambiar: change (to)
cambio (*m.*): change
cambio de humor de repente, cambio de estado de ánimo: sudden mood swings or changes
cambio (*m.*) **de vida** (*f.*): change of life
caminar: walk (to)
cáncer (*m.*): cancer
canceroso(a): cancerous
cansado(a): tired
cantidad (*f.*): quantity
cápsula (*f.*): capsule
cara (*f.*): face
carbohidratos (*m.*): carbohydrates
cardiología (*f.*): cardiology
cardiólogo(a): cardiologist
caries (*m.*), **dientes** (*m.*) **podridos, picaduras** (*f.*): cavities
caro(a): expensive
carro (*m.*): car
carta (*f.*), **gráfico(a)** (*m., f.*): eye chart
casa (*f.*): house
caspa (*f.*): dandruff
casualidad (*f.*)**/por casualidad:** casualty/by chance, by accident
cataratas (*f.*): cataracts
catarro (*m.*) **o resfriado** (*m.*) **en el pecho** (*m.*): chest cold
causar: cause (to)
cauteloso(a): cautious
cebolla (*f.*): onion
ceceo (*m.*): lisping

cefalgia (*f.*), **cefalea** (*f.*), **dolores** (*m.*) **de cabeza persistentes:** persistent headaches
ceja (*f.*): eyebrow
células (*f.*): cells
celulitis (*f.*) **orbital:** orbital cellulitis
cepillo (*m.*) **de dientes** (*m.*): tooth brush
cera (*f.*), **cerumen** (*m.*), **cerilla** (*f.*): ear wax
cerebro (*m.*): brain
cerrar: close (to)
cerveza (*f.*): beer
cesárea (*f.*): cesarean
ceviche (*m.*): raw fish in a tomato base, "cooked" in limes in the sun
chancro (*m.*), **grano** (*m.*): chancre
charlar, platicar (Mex): chat (to)
chele (*m.*): light hair or skin (*El Sal, Nica.*)
chícharos (*m.*) (*Mex.*), **guisantes** (*Sp.*), **petit pois** (*m.*) (*Carib. and C.A.*): peas
chile (*m.*), **ají** (*m.*) (*Carib.*): chile
chocar: crash (to)
chuleta (*f.*): chop, i.e. pork chop
chupar: suck (to)
chupón (*m.*), **bobo** (*m.*) (*P.R.*): pacifier
cianosis, "piel azulada": cyanosis
cicatriz (*f.*): scar
ciego(a): blind
cierto(a)(s): certain
cilantro (*m.*): coriander (tea)
cine (*m.*): movie
cintura (*f.*): waist, lower back (*N. Mex.*)
circular: cycle (to), circulate (to)
circuncisión (*f.*): circumcision
cirugía (*f.*): surgery
cirujano(a): surgeon
cita (*f.*): appointment, date
citología (*f.*): cytology
citólogo(a): cytologist

clamidia (*f.*) o chlamydia: chlamydia
claro(a): light, clear
clavícula (*f.*): clavicle
clítoris (*m.*): clitoris
cloasma (*f.*): chloasma
codeína (*f.*): codeine
codo (*m.*): elbow
colágeno (*m.*): collagen
colesterol (*m.*): cholesterol
cólico (*m.*): colic
cólicos (*m.*): menstrual cramps
coliflor (*f.*): cauliflower
colitis (*f.*): colitis
columna (*f.*) vertebral: spinal column
comadre (*f.*): friend, relationship
    between godchild's parent and
    godmother
comenzar, empezar: begin (to)
comenzó, empezó: began
    (Ud./he/she/it)
comer: eat (to)
comezón (*f.*), picazón (*f.*): itching
¿cómo?: how?
como que: like, as if
¿Cómo se siente?: How do you feel?
complexión (*f.*): physical build
complicación (*f.*): complication
comprar: buy (to)
comprender, entender (ie): understand
    (to)
con: with
con permiso (*m.*): excuse me (when
    leaving room)
con razón: no wonder
condones (*m.*), preservativos (*m.*),
    hules (*m.*): condoms, prophylactics,
    rubbers
conducto (*m.*) lacrimal/conductos (*m.*)
    lacrimógenos: tear duct(s)
confundido(a): confused
congelar: freeze (to)
congestión (*f.*): congestion

conjuntivitis (*f.*): conjunctivitis, pink
    eye
constante, fijo (*Carib.*): constant
consultar: consult (to)
consultorio (*m.*): Doctors or dentist
    office
contagiar: become infected (to)
contagioso(a): contagious
contaminar: contaminate (to)
contar (ue): count (to)
contento(a): content/happy
continuar: continue (to)
contracepción (*f.*): contraception
controlar: control (to)
contusión (*f.*), golpe (*m.*): contusion
convalecencia (*f.*): convalescence
converser: talk (to), converse (to)
convulsiones (*f.*), ataques (*m.*):
    convulsions
corazón (*m.*): heart
cordón (*m.*) umbilical: umbilical cord
córnea (*f.*): cornea
coroiditis (*f.*): choroiditis
corona (*f.*): crown
correr: run (to)
cortada (*f.*): cut (noun)
cortar: cut (to)
cortisona (*f.*): cortisone
corto(a): short (length)
corvo (*m.*), cascorvo (*m.*), "zambo"
    (*m.*): bow-legged
costilla (*f.*): rib
cráneo (*m.*): cranium
creer: believe (to)
crema (*f.*): cream
crónico(a): chronic
crudo(a): raw (a little)
cuadra (*f.*): block (street)
¿cuál?: which?
¿cuál(es)?: which ones?
cuando: when
¿cuándo?: when?

¿**cuánto(a)?**: how much?

¿**cuántos(as)?**: how many?

cubiertos (*m.*): tableware, utensils

cubrir: cover (to)

cuchara (*f.*): spoon (table)

cucharada (*f.*): tablespoonful

cucharadita (*f.*): teaspoonful, dessert spoonful

cucharita (*f.*): teaspoon, dessert spoon

cuchillo (*m.*): knife

cuello (*m.*): neck

cuenta (*f.*): bill, the account

cuero (*m.*) **cabelludo**: scalp

cuidar: care for (to)/take care of (to)

cuñada (*f.*): sister-in-law

cuñado (*m.*): brother-in-law

curandero(a), santero(a) (*Carib.*): medicine man (woman), (folk) healer

curar: cure (to)

cutis (*m.*), **tez** (*f.*): skin complexion

daltónico(a), daltonismo (*m.*): color blind

dañar: harm (to)

dar: give (to)

dar pecho (*m.*), **amamantar**: breast feed (to)

de: of, from

de frente: from the front

de lado: on one's side

de repente, repentinamente: suddenly

de uso extendido: extended wear

dé vuelta: Turn! (command)

deber: must , should, owe (to)

dedo (*m.*): finger

defecar: defecate (to)

defecto (*m.*) **congénito del corazón**: congenital heart defect

degeneración (*f.*) **de la mácula** (*f.*): macular degeneration

dejar: leave behind (to)

dejar de fumar: stop or quit smoking

delgado(a): thin, slim

delicioso(a), sabroso(a), rico(a): delicious

demasiado(a): too much

dentadura (*f.*) **completa**: full denture

depresión (*f.*), **estar triste**: depression

depresor (*m.*): tongue depressor

deprimido(a): depressed

derecho: straight ahead

dermatistis (*f.*): dermatitis

dermatología (*f.*): dermatology

dermatólogo(a): dermatologist

derrame (*m.*) **de bilis**: spilling of bile

descansar: rest (to)

descanso (*m.*): rest, break

desconectar: disconnect (to)

desde: from, since

desear: desire (to)

desechable: disposable

desecho (*m.*), **secreción** (*f.*): discharge

desgarre (*m.*): torn ligament, "pulled muscle"

desinfectar: disinfect (to)

desmayar: faint (to)

desmayos (*m.*): fainting spells

después: afterwards, later, then

después de: after

destetar: wean (to)

destino (*m.*): destination, destiny

desvístase: Undress! (command)

diabetes (*f.*): diabetes

diafragma (*m.*): diaphragm

diarrea (*f.*), **"estómago** (*m.*) **suelto," "chorro** (*m.*)**/chorrillo** (*m.*)**"**: diarrhea, loose bowels

diciembre: December

dientes (*m.*): teeth

dieta (*f.*): diet

dificultad (*f.*) **al respirar**: shortness of breath

difteria (*f.*), **diteria**(*f.*): diphtheria

dinero (*m.*): money

directorio (*m.*): directory

disentería (*f.*), "cursio" (*m.*):
dysentery

dislocación (*f.*): dislocation

dismenorrea (*f.*): dysmenorrheal

dispositivo (*m.*), aparato (*m.*), DUI
(*Cuba*): IUD

doblar: turn (to), bend (to)

doctor(a): doctor

doler (ue): hurt (to)

dolor (*m.*): pain (noun)

dolor de diente (*m.*), muela (*f.*):
toothache

dolor (*m.*) de espalda (*f.*): back pain

dolor de oído (*m.*): earache

dolor (*m.*) en el pecho (*m.*): chest
pain

dolor (*m.*) o presión (*f.*) en el pecho
(*m.*): pain, pressure or tightness
in the chest

dolores (*m.*) de cabeza (*f.*), o jaquecas
(*f.*): headaches

¿Dónde?: Where?

dormir (ue): sleep (to)

dosis (*f.*): dosis

drogas (*f.*): illicit drugs

duchas (*f.*), lavados (*m.*): douches

dulce (*m.*): sweet

durante: during

durar: last (to)

durazno (*m.*) (*Mex.*), melocotón (*m.*):
peach

ectropión (*f.*): ectropion

eczema (*f.*): eczema

edema (*f.*) pulmonar: pulmonary
edema

edificio (*m.*): edifice, building

ejotes (*m.*) (*Mex.*), habichuelas verdes
(*f.*) (*Cuba*), judías verdes (*f.*) (*Sp.*):
string beans

el cuerpo cortado (*Mex., Sp.*): aching all
over, flu-like symptoms

el otro día: the other day

elote (*m.*) (*Mex.*), mazorca (*f.*): ear of
corn

em: uh, um

embarazarse: become pregnant (to)

embarazo (*m.*): pregnancy

embolia (*f.*): embolism, stroke

embriólogo(a): embryologist

emergencia (*f.*): emergency

empacho (*m.*): impaction, obstruction
(intestinal)

empastar, tapar, rellenar (dental): fill
(to) a tooth cavity

en: in or on

en ayunas: fasting, without eating in the
morning

en voz alta: out loud

encefalitis (*f.*): encephalitis

encender: light (to), turn on (lights) (to)

encías (*f.*): gums

encontrar, hallar: find (to)

endodoncia (*f.*): endodontics

endodoncia (*f.*), extraer (sacar) el
nervio, tratamiento (*m.*) de
conductos (*m.*): root canal

enemas (*f.*), lavativas (*f.*): enemas

enero: January

enfermarse: get sick (to)

enfermedad (*f.*) mental: mental illness

enfermedad (*f.*) pulmonar: lung disease

enfermedad (*f.*) venereal: venereal
disease, STDs, STIs

enfermedades (*f.*) del corazón (*m.*):
heart diseases

enfermera(o): nurse

enfermo(a): sick

enfisema (*f.*): emphysema

enrojecimiento (*m.*): reddening,
redness

entablillar: put on a splint (to)

entonces: and so, and then, therefore

entrar: enter (to)

entropión (*m.*): entropion

entumido(a), entumecido(a): numb

enyesar: put a cast on (to)

epazote: Worm Seed

epidemia: epidemic

epidídimo (*m.*): epididymus

epilepsia (*f.*): epilepsy

episcleritis (*f.*): episcleritis

erisipela (*f.*): erysipela

eructar: burp (to)

erupción (*f.*): eruption

es: is, it is, s/he is

es que . . . : It's that . . .

escalofríos (*m.*): chills

escleritis (*f.*): scleritis

escorbuto(a): scurvy

escribir: write (to)

escroto (*m.*): scrotum

escuchar: listen (to)

escupir: spit (to)

esfínter (*m.*): sphincter

esófago (*m.*): esophagus

espalda (*f.*): back

español (*m.*): Spanish

espasmódico(a): spasmodic

espasmos (*m.*): spasms

especial: special

espéculo (*m.*), **pato** (*m.*) (*slang*): speculum

espejo (*m.*): mirror

espinacas (*f.*): spinach

espinilla (*f.*): shin bone, blackhead

espíritu (*m.*): spirit

esponja (*f.*): sponge

esposa (*f.*): wife

esposo (*m.*): husband

esposos (*m.*): spouses, handcuffs

espuma (*f.*): foam

esqueleto (*m.*): skeleton

esquizofrénico(a): schizophrenic

¿Está . . . ?: Are you . . . ?, Is he?, Is she?

estar mal: be sick (to)

esterilidad (*f.*): sterility

esterilización (*f.*): sterilization

esterilizar: sterilize (to)

estetoscopio (*m.*): stethoscope

estítico(a) (*El Salv.*), **estreñido(a):** constipated

estómago (*m.*): stomach

estómago (*m.*) **revuelto** (*m.*): upset stomach

estos problemas (*m.*): these problems

estreñido(a), estítico(a) (*El Salv.*): constipated

estrías (*f.*): stretch marks

estrógeno (*m.*): estrogen

estructura (*f.*): structure

estudiar: study (to)

evitar: avoid (to)

examiner: examine (to)

excepción (*f.*): exception

excremento (*m.*): stool, excrement

excusado (*m.*), **inodoro** (*m.*): toilet

existir: exist (to)

exoftalmos (*m.*): exophthalmos

extender (ie): extend (to)

extraer, sacar, remover: extract (to)

extremidades (*f.*): extremities

falta de respiración (*f.*): shortness of breath

faltar: miss (to)

familia (*f.*): family

familiares (*m.*): family members

faringitis (*f.*): pharyngitis

farmacia (*f.*): drug store, pharmacy

fatigado(a): fatigued

favor (por): favor (please)

febrero: February

fecha de parto (*m.*) **apróximado:** due date

fechas (*f.*): dates

fetoscopio (*m.*): fetoscope
fibra (*f.*): fiber
fibroma (*f.*), **fibroides** (*m.*): fibroids, tumors
fiebre (*f.*), **calentura** (*f.*): fever
fiebre (*f.*) **de escarlatina:** scarlet fever
fiebre de heno (*f.*), **"romadizo"** (*m.*): hay fever
fiebre (*f.*) **del valle, coccidioidomicosis:** valley fever, coccidioidomycosis
fiebre (*f.*) **reumática:** rheumatic fever
firma (*f.*): signature
firmar: sign (to)
físico(a): physical
fisiológico(a): physiological
fístula (*f.*): fistula
flaco(a), esbelto(a): skinny, scrawny/svelte
flan (*m.*): custard
flema (*f.*): phlegm
flojo(a): loose, lazy
flor de azahar (*f.*): orange blossoms
flujo (*m.*): flow
flujo (*m.*) **menstrual:** menstrual flow
folículo (*m.*): follicles
fomentos (*m.*) **de agua caliente:** hot water compresses
fontanela (*f.*) **caída o deprimida, "mollera** (*f.*) **caída":** fallen fontanel
fosa (*f.*) **nasal:** nasal cavity
fósforo (*m.*): matches, phosphorous
fracturado: fractured, broken
frasco (*m.*): jar, container
frecuencia (*f.*): frequency
frenos (*m.*), **frenillos** (*m.*): braces
frente: forehead
frente (*f.*): in front
frentes (*m.*) **estéticos (dental):** veneers
fresa (*f.*): strawberry
fresco(a): fresh
frigidez (*f.*): frigidity
frijoles (*m.*): beans

frío (*m.*): cold
frotar, sobar: rub (to), massage (to)
fuegos (*m.*): chancre sores, fever blisters or cold sores
fuerte: strong
fumar: smoke (to)

gabinete (*m.*): cabinet
galletas (*f.*): cookies
garganta (*f.*): throat
garganta (*f.*) **inflamada:** inflamed, sore throat
gases (*m.*) **en el estómago:** stomach gas
gastar: spend (to), waste (to)
gastritis (*f.*): gastritis
gatear: crawl (to)
gel (*m.*): gel
gelatina (*f.*): gelatin
generalmente: generally
generoso(a): generous
genitalia (*f.*): genitalia
ginecología (*f.*): gynecology
ginecólogo(a): gynecologist
gingivitis (*f.*): gingivitis
glande (*m.*): gland
glándula (*f.*) **tiroides:** thyroid gland
glándulas (*f.*) **inflamadas:** swollen glands
glándulas (*f.*) **sebáceas:** sebaceous glands
glaucoma (*f.*): glaucoma
glúteo (*m.*): gluteus
golpear: beat up (to)
gonorrea (*f.*), **purgación** (*f.*), **blenorragia** (*f.*): gonorrhea
gordo(a): fat
gordolobo: mullein
gota (*f.*), **podagra** (*f.*): drop, gout; podraga = gout
gotero (*m.*): dropper
gragea (*f.*): coated pill

gramo (*m.*): gram
grande: big, large
grano (*m.*)**, enterrado, nacido,**
"tacotillo" (*m.*): boil, carbuncle
grasa(s) (*f.*): fat(s)
grasoso(a): oily
grieta (*f.*): chapped skin, cracks
gripe (*f.*): cold or flu
gris: grey
guardar: keep (to)
guardar cama (*f.*): stay in bed (to)
güero(a): blond, light hair or skin
(*Mex.*)
guisado (*m.*): stew

hablar: speak (to), talk (to)
hace dos días: two days ago
hacer (g): make (to), do (to)
hacerlo: do it (to)
hacia: towards
hacia atrás: backward, as in "camine
hacia atrás" = walk backward
¡Haga esto!: Do this!
halitosis (*f.*): halitosis
hambre (*m.*): hunger
hamburguesa (*f.*): hamburger
hay/¿Hay?: there is, there are/Is there?,
Are there?
¿Hay algo que alivia el dolor?: Is there
anything that alleviates the pain?
**¿Hay algo que le hace sentir
mejor?/¿Con qué se siente mejor?:**
(Is there anything that) What makes
it feel better?
**¿Hay algo que le hace sentir
peor?/¿Con qué se siente peor?:** (Is
there anything that) What makes it
feel worse?
helado (*m.*): ice cream
hematología (*f.*): hematology
hematólogo(a): hematologist
hembra (*f.*): female

hemorroides (*f.*)**, almorranas** (*f.*)**:**
hemorrhoids, piles
hepatitis (*f.*) **A, B, C:** hepatitis A, B, C
herido(a)/herida (una) (*f.*)**:**
wounded/wound (a)
hermano(a): brother/sister
hermanos: siblings
hernia (*f.*): hernia
herpes (*m.*): herpes
hidrocele (*f.*): hydrocele
hiel (*f.*)**, bilis** (*f.*)**, "yel"** (*m.*)**:** gall, bile
hielo (*m.*): ice
hígado (*m.*): liver
hijo(a): son (daughter)
himen (*m.*): hymen
hinchado(a): swollen
hinchazón (*f.*): swelling
hiperglucemia (*f.*): hyperglycemia
hiperópico (*m.*): far sighted
(hyperopic)
hipertensión (*f.*): hypertension
hipocondría (*f.*): hypochondria
hipoglucemia (*f.*): hypoglycemia
histerectomía (*f.*): hysterectomy
histeria (*f.*): hysteria
histólogo(a): histologist
hombre (*m.*): man
hombro (*m.*): shoulder
hora (*f.*): time
hormigueo (*m.*): tingling
hormonal: hormonal
hormonas (*f.*): hormones
hospitalizaciones (*f.*): hospitalizations
hoy: today
huachinango (*m.*)**, pargo** (*m.*)**:** red
snapper
hueso (*m.*): bone
huevos (*m.*)**, blanquillos** (*m.*) (*N.
Mex.*)**:** eggs
hule (*m.*) **protector** (dental): rubber
dam
humor (*m.*): mood, humor

ictericia (*f.*), **piel** (*f.*) **amarillenta:**
  jaundice
identidad (*f.*): identity
implantes (*m.*): Norplant®, implants
importancia (*f.*): importance
impotencia (*f.*): impotence
incómodo(a): uncomfortable
incordio (*m.*), **encordio** (*m.*): swollen
  glands (in groin)
indicación (*f.*): indication
indicar: indicate (to)
indigestión (*f.*), **indigesto** (*m.*):
  indigestion
infarto (*m.*): infarct
infarto (*m.*), **derrame**(*m.*) **cerebral:**
  infarction, cerebral infarct
infección (*f.*) **por hongos** (*m.*): yeast
  infection
infeccioso(a): infectious, contagious
infectar: infect (to)
inflado(a), aventado(a): inflated,
  bloated
inflamación (*f.*): imflammation
inflamación (*f.*) **del estómago** (*m.*):
  gastritis
inflar: inflate (to)
ingle (*f.*): groin
ingresar: admit (to), hospitalize (to)
inmunización (*f.*): immunization,
  vaccination
inmunizar: immunize (to), vaccinate
  (to)
inmunología (*f.*): immunology
inquieto(a): uneasy, restless
insistencia (*f.*): insistence
insistir: insist (to)
insuficiencia (*f.*): insufficiency
insulina (*f.*): insulin
intermitente: intermittent
internar: admit (to), hospitalize (to)
intestino (*m.*) **delgado:** small intestine
intestino (*m.*) **grueso:** large intestine

introducir (*z*): insert (to)
inyección (*f.*): injection, shot
inyecciones (La Dosis), Depo (*f.*): Depo
  Provera®
inyectar: inject (to), give a shot (to)
ir: go (to)
iridectomía (*f.*): iridectomy
iris (*f.*): iris
iritis (*f.*), **inflamación de la iris:** iritis
irregular: irregular
irregularidades (*f.*): irregularities
irrigar: irrigate (to)
irritación (*f.*): irritation

¿Jadea cuando camina?: Do you pant
  (wheeze) when you walk?
jalar: pull (to)
jamón (*m.*): ham
jarabe (*m.*): syrup
jeringa (*f.*): syringe
joven (*m.*, *f.*): young, youth
juanete (*m.*): bunion
jugo (*m.*), **zumo** (*m.*): juice
julio: July
junio: June

la última vez: the last time
labihendido(a), labio (*m.*) **leporino,**
  "comido de la luna": cleft lip,
  harelip
labios (*m.*): lips
labios (*m.*) **vaginales:** labia
laboratorio (*m.*): laboratory
laceración (*f.*): laceration
langosta (*f.*): lobster
largo(a): long (length)
laringe (*f.*): larynx
laringitis (*f.*): laryngitis
lastimado(a): hurt
latido (*m.*): heart beat, (hunger pang)
lavar: wash (to)
lavarse: wash oneself (to)

laxante (*m.*): laxative

¿Le duele cuándo pongo (aplico) presión?: Does it hurt when I apply pressure?

¿Le duele cuándo suelto (quito) la presión?: Does it hurt when I remove the pressure?

leche (*f.*): milk

lechuga (*f.*): lettuce

leer: read (to)

lengua (*f.*): tongue, language

lengua (*f.*) sucia: coated "dirty" tongue

lenguado (*m.*): sole fish

lentes (*m.*), gafas, anteojos (*m.*), espejuelos (*m.*) (*Carib.*): glasses

lentes (*m.*) de contacto, pupilentes (*m.*): contact lenses

lento(a): slow

lesionado(a): injured

levantarse: stand up (to), get up (to)

levanter: raise (to), lift (to)

libro (*m.*): book

licuado (*m.*) (*Mex.*), batida (*f.*) (*Carib.*), batido (*m.*) (*C.A.*): smoothie (natural fruit drinks made with milk)

ligadura (*f.*) de trompas (*f.*): tubal ligation

ligamentos (*m.*): ligaments

lima (*f.*), limón (*m.*) (*Mex.*): lime

limón (*m.*): lemon, lime (*Mex.*)

limpiar: clean (to)

linimento (*m.*): liniment

líquido(s) (*m.*): liquid(s), fluid(s)

llaga (*f.*): bed sore, open oozing wound

llamarse: call oneself (to), be named (to)

llevar: carry (to), wear (to), take someone somewhere (to)

lo siento mucho: I'm very sorry

loción (*f.*): lotion

lombrices (*f.*): intestinal worms

lombriz (*f.*) solitaria: tapeworm

lomo (*m.*): loin, i.e. pork loin

los dos, ambos: both

lubricar: lubricate (to)

luego: then (in a series), later

lunar (*m.*): mole

machos (*m.*), varones (*m.*), hombres (*m.*): males

madre (*f.*): mother

madres (*f.*): mothers (in general)

maduro(a): ripe

maíz (*m.*): corn

mal (*m.*): bad, sick

mal aliento (*m.*): bad breath

Mal de Orin (*m.*), chistata (Nica.): urinary tract infection

malaria (*f.*), paludismo (*m.*): malaria

maleta (*f.*): suitcase

malpartos (*m.*) (abortos (*m.*) naturales o espontáneos): miscarriages

maltratado(a): abused

mañana por la mañana (*f.*): tomorrow morning

manejar: drive (to), manage (to)

mano (*f.*): hand

mantel (*m.*): table cloth

mantequilla (*f.*): butter

manzana (*f.*): apple

máquina (*f.*): machine

marca de nacimiento/"mancha (*f.*) de nacimiento": birth mark

mareado(a): dizzy

mareos (*m.*): dizziness

mariscos (*m.*): shellfish

martillo (*m.*): hammer

marzo: March

más o menos: more or less, sort of

masajear: massage (to)

masticar, mascar: chew (to)

maternidad (*f.*): maternity

mayo: May

mayor: older

¿Me explico?: Do you understand?, Does that make sense? (literally, Am I explaining myself?)

me parece, se me hace: it seems to me

medicamento (*m.*): medication

medicina (*f.*): medicine

médico(a): medical, doctor

medir (i): measure (to)

mejorar: better (to), get better (to)

menopausia (*f.*): menopause

menor: younger

mesa (*f.*): table

mesero(a): waiter, waitress, server

método (*m.*) **del ritmo** (*m.*): rhythm method

Mi esposo me cuida: withdrawal (coitus interruptus)/My husband takes care of me (*lit.*)

microscopio (*m.*): microscope

miedo (*m.*): fear

migraña (*f.*): migraine

milanesa (*f.*): breaded veal

mililitro (*m.*), **ml.:** milliliter

minimizar: minimize (to)

miope (*m.*): near sighted (myopic)

miopía (*f.*): myopic

mirar: look at (to)

mojar: wet (to)

mole (*m.*): sauce for chicken (made of chocolate, peanuts, and chiles)

molestias (*f.*): discomforts, problems, bothers

momento (*m.*): moment

morado(a): purple

morder: bite (to)

moreno(a): dark skin color

moreteado(a): bruised

moretón (*m.*): bruise

morir (ue): die (to)

mormado(a), tupido(a) (*Carib.*): stuffed-up nasally

mortalidad (*f.*): mortality

mortificado(a): mortified, upset

mostrador (*m.*): counter

mostrar: show (to)

mover (ue): move (to)

mucho(a): a lot, much

muela (*f.*) **de atrás:** back molar

muela (*f.*) **del juicio:** wisdom tooth

muelas (*f.*): molars, teeth (slang)

muestra (*f.*): sample

mujer (*f.*): woman

muñeca (*f.*): wrist, doll

museo (*m.*): museum

muslo (*m.*): thigh

muy bien: very good

nacidos a tiempo (*m.*): full term

nacidos muertos: still born

nada más: only, nothing more

nada más, no más, solamente: it just/it only

nada más que: it's just that

nadar: swim (to)

nalgas (*f.*): butt cheeks

naranja (*f.*): orange

narcótico (*m.*): narcotic

nariz (*f.*): nose

nariz (*f.*) **suelta:** runny nose

nariz (*f.*) **tapada, tupida** (*Carib.*): stuffed up nose

náusea (*f.*), **asco** (*m.*), **basca** (*f.*): nausea

nebulizador (*m.*), **tubito** (*m.*): nebulizor, small tube

necesitar: need (to)

negro(a): black

nervio (*m.*): nerve

nervioso(a): nervous

neurología (*f.*): neurology

neurólogo(a): neurologist

neurótico(a): neurotic

ni . . . ni: neither . . . nor

nieto(a): grandson (granddaughter)

niño(a): boy (girl)

niños (*m.*): children

¡No se preocupe!: Don't worry!
nódulo (*m.*): nodule
nombre (*m.*): name
normal: normal
novia(o): girl/boyfriend, bride/groom
noviembre: November
nuca (*f.*): nape
nuera (*f.*): daughter-in-law
nunca: never
nutricionista (*f.*), **nutriólogo** (*m.*):
    nutritionist

o, ó: or
o sea: in other words, that is to say
obrar, defecar: bowel movement (to
    have a)
observer: observe (to)
obstétrico(a): obstetrical
oclusión de la arteria (*f.*)**/vena** (*f.*):
    retinal, retinal artery, (vein)
    occlusion
octubre: October
oftalmología (*f.*): ophthalmology
oftalmólogo(a): ophthalmologist
oído (*m.*): inner ear, ear (*Mex.*)
ojo (*m.*): eye
ojo (*m.*) **de venado** (*m.*): deer's eye (*lit.*)
    amulet to protect against the Evil
    Eye
ojos (*m.*) **cansados/fatigados:** tired
    eyes, eye strain
ojos (*m.*) **llorosos:** watery eyes
ojos (*m.*) **secos:** dry eyes
ombligo (*m.*): belly button, umbilicus
operaciones (*f.*): operations
operar: operate (to)
oreja (*f.*): outer ear
orina (*f.*): urine
orinar: urinate (to)
ortodoncia (*f.*): orthodontics
orzuelo (*m.*), **perrilla** (*f.*): sty
oscuro(a), obscuro(a): dark

ostras (*f.*), **ostiones** (*m.*): oysters
otoscopio (*m.*): otoscope
otro(a): other, another
otros(as): others
ovario (*m.*): ovary

padecer (z): suffer from (to)
padre (*m.*): father
padres (*m.*): parents
padres (*m.*) **de familia:** fathers (in
    general)
pagar: pay (to)
paladar (*m.*): palate
paladar (*m.*) **hendido, grietas** (*f.*) **en el
    paladar:** cleft palate
palidez (*f.*), **pálido:** paleness, pale
palma (*f.*): palm
palmas hacia abajo: palms down
palmas hacia arriba: palms up
palpar: palpate (to)
palpitaciones (*f.*): palpitations
pan (*m.*): bread
pan (*m.*) **dulce, pan de dulce:** sweet
    rolls
páncreas (*m.*): pancreas
paño (*m.*): facial discoloration
pantorrilla (*f.*): calf
papas (*f.*): potatoes
paperas (*f.*), **bolas** (*f.*), chanza (*f.*):
    mumps
para: for, in order to
para mañana: for tomorrow
parálisis (*f.*) **facial:** facial paralysis
parar(se): stand (to)
parar, dejar de: stop (to)
parásitos (*m.*): parasites
parche (*m.*): patch, plaster
parecer (z): appear (to), seem (to)
paregórico: paregoric
pareja (*f.*): partner (romantic), couple
parpadear: blink (to)
párpado (*m.*): eyelid

párpados (*m.*) **inflamados:** inflamed eyelids

párrafo (*m.*): paragraph

partes (*f.*) **genitals:** genitalia

parto (*m.*): delivery

pasado mañana: day after tomorrow

pasar: pass (to), happen (to)

pastel (*m.*) (*Mex.*), **bizcocho** (*m.*), **torta** (*f.*), **queque** (*m.*) (*Cuba and N. Mex.*): cake

patizambo(a), chueco(a): defect of foot, ankle, knee

pato (*m.*): duck, speculum (slang)

patología (*f.*): pathology

patólogo(a): pathologist

pavo (*m.*), **guajolote** (*m.*) (*Mex.*), **guanajo** (*m.*) (*Cuba*): turkey

pay (*m.*) (*Mex.*), **tarta** (*f.*): pie

pecho (*m.*)/**pechos:** chest/breasts

pegar: hit (to), glue (to), stick (to)

pellizcar: pinch (to)

pelo (*m.*), **cabello** (*m.*): hair

pelos (*m.*) **o cabellos** (*m.*) **de elote** (*m.*): corn silk (tea)

pelvis (*m.*): pelvis

pene (*m.*): penis

penicilina (*f.*): penicillin

pensando a solas: thinking to oneself

pensar: think (to)

peor ataque (*m.*): worst attack

pequeña úlcera (*f.*) **en la boca** (*f.*), **fuego** (*m.*), **chancro** (*m.*): canker sore, chancre

pequeñito(a): little one

pequeño(a), chico(a): little, small

pera (*f.*): pear

perder: lose (to)

pérdida (*f.*): loss

pérdida (*f.*) **del conocimiento:** unconsciousness

periodontal: periodontal

peritonitis (*f.*): peritonitis

pero: but

pesar: weigh (to)

pesarse: weigh oneself, yourself, himself, herself (to)

pescado(s) (*m.*): fish

peso (*m.*): weigh, a coin

pestaña (*f.*): eyelash

petit pois (*m.*) (*Carib. and C.A.*), **chícharos** (*m.*) (*Mex.*), **guisantes** (*m.*) (*Sp.*): peas

pezón (female) (*m.*), **tetilla (male)** (*f.*): nipple

picazón (*f.*), **comezón** (*f.*): itch

pie (*m.*): foot

pie (*m.*) **de atleta:** athlete's foot

pie (*m.*) **plano:** flat foot

piel (*f.*): skin

piel (*f.*) **grasosa (cara):** oily skin (face)

piel (*f.*) **seca, piel reseca:** dry skin

pierna (*f.*): leg

píldora (*f.*), **pastilla** (*f.*): pill

píldora (*f.*), **pastilla** (*f.*) **anticonceptiva:** birth control pill

pimienta (*f.*): pepper

piña (*f.*), **ananás** (*Arg.*): pineapple

pintando(a): painting

piojos (*m.*) **púbicos** (*m.*): pubic lice

plátano (*m.*) (*Mex.*), **banana** (*f.*), **banano** (*m.*), **guineo** (*m.*) (*C.A. and Carib.*): banana

plátano (*m.*) **macho** (*Mex.*), **plátano** (*m.*) (*Carib. and C.A.*): plantain

plato (*m.*): dish

pleuresía (*f.*): pleurisy

pluma (*f.*): pen, feather

pobrecito(a): poor little one

poco(a): a little/a little bit, slightly

poder: be able (to)

poliomielitis (*f.*): polio

pólipos (*m.*), **fibromas** (*f.*) **en la matriz** (*f.*): polyps in the uterus

político(a): political, politician
pollo (*m.*), **gallina** (*f.*): chicken
pomada (*f.*): balm, ointment, salve
pompis (*f.*): tush
pómulo (*m.*): cheekbone
poner (g): put (to)
ponzoñoso(a): poisonous
popotes (*m.*) (*Mex.*), **pajillas** (*f.*):
   straws
por: by, for, through
por día, al día: per day
por dos días: for two days
por eso: that's why, due to that
por lo menos: at least
por primera vez: for the first time
¿Por qué?: Why?
poro (*m.*): pore
porque: because
postemillas o fuego (*m.*): abscessed
   tooth, chancre
potasio (*m.*): potassium
prebiopia (*f.*): presbyopia
preguntar: ask (to)
prematuro(a): premature
prender: pin (to), turn on (to)
preocupado(a): preoccupied, worried
preparación (*f.*) **antibiótica:** antibiotic
   preparation
preparer: prepare (to)
prepucio (*m.*): foreskin
presión (*f.*): pressure
presión (*f.*) **arterial:** blood pressure,
   arterial pressure
primer(o)(a): first
primera vez: first time
primo(a): cousin
principios (*m.*): beginnings
probar: try on (to), test (to), try for first
   time (to)
problemas (*m.*), **molestias** (*f.*):
   problems
producir (z): produce (to)

prometido(a): fiancé(e)
propina (*f.*): tip
próstata (*f.*): prostate
proteger: protect (to)
protéinas (*f.*): proteins
pruebas (*f.*): tests
psicólogo(a), sicólogo(a): psychologist
ptosis, caída de párpado (*m.*): ptosis
puede vestirse ahora: you can get
   dressed now
puente (*m.*) **fijo (dental):** bridge
puente (*m.*) **removible (dental):** partial
   bridge
puerco (*m.*): pig, pork
puerta (*f.*): door
pues, 'pos (*slang Mex.*): well
pulmón (*m.*): lung
pulmonía (*f.*), **neumonía:** pneumonia
pulmonía doble (*f.*): double pneumonia
pulmonía (principios de): walking
   pneumonia
pulpo (*m.*): octopus
pulsativo(a): pulsating, throbbing
pulso (*m.*): pulse
puntas (*f.*) **del pie:** tiptoes
punto (*m.*): point
puntos (*m.*) **o puntadas** (*f.*): stitches
punzante como una navaja (*f.*) **o**
   cuchillo (*m.*): stabbing like a blade
   or knife (shooting pains)
pupila (*f.*), **niña** (*f.*) **del ojo** (*m.*): pupil
purgante (*m.*): purgative

¿Qué?: What?
¡Qué bueno!: That's good!
que he sufrido: that I have had
   (suffered)
¡Qué pena!: How embarrassing!
que sufrí: that I had (that I suffered)
quedar: remain (to)
quemado(a): burned, burnt
quemadura (*f.*): burn

quemar: burn (to)
querer (ie): want (to), love (to)
quesadilla (*f.*): melted cheese in a
tortilla
queso (*m.*): cheese
¿Quién?: Who?
quimioterapia (*f.*): chemotherapy
quiste (*m.*): cyst
quitar: take off (to), remove (to)
Quítese la ropa (*f.*): Take off or Remove
your clothing. (*command*)

radiaciones (*f.*): radiation treatment
radiología (*f.*): radiology
rápido(a): fast, quick, rapid
raquítico(a): scrawny
rascar: scratch (to)
rasguña (*f.*): scratch
raspadura (*f.*): abrasion
rayos X (*m.*), **radiografías** (*f.*), **placas**
(*f.*): X rays
reacción (*f.*): reaction
recepcionista (*f.*): receptionist
receta (*f.*): prescription, recipe
receta (*f.*) **médica:** medical prescription
recetar: prescribe (to)
reconstruir: reconstruct (to)
recorder: remember (to)
recto (*m.*): rectum
recuperación (*f.*): recuperation
regla (*f.*): ruler, rule
regla (*f.*), **período** (*m.*), **menstruación**
(*f.*), **"mes"** (*m.*): menstrual period
regresar, volver: return (to)
regular: moderate, moderately
regular, normal, así así: regular
relajación (*f.*): relaxation
relajarse: relax (to)
remedios (*m.*) **caseros:** home remedies
repisa (*f.*): shelf
reseca(o): dry (noun)
resistir: resist (to)

respiración (*f.*) **asmática:** asthmatic
respiration
respiración (*f.*) **dificultosa, dificultad
al respirar:** difficulty breathing
respirar: breathe (to)
**respirar con silbidos, respirar con
chiflidos** (*m.*): wheezing, to
wheeze
responder: answer (to), respond (to)
resultado (*m.*): result
resultar: result (to)
retinopatía (*f.*) **diabética:** diabetic
retinopathy
retortijones, retorcijones (*m.*): cramps
(abdomen)
retrocediendo: receding
reumatismo (*m.*) **del corazón** (*m.*):
rheumatic heart
reventar: burst open (to)
rico(a): rich, delicious
riñón (*m.*): kidney
rociar, enjuagar: rinse (to)
rodilla (*f.*): knee
rojo(a): red (color)
ronchas (*f.*), **erupciones** (*f.*) **de la piel:**
rash
ronco(a): hoarse
ronquera (*f.*): hoarseness
rosa (*f.*): pink
Rosa de Castillo (*f.*): rose (tea)
rubio(a): blond
ruda (*f.*): rue (tea)
ruido (*m.*): noise

sabañones (*f.*), **"saballones"** (*f.*):
chilblains
saber: know (to)
sábila (*f.*): aloe, aloe vera
sacar: take out (to), take (as in photos
or Xrays) (to)
sal (*f.*): salt
saliva (*f.*): saliva

salpullido (*m.*)/**sarpullido** (*m.*): rash (mild)

salsa (*f.*) **picante:** hot sauce

salvar: save (as in a life) (to)

salvia (*f.*): sage

sandía (*f.*): watermelon

sangrado, desangramiento, pérdida de sangre: bleeding

sangrar: bleed (to)

sangrar de las encías (*f.*): bleeding of the gums

sangre (*f.*): blood

sangre (*f.*) **en el esputo** (*m.*): blood in the sputum

sarampión (*m.*) **o rubéola** (*f.*): measles

sarampión (*m.*), **rubéola** (*f.*): rubella

sarna (*f.*): scabies

sarro (*m.*): tartar

¿Se siente . . . ?: Do you feel . . . ?

secar: dry (to)

seco(a): dry or stale

secreción (*f.*): secretion

sed (*f.*): thirst

sedante (*m.*): sedative

según: according to

segundo(a): second

seguro médico (*m.*), **aseguranza** (*f.*) (*slang*): medical insurance

semana (*f.*) **pasada:** last week

seno (*m.*): sinus

senos (*m.*), **mamas** (*f.*): breasts

senos/pechos (*m.*) **adoloridos:** tenderness in the breasts

sentar: seat (to)

sentarse: sit (oneself) (to), sit down (to), sit up (to)

sentirse: feel (oneself) (to)

separar: separate (to)

se(p)tiembre: September

ser: be (to)

serio(a): serious

servicio (*m.*): service

servilleta (*f.*): napkin

sexualidad (*f.*): sexuality

si: if

sí: yes

sialorrea (*f.*), **mucha saliva** (*f.*): salivation

sicótico(a), psicótico(a): psychotic

SIDA (*m.*): AIDS

siempre: always

sífilis (*f.*), **"sangre mala"** (*f.*): syphilis

silla (*f.*)/**silla de ruedas:** chair/wheelchair

sin: without

sin fuerzas/débil: weak

síndrome (*m.*) **de Down:** Down syndrome

síndrome (*m.*) **fetal de alcohol** (*m.*): fetal alcohol syndrome

sinusitis (*f.*): sinusitis

sobre: over, envelope

sobrino(a): nephew/niece

socio(a): partner (business)

soda (*f.*), **refresco** (*m.*), **frescos** (*m.*) (*C.A.*): soft drink

sodio (*m.*): sodium

solución (*f.*): solution

sombrero (*m.*): hat

son: are, they are

sonda (*f.*), **catéter** (*m.*): catheter

sonrisa (*f.*): smile

sopa (*f.*), **caldo** (*m.*): soup

soplo del corazón (*m.*): heart murmur

sordera (*f.*): deafness

sordo(a): deaf, dull (as in a dull pain)

sordomudo(a): deaf-mute

sorprendido(a): surprised

subir: go up (to), get on (to), ascend (to)

subir de peso (*m.*): gain weight (to)

subirse: getup on, (to)

sudores (*m.*): sweats

suegra (*f.*): mother-in-law

suegro (*m.*): father-in-law

suero (*m.*): I. V.

suero (*m.*), **alimentación** (*f.*)
intravenosa: intravenous feeding,
Pediolite® is also referred to as
"suero"

sufrir: suffer (to)

sugerir: suggest (to)

sulfa (*f.*): sulfa

supositorio (*m.*): suppository

susto (*m.*): fright, a scare

suyo(a): his, hers, yours

tabique (*m.*): nasal septum

tableta (*f.*): tablet

taco (*m.*): taco

taladro (*m.*): drill

talón (*m.*): talus, heel

también: also, too

tambor (*m.*) **o tímpano** (*m.*) **roto**:
perforated eardrum

tanto/tanto como: so much/as
much as

tapadera (*f.*): cover, cap

tapar, cubrir: cover (to), coverup (to)

tarde: late

tarea (*f.*): homework, task

tartamudear: stutter (to), stammer
(to)

té (*m.*): tea

té (*m.*) **de manzanilla**: chamomile tea

técnico(a): technician

tejidos (*m.*): tissues

teléfono (*m.*): telephone

temperatura (*f.*): temperature

temprano: early

tenedor (*m.*): fork

tener (g): have (to)

tener gas (*m.*), **echar un pedo** (*m.*)
(slang), **tirar un pedo**: expel gas
(to), to fart

terapia (*f.*): therapy

tercer(o)(a): third

terminar: terminate (to), end (to)

termómetro (*m.*): thermometer

testículos (*m.*), **"bolas"** (*f.*), **"huevos"**
(*m.*), **"talagas"** (*f.*): testicles

testigo(a): witness

textura (*f.*): texture

tía (*f.*): aunt

tiburón (*m.*): shark

¿Tiene apetito (*m.*)?: Do you have,
Does she/he have an appetite?

tifoidea (*f.*): typhoid

tila (*f.*): linden

tímpano (*m.*): eardrum

tintineo (*m.*), **zumbido** (*m.*) **de/en**
los oídos (*m.*): ringing, buzzing in
the ears

tío(a): uncle/aunt

tíos (*m.*): aunt and uncle (as a unit)

toalla (*f.*): towel

tobillo (*m.*): ankle

tocar: knock (to), play and instrument
(to), touch (to)

tocino (*m.*): bacon

todavía: still

todavía no: not yet

todos: all (plural)

toma: takes

tomar: drink (to), take (to)

tomate (jitomate) (*m.*) (*Mex. City, S.*
Mex.): tomato

tónico (*m.*): tonic

tórax (*m.*) **o pecho** (*m.*): thorax

torcedura (*f.*), **"falseado"** (as in "me
falseé"): twist, sprain

torcer, descoyuntar, dislocar,
desconcertar: twist (to)

toronja (*f.*), **pomelo** (*m.*) (*Arg., Sp.*):
grapefruit

torsión (*f.*) **de los testículos** (*m.*):
torsion/twisting of testicles

tortícolis (*f.*), **"cuello tieso"** (*m.*): stiff
  neck
tortilla (*f.*): tortilla (flour or corn),
  potato omelet (*Sp.*)
tos (*f.*): cough
tos (*f.*), **tos seca:** cough, dry
tos con flema (*f.*), **"desgarrando":**
  cough with phlegm, wet cough
tos de perro: seal's bark, dog's cough
  (lit.)
toser: cough (to)
tosferina (*f.*), **tos ferina** (*f.*),
  "coqueluche": whooping cough
trabajador(a) social: social worker
trabajar: work (to)
tragar (ue): bolt down food (to),
  swallow (to)
tragar/pasar saliva (*f.*): swallow (to)
tranquilizantes (*m.*), **calmantes** (*m.*):
  tranquilizers
transfusión (*f.*) **de sangre** (*f.*): blood
  transfusion
tráquea (*f.*): traquea
tratamiento (*m.*) **hormonal:** hormone
  treatment
tratamiento del láser (*m.*): laser
  treatment
tratar: treat (to)
triste : sad
trocitos (*m.*), **pastillas** (*f.*) **para chupar:**
  lozenges
trombosis (*f.*): thrombosis
trompa (*f.*), **tubo** (*m.*) **de Falopio:**
  fallopian tube
tuberculosis (*f.*), **"tisis," "tis":**
  tuberculosis, T. B.
tumor (*m.*): tumor
tumores (*m.*): tumors

úlcera (*f.*): ulcer, sore
úlceras (*f.*) **en la córnea** (*f.*): corneal
  ulcers

última (*f.*) **vez:** last time
uña (*f.*): nail
uña (*f.*) **enterrada:** ingrown nail
ungüento (*m.*): ointment
universidad (*f.*): university
uréter (*m.*): ureter
uretra (*f.*): urethra
urología (*f.*): urology
urólogo(a): urologist
urticaria (*f.*): hives
usar, utilizar: use (to), utilize (to)
útero (*m.*): uterus
uvas (*f.*): grapes

va y viene: it comes and goes
vacunar: vaccinate (to)
vagina (*f.*): vagina
variante (*f.*): variation
varicocele (*f.*): varicocele
vasectomía (*f.*): vasectomy
vaso (*m.*): glass, vessel
vaso (*m.*) **deferente, conducto
  deferente:** vas deferens
vaso (*m.*) **sanguíneo:** blood vessel
veces: times (series)
vegetales (*m.*), **verduras** (*f.*),
  legumbres (*f.*): vegetables
vejiga (*f.*): bladder
vello (*m.*): body hair, pubic hair
velocímetro (*m.*): speedometer
vena (*f.*): vein
venas (*f.*) **varicosas, várices** (*f.*):
  varicose veins
venda (*f.*), **vendaje** (*m.*): bandage
vender: sell (to)
venir (g): come (to)
ventana (*f.*): window
ventanas (*f.*) **de la nariz** (*f.*), **narices**
  (*f.*): nostrils
ventanilla (*f.*): little window
ver: see (to)
verde: green

verrugas (*f.*) **genitals:** genital warts
vesícula (*f.*) **biliar:** gall bladder
vestirse: dress oneself (to)
vez: time (sequence)
vigilar: watch (to), guard (to)
VIH (*m.*): HIV
viruela (*f.*): small pox
viruela (*f.*) **loca o varicela** (*f.*): chicken
   pox
visitar: visit (to)
vista (*f.*) **borrosa, nublada, empañada:**
   blurred vision
¡Vístase!: Get dressed! (*command*)
vitaminas (*f.*): vitamins
vivir: live (to)
voltear: turn around (to)
voltear(se): turn over (to)

vomitar: vomit (to)
vómito (*m.*): vomit
vómitos (*m.*): vomiting

y: and
¡Ya!: Now!, Enough!, Already!
ya casi, ya mero (*Mex.*): almost done
ya no: no longer
yemas (*f.*): finger pads
yerba (*f.*) **o hierba buena (té de):** mint
   (tea)
yerbero(a), hierbero(a): one that uses
   herbs for healing, medicine person
yerno (*m.*): son-in-law

zanahoria (*f.*): carrot
zumbido (*m.*): buzzing (in ears)

Index